PETER IN THE NEW TESTAMENT

Peter in
the New Testament

A Collaborative Assessment by Protestant and
Roman Catholic Scholars

Edited by

Raymond E. Brown, Karl P. Donfried, and John Reumann

From Discussions by

PAUL J. ACHTEMEIER
MYLES M. BOURKE
P. SCHUYLER BROWN
RAYMOND E. BROWN
JOSEPH A. BURGESS

KARL P. DONFRIED
JOSEPH A. FITZMYER
KARLFRIED FROEHLICH
REGINALD H. FULLER
GERHARD KRODEL

JOHN REUMANN

Sponsored by
the United States Lutheran—Roman Catholic Dialogue
as Background for Ecumenical Discussions
of the
Role of the Papacy in the Universal Church

1973
Augsburg Publishing House • Minneapolis
Paulist Press • New York/Paramus/Toronto

Copyright © 1973 Augsburg Publishing House

Library of Congress Catalog Card No. 73-83787

International Standard Book No. 0-8066-1401-3

Published by
Augsburg Publishing House
Minneapolis, Minnesota

and

Paulist Press
New York/Paramus/Toronto

Manufactured in the United States of America

PREFACE

As will be described more fully in Chapter One, this discussion of *Peter in the New Testament* originated as background for a forthcoming study of *Papal Primacy,* the fifth volume in the series *Lutherans and Catholics in Dialogue.* The whole tone of the theological discussion in this National Dialogue has been set by an effort to see in a *new* light the old problems that have separated the churches.

When we who were involved in the National Dialogue approached the subject of the papacy in the context of the ministry to be exercised toward the church as a whole, we saw quickly that it would be essential for our task to have a thorough reassessment of the role of Peter in the New Testament according to modern critical scholarship. We were aware that some in Christendom have questioned both the propriety and the reliability of this critical approach to biblical research, and we ourselves recognized its limitations in reaching final theological conclusions. Nevertheless, we believed that responsible enquiry into original source materials was a necessary task and would greatly further mutual understanding of a central issue that has vexed Christian relationships over many centuries.

In order that this biblical study might be done with care and expertise, a task force of New Testament scholars was sponsored by the National Dialogue group for a period of two years. The membership, while predominantly Lutheran and Roman Catholic, was broadened to include scholars of several churches with the hope that the work done might serve other ecumenical dialogues and discussions as well.

While the New Testament study has been carried on with all

the techniques of scholarship, the editors have sought to phrase the results with an eye toward general intelligibility and pedagogy. The scholars on this New Testament task force have understood that they are speaking not only to other scholars but also to the parish clergy and knowledgeable laity of the churches. Precisely because the study is fundamental and of wide utility, we in the National Dialogue have decided to publish it separately, rather than to include it in the forthcoming dialogue volume. We hope that this wider exposure will make it the subject of study in ecumenical discussion groups and the text for adult education classes. Ample documentation and footnotes have been provided, so that the text can serve as a resource in college religion classes and in seminars at theological schools.

All those who take advantage of it will share our debt to the eleven contributing scholars who worked without remuneration or royalty. To a man they reported that they found the stimulation of working together in friendship and openness to be sufficient reward, and we think that their joy in harmonious discovery is attested in the results. At no period since the Reformation has such a joint effort on a divisive topic been possible. Finally, on behalf of the National Dialogue we express our appreciation to the Auburn Program of Union Theological Seminary (N.Y.C.) for having placed its library reading room at the disposal of the task force for its meetings.

Paul C. Empie   ✠ T. Austin Murphy
Former General Secretary   *Auxiliary Bishop of Baltimore*
U.S.A. National Committee   Bishop's Committee for
Lutheran World Federation   Ecumenical and Inter-
                                      religious Affairs

CONTENTS

CHAPTER ONE:
ORIGINS OF
THE STUDY[1]

A National Dialogue between Lutheran and Roman Catholic theologians began in July 1965 under the sponsorship of the U.S.A. National Committee of the Lutheran World Federation and the Committee for Ecumenical and Interreligious Affairs of the National Conference of Catholic Bishops. The first five years of these discussions produced joint statements on such sensitive topics as the creed, baptism, the eucharist, and ministry.[2] Scholars, responsible to their own traditions, were able in dialogue to reach a remarkable degree of agreement on basic points that have long divided the respective churches. Emboldened by this harmony, in their 1971 meetings[3] they began to discuss one of the thorniest problems arising from the Reformation: the problem of ministry in the universal church, with special emphasis on papal primacy.

---

[1] This chapter was composed by John Reumann and R. E. Brown.

[2] *Lutherans and Catholics in Dialogue,* Published Jointly by Representatives of the U.S.A. National Committee of the Lutheran World Federation (New York) and the Bishops' Commission for Ecumenical and Interreligious Affairs (Washington, D.C.): *I. The Status of the Nicene Creed as Dogma of the Church* (1965); *II. One Baptism for the Remission of Sins* (1966); *III. The Eucharist as Sacrifice* (1967); *IV. Eucharist and Ministry* (1970).

[3] The decision on the general topic was taken in the eleventh meeting of the National Dialogue at Chicago in October 1970; and the decisions leading directly to the task force on "Peter in the New Testament" were taken at the meetings of February 1971 (twelfth meeting, Miami) and of September 1971 (thirteenth meeting, Greenwich, Conn.).

1

It was quickly recognized that, in addition to the papers presented by the theologians involved in the National Dialogue, specialized studies would be needed in the history leading to the emergence of the papacy in the Western Church. In order that the work of the National Dialogue not become impossibly long, it was decided that smaller task forces of specialists be appointed to work on two particularly sensitive historical periods, namely, the New Testament and the Patristic periods.[4]

Two members of the National Dialogue, New Testament scholars themselves, Raymond E. Brown and John Reumann, were appointed respectively by the Roman Catholics and the Lutherans to organize and chair the task force on "Peter in the New Testament." Knowing that the subject of the Petrine office and the papacy would be of interest to many different ecumenical dialogues, they decided to invite scholars from traditions other than the Lutheran and Roman Catholic to join the members officially appointed by the National Dialogue. As a result the task force consisted of the following eleven members:

Lutherans Appointed by the National Dialogue

1. Rev. Dr. John Reumann (co-chairman), Lutheran Theological Seminary, Philadelphia.[5]
2. Rev. Dr. Joseph A. Burgess, Pastor of Zion and English Lutheran Churches, Regent, North Dakota.[6]
3. Rev. Dr. Karl P. Donfried, Smith College, Northampton, Massachusetts.

---

[4] The Patristics task force, co-chaired by the Rev. Dr. A. C. Piepkorn of Concordia Seminary, St. Louis, Missouri, and by Professor J. McCue of the School of Religion at the State University of Iowa (Iowa City), will make a separate report on the evidence pertaining to the first five centuries.

[5] Dr. Reumann was on sabbatical leave in India beginning in the fall of 1972 and so was not present for the final sessions of the task force. During his absence, Dr. Froehlich was designated as acting co-chairman for the Lutheran side.

[6] Dr. Burgess wrote his doctoral dissertation on *A History of the Exegesis of Matthew 16:17-19 from 1781 to 1965* (Basel, 1965). Geographical distance permitted him to attend only the sessions on "Peter in the Gospel of Matthew"; his place at the other sessions was taken by Dr. Krodel.

Roman Catholics Appointed by the National Dialogue

4. Rev. Dr. Raymond E. Brown, S.S. (co-chairman), Union Theological Seminary and Woodstock College, New York City.
5. Rev. Msgr. Myles M. Bourke, Rector of Corpus Christi Church and Adjunct Professor at Fordham University, New York City.
6. Rev. Dr. Joseph A. Fitzmyer, S.J., Fordham University, New York City.

Invited Scholars

7. Rev. Dr. Paul J. Achtemeier, Union Theological Seminary, Richmond, Virginia.
8. Dr. (Theol.) Karlfried Froehlich, Princeton Theological Seminary, Princeton, New Jersey.[7]
9. Rev. Dr. Reginald H. Fuller, Protestant Episcopal Seminary, Alexandria, Virginia.[8]
10. Rev. Dr. Gerhard Krodel, Lutheran Theological Seminary, Philadelphia, Pennsylvania.[9]
11. Rev. Dr. P. Schuyler Brown, S.J., Woodstock College, New York City.[10]

Between October 1971 and March 1973 the task force held some fifteen sessions, usually of about three hours duration, in the Auburn Library of Union Theological Seminary (N.Y.C.). As background the task force had available three unpublished papers on Peter that had earlier been presented to the National Dialogue,[11] and a number of observations from those papers

---

[7] A member of the National Lutheran-Roman Catholic Dialogue, Dr. Froehlich participated as a liaison with the Patristics Task Force. See notes 4 and 5 above.

[8] During the 1971-72 academic year Dr. Fuller was on the faculty of Union Theological Seminary, New York City.

[9] See note 6 above.

[10] Provisionally assigned to draft a paper on Peter's role in the New Testament for another national dialogue, Dr. Schuyler Brown began to participate only in the April 1972 (eighth) session.

[11] These papers (presented at Miami in February 1971) consisted of: Raymond E. Brown, "Peter and the New Testament"; Jerome Quinn, "To

found their way into this final study. But the task force's proper work consisted in the detailed study of the New Testament evidence, roughly in chronological order, beginning with Paul's letters. One or more sessions were devoted to each section of the New Testament, as reflected in the chapters of this book. A member of the task force was asked to compose beforehand a list of questions that would point up the most important issues to be considered, and then to lead the discussions at the actual sessions which dealt with his questions.[12]

Detailed minutes, and sometimes tapes, of the discussions were recorded,[13] and these minutes were subsequently circulated for correction. After approval of the minutes, K. Donfried used them to compose a rough draft of what would become a final statement. This initial draft was circulated for comments, in the light of which a committee[14] rewrote it. The rewritten draft, which constituted a truly formative stage in the history of the document, was then recirculated for reactions. These reactions were given to R. E. Brown who completely rewrote the draft a second time. All the participants saw this second draft and submitted suggestions. R. E. Brown and K. Froehlich incorporated these suggestions into the final typescript, submitting to the last meeting of the task force (March 1973) points that required fuller discussion.

It is significant that all those engaged in the task force enjoyed this form of collaborative study and learned immensely from it. The interchange opened new horizons for all, so that the end product was achieved, not so much by way of com-

---

Visit Cephas"; John Reumann, "Comments on Peter in the New Testament."

[12] The first footnote in each chapter will report how many sessions were devoted to the material under discussion and who led the discussion.

[13] Throughout most of the academic year 1971-72 J. Reumann served as secretary, taking the minutes. When he was absent and during his sabbatical (note 5 above), minutes were taken by P. Achtemeier, J. A. Fitzmyer, G. Krodel, and R. E. Brown.

[14] Redrafting sessions were held in May 1972 at Philadelphia; in August 1972 at Claremont, California; and in December 1972 at New York City. R. E. Brown and K. P. Donfried took part in all of them; J. Reumann participated in the Philadelphia session, and P. Achtemeier in part of the Claremont session.

promise and concession, but by way of mutual and creative discovery. Indeed, the comment was often made that we should continue something like this because we were profiting from it more than we profited from professional biblical meetings. There was no embarrassment about making suggestions and having them roundly rejected. Perhaps, after all, we caught a bit of the spirit of our apostolic saint who accomplished so much for the church, but only after he had been guilty of some of the most memorable blunders in the New Testament.

Before we begin the report itself, we must emphasize that it has emerged as *a collective study,* i.e., a study truly representative of discussions by a group of scholars. Each member of the task force contributed to it in different ways, but the end product is not what anyone of us would have written personally. In the publication of our collaborative effort, individuals have at times agreed to the serious consideration of views that they would not choose to make their own. The norm was not total agreement, but a consensus about the reasonable limits of plausibility. The editing, which consisted largely in giving intelligible expression and order to this variety of views, has also respected the collaborative nature of the project.

CHAPTER TWO:
PRESUPPOSITIONS FOR
THE STUDY[15]

Our study of the role of Peter in the New Testament will presuppose the attitudes and methods common in contemporary biblical criticism. We have found it useful to spell these out at the beginning, so that the reason for and the consistency of our later procedures will be clear.

A. The Nature of the New Testament Writings

The New Testament writings, composed within a range of approximately twenty to one hundred years after the ministry of Jesus of Nazareth, are not documents whose purpose is to present us with scientific history.[16] This is obvious in the case of the New Testament letters which are aimed at community

---

[15] The material for the chapter was supplied by John Reumann from the paper he had prepared for the National Dialogue meeting in Miami (note 11 above); it was rewritten by R. E. Brown.

[16] This recognition of the implications of historical criticism was first achieved by Protestant scholars and has produced an enormous literature. More recently it has been accepted by Roman Catholic scholars, particularly under the rubric of acknowledging the different literary forms present in the New Testament (a principle proposed by Pope Pius XII in his 1943 encyclical *Divino Afflante Spiritu*). In particular, see Augustin Cardinal Bea, *The Study of the Synoptic Gospels: New Approaches and Outlooks,* Eng. version ed. J. A. Fitzmyer (New York: Harper & Row, 1965); and *The Jerome Biblical Commentary,* ed. R. E. Brown, J. A. Fitzmyer, R. E. Murphy (Englewood Cliffs: Prentice Hall, 1968), especially articles 41 and 71.

needs and problems, but it is also true of writings that have a narrative content, e. g., the Gospels and Acts. Even these are not impartial records, but documents in which faith has shaped the presentation. Students of the Scriptures are familiar with the "quest of the historical Jesus," a quest that implies a development from what obtained in the actual ministry of Jesus to the post-resurrectional pictures of Christ that appear in the New Testament writings. Similarly, in the present study we do not neglect a quest for the historical Simon (Cephas, Peter).[17] But our primary concern will be to trace how the historical facts about this companion of Jesus have been developed into the New Testament portrait of the best known of the Twelve apostles.

A stress on the New Testament writings as documents reflecting the faith and milieu of early Christians warns us to be careful not only about their relation to earlier history (the ministry of Jesus) but also about their relation to later history, i.e., the life and problems of the subsequent church. We have stated that we are making this assessment of the role of Peter in the New Testament as a background for modern ecumenical discussion of the role of the papacy in the universal church. However, that does not mean that we can read the New Testament in the light of such a later problem. No matter what one may think about the justification offered by the New Testament for the emergence of the papacy, this papacy in its developed form cannot be read back into the New Testament; and it will help neither papal opponents nor papal supporters to have the model of the later papacy before their eyes when discussing the role of Peter. For that very reason we have tended to avoid "loaded" terminology in reference to Peter, e.g., primacy, juris-

---

[17] The similarity between the quest for the historical Jesus and the quest for the historical Simon carries over into nomenclature. Jesus has become known by the title given him in Christian faith: "Christ" (from *Christos,* the Greek translation of the Hebrew title "Messiah"). Similarly Simon, son of Jonah or John (Matt 16:17; John 1:42), has become known by the surname or sobriquet: "Cephas" or "Peter" (reflecting the Aramaic and Greek words for "rock," respectively *Kēphā'* and *Petra*). And just as we find in the New Testament the combined personal name and title "Jesus Christ," so we find "Simon Peter," with special frequency in John.

diction. Too often in the past, arguments about whether or not Peter had a "universal primacy" have blinded scholars to a more practical agreement about such things as the widely accepted importance of Peter in the New Testament and his diversified image.

B. The Composition of the New Testament Books Used in This Study

We have decided to study the role of Peter in the New Testament in a roughly chronological fashion, starting with the picture of Peter in the oldest New Testament writings (the Pauline letters) and ending with the evaluation of him in the latest works (concluding with II Peter). Such a method implies judgments about when and how the writings were composed.

1. *The Letters of Paul.* There are important references to Peter in Galatians and I (and perhaps II) Corinthians, letters from about the mid-50's.[18] The antiquity of these references is underlined by the fact that Paul is sometimes referring to dealings with Peter that occurred very much earlier, in which he himself was involved. Of course, even such eyewitness references must be seen in the setting of the Pauline letters where Paul is using them to establish his point (e.g., his references to Peter in Galatians are part of Paul's defense of his gospel and his apostleship).

2. *The Book of Acts.* Treating Acts in second place constitutes our main departure from chronological sequence, for we accept the common scholarly view that Luke-Acts was written toward the end of the first century and, thus, after the Gospel of Mark. It is maintained by many scholars that Luke used more ancient sources in composing the Book of Acts, but it is *not* for that reason that we put Acts after the Pauline letters; for we recognize that, even if and when he did use sources, Luke reshaped them into a programmatic theological

---

[18] Paul refers to "Cephas" in Gal 1:18; 2:9, 11, 14 and in I Cor 1:12; 3:22; 9:5; 15:5, but to "Peter" only in Gal 2:7-8. The possible references to Peter in II Corinthians are by implication; see note 81 below.

history *(Heilsgeschichte)*. Thus our sequence does not imply in any way that Acts has a historical value equal to that of Paul's letters when they are both describing the same events. Our sequence in this instance is topical, i.e., it is based on the fact that often Paul and Acts describe the same or roughly contemporary events pertaining to Peter. To have put Acts in its proper chronological order (after the Gospel of Luke) would also have had the unhappy effect of breaking up our sequence of treating Peter as he appears in the four Gospels.

The judgment that Acts cannot be treated as "straight history," reporting in every case things "as they actually happened" (*wie es eigentlich gewesen ist*), will constitute for many of our readers one of the major departures from past evaluations of Peter. Luke's picture of Peter and Paul as the two chief figures in early church history, with roughly half of Acts devoted to Peter, and the second half devoted to Paul, reflects Luke's skill as a theological writer: he has chosen this method of unifying his picture of how the word of God advanced into the Roman Empire. Acts contains facts about Peter's role in this advance, but it also reflects the "tendencies of the Lucan writing of history";[19] and we shall have to attempt to distinguish between these aspects.

3. *The Gospels.* Peter appears prominently in all four Gospels. We shall work with the assumption that Mark was the first of our Gospels, and was used as a source in the composition of the Gospels of Matthew and Luke. We shall treat John as the last of the four Gospels to be completed. We have already stressed that the Gospels give us a picture that has developed beyond the historical ministry of Jesus. But besides distinguishing between the historical level and the Gospel level, precisely because we accept the thesis of pre-Gospel sources or material, we shall have to subdivide the Gospel level into the level of the pre-Gospel sources and their theological outlook, and the level of the evangelist and his theological outlook in the process of redacting his sources and fitting the whole Gospel together. And so, when we treat the picture of Peter in

---

[19] E. Dinkler, "Petrus, Apostel," *Die Religion in Geschichte und Gegenwart,* vol. 5 (3rd ed.; Tübingen: Mohr, 1961), col. 248.

the individual passages of the Gospels, we shall generally find ourselves asking questions on three levels: (a) the level of history: Are we dealing with a scene or saying that wholly or partially stems from the ministry of Jesus; and if so, what import did it have in that history? (b) the level of pre-Gospel source or tradition: Did the scene or saying come to the evangelist from an earlier source on which he is dependent; and if so, what was the interpretation of it in that source? (c) the level of the evangelist or of redaction (*Redaktionsgeschichte*): To what extent has the scene been influenced or even created by the evangelist himself, and what does he mean to convey by it in the context of the whole Gospel?

The identification of pre-Gospel sources is often tentative. This affects not only conclusions about the theological outlook on Peter in the sources, but even, to some extent, conclusions about the theological outlook in the Gospels; for some judgments about the mind of the evangelist are made on the basis of our evidence of how he treated and modified his sources. Nevertheless, one is usually on firmer ground in determining what the evangelist meant than in determining the meaning of a pre-Gospel source, written or oral.

We shall deal with the likelihood of a specific picture of Peter in each Gospel. The view that "there is no difference between the individual Synoptists in their treatment of Peter," though "we find a rather different picture in John's Gospel,"[20] has been superseded in more recent study by the recognition that there are different accents in each Gospel.[21]

4. *The Gospel of Mark.* Since we accept Marcan priority, the question of this evangelist's sources and of his own attitude toward Peter is highly significant for our study. While it has been recognized from antiquity that the evangelist himself was not an eyewitness, it has been held on the basis of a second-century statement from Papias[22] that Mark was "Peter's inter-

---

[20] O. Cullmann, *"Petros," Theological Dictionary of the New Testament*, ed. G. Kittel and G. Friedrich, vol. 6 (Grand Rapids: Eerdmans, 1968, from German, 1959), p. 102.

[21] E.g., Dinkler (note 19 above), col. 248.

[22] Eusebius, *Church History*, III, 39:14-15.

preter" and thus incorporated Peter's own testimony.[23] Many today, while still allowing the possibility that Peter stands behind some material in Mark (e.g., the healing of Simon's mother-in-law, 1:30-31), are not inclined to rate the Papias tradition so highly.[24] In particular, the view of direct dependency upon Peter is brought into doubt by form criticism which detects material in Mark that for some time circulated orally in short units, serving church interests, and was probably of anonymous, often communitarian, origin or shaping. And so, for instance, we shall have to ask whether a scene such as Mark 8:27-33 (Peter's confession of Jesus at Caesarea Philippi) constitutes a verbatim transcript, as was traditionally held, or is the product of a complicated development, involving some historical memories about Peter, post-Easter reflection by the Christian community, and editing by Mark the evangelist.[25] Finally, after

---

[23] See V. Taylor, *The Gospel According to St. Mark* (London: Macmillan, 1955), pp. 26ff., 74-75, 82, 168, and passim. But even Taylor (p. 3) admits that "the Papias tradition ... ought not to be taken as covering everything contained in Mark, and not necessarily the greater part of the Gospel, for there are clear signs that the Evangelist used other traditions in both narratives and sayings."

[24] W. G. Kümmel, *Introduction to the New Testament* (Nashville: Abingdon, 1966), p. 69, characterizes it as "untrustworthy." Such a critical judgment may sound arbitrary, but a careful scrutiny of the Papias statement reveals nuances that must be taken into account. One has to distinguish between what Papias says on his own and what he attributes to "the elder" (*ho presbyteros*—whoever that may be). To the latter Papias attributes the following statement: "When Mark became Peter's interpreter, he wrote down accurately, though not in order (*ou mentoi taxei*), as much as (*hosa*) he remembered of what had been said or done by the Lord." Papias then explains that Mark "had not heard the Lord or followed him," but later followed Peter. Papias concludes, "So Mark wrote down some of the things as he remembered them; for he made it his sole concern to omit nothing (*mēden*) of what he had heard nor to falsify anything in that." The real question is centered on what basis Papias had for his last claim, which to a modern reader may sound naive. Contrast the "as much as" (*hosa*) of the earlier statement with the "nothing" (*mēden*) here. Again, it is not clear what is meant by "not in order"; it could possibly refer to a chronological ordering of details of the ministry of Jesus or to a literary order (e.g., not in the order given by Matthew). Consequently, little is gained by stressing the reliability of the Papias testimony or the extent to which it may be applicable.

[25] Indeed, radical scholarship might dispense altogether with a basis in historical memories about Peter. Roman Catholic readers of this study may wonder whether a theory of creative Gospel development is conso-

discussing such questions, we shall have to assess the general attitude of the Gospel of Mark toward Peter: is it pro-Petrine, or anti-Petrine, or both, or neither?[26]

5. *The Gospel of Matthew.* Despite the name attached to this Gospel, we accept the now almost-universal opinion of scholars that the evangelist was not Matthew (or Levi), one of the Twelve companions of Jesus, but a "second-generation" Christian, living late in the first century. Not an eyewitness himself, the evangelist drew upon the Gospel of Mark, upon "Q" (a collection of sayings material common to Matthew and Luke),[27]

---

nant with their Church's position. Two Roman Church documents offer guidance on this: the 1964 Instruction from the Pontifical Biblical Commission entitled "On the Historical Truth of the Gospels" (published with a commentary by J. A. Fitzmyer [Paramus: Paulist Press, 1964]); and the 1965 Constitution of Vatican II on Divine Revelation (*Dei Verbum,* especially V, 19). These documents distinguish three stages of development in the Gospel tradition. First, the tradition begins with the words and deeds of the *historical Jesus;* second, it passes through a period of *apostolic preaching,* where there is already considerable growth because faith now colors the memory of what Jesus said and did; and third, it is written down by the *sacred writers* who select, synthesize, and "explicate" material taken from the apostolic preaching. The hint that the sacred writers are separated from Jesus by a generation of apostolic preachers, together with the reference to their "explicating" (expanding) the tradition, has encouraged many Catholic scholars to posit considerable creativity within the process of Gospel development. Indeed, the Biblical Commission Instruction itself goes so far as to tell Catholics that the Gospels do not necessarily relate the sayings of Jesus literally (IX), and that his doctrine and life were not simply reported to be remembered, "but were 'preached' so as to offer the Church a basis of faith and morals" (X).

[26] R. Bultmann, *The History of the Synoptic Tradition* (New York: Harper & Row, 1963, from the German 2nd ed., 1931), p. 258, argues that Mark has suppressed some older Jewish-Christian pro-Petrine material (now found in Matthew, e.g., Matt 16:17-19) and, under the influence of a Hellenistic Christianity represented by Paul, has introduced a polemic against Peter. See also *Zeitschrift für die neutestamentliche Wissenschaft* 19 (1919-20), p. 170. On the other hand, M. Goguel, *The Primitive Church* (New York: Macmillan, 1964, from French, 1949), p. 187, maintains: "There is no trace of anti-Petrinism in Mark." For further discussion see the references in notes 136 and 137 below.

[27] Only in Matt 18:21 (parallel Luke 17:4) and in Luke 12:40-42 (parallel Matt 24:44-45) are there possible instances of a reference to Peter in material generally assigned to "Q." However, as we shall see on pp. 78 and 113 below, in each instance the reference to Peter is found in the one Gospel but not in the other, and so is probably a redactional addition, by Matthew and Luke respectively, to the "Q" material.

and upon some special material.[28] Each of these non-Marcan sources may have had its own particular accent regarding Peter, and the evangelist may have taken over such accents and/or imposed his own outlook.[29]

6. *The Gospel of Luke.* We assume that, like the Gospel of Matthew, this Gospel was composed late in the first century and that the evangelist drew upon the Gospel of Mark, upon "Q," and upon some special material.[30] The fact that Luke and Acts are meant to be complementary must be taken into con-

---

[28] The special Matthean source is sometimes called "M." There are three important scenes (or parts of scenes) involving Peter that are peculiar to Matthew: Peter's walking on the water (Matt 14:28-31); Peter's confession of Jesus as the Son of the living God and Jesus' commending him (Matt 16:16b-19); Peter and the coin in the fish's mouth (Matt 17:24-27).

[29] It has been argued (already in Origen) that in Matthew's Gospel Peter takes on a symbolic significance as a model of what discipleship involves. See J. Reumann, *Jesus in the Church's Gospels* (Philadelphia: Fortress, 1968), pp. 309-13 (cf. 265) and notes; G. Strecker, *Der Weg der Gerechtigkeit: Untersuchung zur Theologie des Matthäus* (Forschungen zur Religion und Literatur des Alten und Neuen Testaments, 82; 3rd ed.; Göttingen: Vandenhoeck, 1971), pp. 198-206, 254; E. Haenchen, "Die Komposition von Mk. viii 27—ix 1 und Par.," *Novum Testamentum* 6 (1963), pp. 102, 109; W. Trilling, "Amt und Amtsverständnis bei Matthäus," *Mélanges bibliques en hommage au R. P. Béda Rigaux*, ed. A. Descamps and A. de Halleux (Gembloux: Duculot, 1970), pp. 42-44. While the task force was sympathetic to this approach to Peter as a model of discipleship, the group as a whole did not regard it as the only, or even as the major, key to the Matthean Petrine material.

[30] The question of Luke's special source(s) is a complicated one in the light of the "Proto-Luke" hypothesis advanced by B. H. Streeter (1924). Streeter maintained that Luke drew upon an ancient narrative source, independent of Mark, into which the "Q" material had already been fused. He regarded Proto-Luke and Mark as of approximately equal historical value. Without committing ourselves to such a theory, we have recognized the possibility of material independently available to Luke ("L"). The pertinence of this special Lucan material to a discussion of Peter is more limited than in the case of the special Matthean material. It involves details about the miraculous catch of fish in Luke 5:1-11; the prayer of Jesus in 22:31-32 that Simon will turn again to strengthen his brethren; and the affirmation in Luke 24:34 ("The Lord ... has appeared to Simon"). For a recent discussion of Luke's sources, see J. A. Fitzmyer, "The Priority of Mark and the 'Q' Source in Luke," *Jesus and Man's Hope*, vol. 1 (Pittsburgh Theological Seminary; *Perspective* 11 [1970]), pp. 131-70.

sideration when we consider the special Lucan portrait of Peter in the Gospel.

7. *The Gospel of John.* Once more, despite the name attached to this Gospel, we have accepted the increasingly common opinion that the evangelist was not John, son of Zebedee and companion of Jesus, but an unknown "second-generation" Christian.[31] While the Fourth Gospel was probably completed after the Synoptic Gospels, we have not posited any necessary Johannine dependence upon the Synoptics and have left open the possibility that this evangelist may have drawn upon (relatively old) sources independent of even the pre-Synoptic sources.[32] The Johannine portrait of Simon Peter requires special attention because, besides a half-dozen references akin to Synoptic references,[33] there are a number of important scenes involving Peter that are peculiar to the Fourth Gospel.[34] In particular, Simon Peter is frequently associated with the "disciple whom Jesus loved,"[35] a mysterious figure whose historical sig-

---

[31] For our purposes it has not been necessary to take any position on whether or not the "Beloved Disciple" (mentioned in John 19:35 and 21:24 as a source of the Gospel's testimony) was John, son of Zebedee, or on whether the evangelist was a follower of the Beloved Disciple, a theory that might establish a chain of eyewitness tradition. While Roman Catholic scholars continued to identify John, son of Zebedee, as the evangelist throughout the first half of this century, that position has been abandoned in the two most recent commentaries by Catholics: R. E. Brown, *The Gospel According to John,* I-XII (Anchor Bible, 29; Garden City: Doubleday, 1966), pp. xcviii-cii; R. Schnackenburg, *The Gospel According to St. John* (New York: Herder and Herder, 1968), pp. 75-104.

[32] The thesis of basic Johannine independence of the Synoptics has become the majority opinion in Fourth Gospel research. Especially influential for English-speaking scholarship were the works of P. Gardner-Smith, *Saint John and the Synoptic Gospels* (Cambridge University, 1938) and of C. H. Dodd, *Historical Tradition in the Fourth Gospel* (Cambridge University, 1963).

[33] E.g., Simon Peter is called a disciple; his name is changed from Simon to Cephas (John 1:42); he confesses Jesus, serving as a type of spokesman of the Twelve (6:67-69); Jesus predicts his denial (13:36-38); and he actually denies Jesus three times (18:17-18, 25-27).

[34] The peculiarly Johannine scenes that do not involve Simon with the Beloved Disciple include the footwashing (13:6-11) and Simon's cutting off the ear of the servant of the high priest at the time of Jesus' arrest (18:10-11).

[35] Simon Peter and the Beloved Disciple are associated at the Last Supper (13:23-25), at the empty tomb of Jesus (20:2-10), and at the

nificance and whose importance to the Johannine community are variously assessed. Moreover, in evaluating the conception of Peter in the Gospel of John, we must keep in mind overall problems about the Johannine concept of the church (and its structure) and the absence of the term "apostle(s)" in John.[36]

8. *The Two Epistles of Peter.* The author of I Peter identifies himself as "Peter, an apostle of Jesus Christ"; the author of II Peter identifies himself as "Simeon Peter, servant and apostle of Jesus Christ." Yet the claim of Petrine authorship for both epistles is under varying degrees of suspicion.

Many serious scholars still accept a Petrine authorship of I Peter, at least in the sense that Peter stands behind the letter, with Silvanus as his amanuensis or secretary (5:12).[37] Increasingly, however, the weight of biblical scholarship has moved toward regarding the work as pseudonymous and attributing to it a date considerably later than Peter's lifetime.[38] (Presumably Peter died in the 60's.) While the question of authorship and dating has importance for our study, of more importance is the indisputable existence of a tradition that reveres Peter, has him address significant geographical areas where Paul had been influential, and has him speak to the presbyters of the churches as "a fellow presbyter and a witness of Christ's sufferings" (5:1). The fact that the epistle conveys greetings from "the woman who dwells in Babylon" (the church of Rome?—5:13) is important as part of the tradition connecting Peter with Rome.

We have accepted the almost unanimous verdict of critical

---

post-resurrectional appearance on the shore of the Sea of Tiberias (21:7, 20-23). See also the scene involving Simon Peter with an unnamed disciple who was known to the high priest (the Beloved Disciple? —18:15-16).

[36] For a discussion of whether or not there is a theology of the church in John, see Brown (note 31 above), pp. cv-cxi, and the literature cited there. The Fourth Gospel mentions the Twelve (but gives no list of their names); it never speaks of "apostles" as a specific designation (cf. John 13:16); it does refer to a "sending" (*apostellein,* 4:38; *pempein,* 20:21).

[37] See J. A. Fitzmyer, *Jerome Biblical Commentary* (note 16 above), article 58, #2; E. G. Selwyn, *The First Epistle of St. Peter* (London: Macmillan, 1958), pp. 9-33.

[38] Kümmel (note 24 above), pp. 298-99: "a pseudonymous writing," A.D. 90-95; F. W. Beare, *The First Epistle of Peter* (3rd ed.; Oxford: Blackwell, 1970): early second century.

scholarship that II Peter is not authentically Petrine and that it may have been the last of the New Testament works to be composed (first half of the second century?). Of significance is its appeal to Peter as an eyewitness authenticator of Gospel-like tradition about the historical Jesus (1:16-18, presumably a reference to the Transfiguration) and as an authority who can correct misinterpretations of Paul (3:14-16).

C. Theological Methodology in Evaluating the New Testament Evidence

Even after scholars have discussed and agreed upon positions in relation to the composition of pertinent New Testament books, there remain more general problems of a theological nature that emerge again and again. It is well to call the reader's attention to some of these at the outset, with a caution that they are not settled in scholarly and ecumenical circles today.

1. *The Role of the New Testament Canon.* The authors of this book (and the confessions of which they are members) are at one in acknowledging which books constitute the canonical New Testament scriptures. Much more difficult is the issue of a "canon within the canon"—a modern designation for a select group of New Testament writings which (for historical and/or theological reasons) are regarded as more central or normative than others. Are all New Testament books or traditions, just because they are in the canon, to be regarded as of equal weight? Or are some to be rated above, and thus "more canonical" than, others (e.g., the "genuine" Pauline letters over the dubiously Pauline or deutero-Pauline letters)? If so, what is the criterion for determining which books or traditions are the more normative?[39] Since this study was prompted by the

---

[39] For discussions in English of this complicated problem, see E. Käsemann, "The Canon of the New Testament and the Unity of the Church," *Essays on New Testament Themes* (Studies in Biblical Theology, 41; London: SCM, 1964); R. E. Brown, *Jerome Biblical Commentary* (note 16 above), article 67, ##92-97; W. Marxsen, *The New Testament as the Church's Book* (Philadelphia: Fortress, 1972).

National (U. S. A.) Dialogue between Lutherans and Roman Catholics, it is worth recalling that among the twenty-three (of the twenty-seven) New Testament works numbered by Luther in his 1522 German edition were all the books we have listed above as forming the basis of our study,[40] including books about whose apostolic authorship there is now doubt. The modern problem of the "canon within the canon" would affect such points as the discrepancies or theological differences between the Pauline letters and Acts, or between the Pauline letters and II Peter.

2. *Pluralism within the New Testament.* As the last sentence indicates, the problem of the more-or-less normative character of a New Testament book is closely related to that of diversity in theological outlook among the biblical authors and in early Christianity. One can no longer ask about *the* New Testament view of Peter, but rather about New Testament views. It is very likely that some sections of the early church attributed greater prestige and authority to Peter than to any other church leader. But this was not necessarily true of all segments of early Christianity (or of the New Testament). It is more than likely that other segments of the church revered another disciple or other disciples as much as they revered Peter or even more than Peter if they were founded by another apostle. What implications does this have for the question of Peter's preeminent ministry to the church as a whole? Were some sections of Christianity (as reflected in New Testament traditions?) even anti-Petrine? Recent scholarship has become aware of all these pluralistic possibilities within canonical Scripture; and in our study of the traditions about Peter, we have had to contrast traditions with one another and with possible rival traditions.[41]

---

[40] The unnumbered books were Hebrews, James, Jude, and Revelation. In his Preface to this edition, where he speaks about "the truest and noblest books of the New Testament," Luther identifies some of the twenty-three numbered books as "the true kernel and marrow of all the books." Acts and II Peter would not belong to this thus further refined group. See *The Reformation Writings of Martin Luther,* vol. II: *The Spirit of the Protestant Reformation,* ed. B. L. Woolf (London: Lutterworth, 1956), p. 283.

[41] In particular the thesis that James was a rival of Peter for first position in the church or even superseded him—cf. E. Stauffer, *New*

At this juncture it may be pertinent to remark that a naive appeal to "the unity of the New Testament Scriptures" cannot be allowed to obscure the plurality of nuances about Peter in the various New Testament traditions concerning him. To admit such pluralism does not constitute the denial of a unity; but it forces the critical Christian theologian to rethink the form of that unity and to consider the interaction of pluralism and unity in the light of his convictions about God's provident direction of the Christian church.

3. *The Relation between Historicity and Tradition.* We have already stated our acceptance of the thesis that not all the New Testament books, not even all the Gospels, can be thought to give us "straight history"; and we have alerted the reader that often, even though they bear titles that mention companions of Jesus, the New Testament books were written by second- or third-generation Christians who were not eyewitnesses and *sometimes* were not able to authenticate the factual character of what they recorded. In an older approach to the Scriptures our increasing inability to affirm the absolute historicity of Peter's deeds and words would have deprived much of our material of any value, since the debate about such problems as Peter's role always centered on what had really happened in the ministry of Jesus or in the Jerusalem church (i.e., in the decades of the 20's and 30's). This is no longer true; for even when we are sure that we are not dealing with exact history or genuine sayings, the Petrine material may still have much to tell us about the role of Peter. Whether historical or not, what the New Testament writers report about Peter represents at least Christian thought about Peter—it represents what the writers or their sources believe to have happened and thus the role which was being given to Peter at the time the particular New

---

Testament Theology (London: SCM, 1955), p. 34. Specifically, J. Jeremias, *New Testament Theology, Part One* (New York: Scribner's, 1971), p. 307, thinks that "radical groups in Palestinian Jewish Christianity" took offense at the universalistic ideas of Peter (Gal 2:12b; Acts 11:2), even to the point of suppressing the account of the first appearance of the risen Lord to Peter (I Cor 15:5; Luke 24:34) by assigning that appearance to James, as recorded in the *Gospel to the Hebrews.* See notes 70, 71, and 79 below.

Testament books were written (the period from the 50's to the early second century). Even if one were to conclude that Jesus did not say, "You are Peter and on this rock I will build my church . . ." in July of A.D. 29 at Caesarea Philippi,[42] that would not settle the issue. This tradition, embedded in Matt 16:18, was maintained somewhere in the first-century church and represents a Christian evaluation of Peter's position with which we must cope.

D. Early Extra-Biblical Evidence

We have no intention of carrying our study of Peter into the Patristic period,[43] but we must call attention to some extra-biblical evidence that is pertinent to the New Testament period.

First, there are early Christian writings that are contemporary with the latest New Testament works. While they do not add much to our historical knowledge about Peter, they may be helpful in clarifying some points of the New Testament tradition. For instance, the New Testament makes no express reference to Peter's presence or residence in Rome and his Roman martyrdom, and indeed these incidents are not explicitly attested before the second half of the second century.[44] Yet, strong circumstantial evidence for Peter's martyrdom in Rome under Nero results from combining New Testament *hints* about Peter's death (John 21:18-19)[45] and about Peter's presence in Rome (I Peter 5:13) with the implications of *I Clement*

---

[42] This dating is given by H. Daniel-Rops, *The Life of Our Lord* (Twentieth Century Encyclopedia of Catholicism, 68; New York: Hawthorn, 1964), p. 173. E. Stauffer, *Jesus and His Story* (London: SCM, 1960), p. 76, dates Peter's confession to the fall A.D. 31, specifically to the 10th of Tishri (the Day of Atonement), without, however, referring to Matt 16:17-19.

[43] See note 4 above.

[44] Cullmann, *"Petros"* (note 20 above), p. 111.

[45] Cullmann, *Peter—Disciple, Apostle, Martyr* (2nd ed.; Philadelphia: Westminster, 1962), pp. 84-91, adds II Peter 1:14 and Rev 11:3ff. as possible allusions to Peter's martyrdom, but finds equivocal the reference to Peter as a "witness" (*martys*) in I Peter 5:1.

5:1—6:1[46] and Ignatius, *Romans* 4:3[47]—thus, with implications of extra-biblical testimony from *ca.* A.D. 100.

Second, the archaeological evidence for the presence of Peter in Rome, his martyrdom and burial there, must be taken into consideration. Given the present state of the discussion, it is most probable, in our opinion, that Peter did get to Rome late in his career and was martyred and buried there. The same cannot be said about the question of whether he served as local "bishop" of the Roman community and whether he appointed his successors in the Roman bishopric.[48] This judgment of probability decides, on the one hand, against those who claim that Peter never reached Rome,[49] and, on the other hand, against a simplistic acceptance of later traditions concerning what Peter did in Rome. The precise results of recent excavations under St. Peter's basilica in Rome continue to be debated.[50]

---

[46] M. Smith, "The Report about Peter in I Clement V.4," *New Testament Studies* 7 (1960-61), pp. 86-88, suggests that this key report can be explained entirely from materials in the Book of Acts. Such a view of *I Clement* has not found a wide following; nevertheless, it should make us cautious in drawing upon later or extra-canonical traditions for Petrine data not found in the New Testament.

[47] Cf. also the *Ascension of Isaiah* 4:2-3. In general, we have no intention of entering the field of Christian apocrypha, a study that properly belongs to Patristic enquiry. There are extensive references in the apocrypha to Peter's missionary activities, his visions, and his martyrdom. In E. Hennecke, *New Testament Apocrypha*, ed. W. Schneemelcher (2 vols.; Philadelphia: Westminster, 1963, 1965), see *The Gospel of Peter* (I, pp. 179-87); *The Kerygma(ta) Petrou* (II, pp. 94-127); *The Acts of Peter* (II, pp. 259-321); *The Pseudo-Clementines* (II, pp. 532-70); *The Apocalypse of Peter* (II, pp. 663-83); also II, pp. 572-75. In the Nag-Hammadi finds, there is also Petrine material: *The Acts of Peter and the Twelve Apostles* (Codex VI, Tractate 1); *The Apocalypse of Peter* (Codex VII, Tractate 3); *The Letter of Peter which He Sent to Philip* (Codex VIII, Tractate 2)—cf. J. M. Robinson, "The Coptic Gnostic Library Today," *New Testament Studies* 14 (1967-68), pp. 397, 399-400.

[48] O. Cullmann, *Peter* (note 45 above), especially pp. 113-23; D. W. O'Connor, *Peter in Rome: The Literary, Liturgical, and Archaeological Evidence* (New York: Columbia University, 1969), especially p. 209.

[49] K. Heussi, *Die römische Petrustradition in kritischer Sicht* (Tübingen: Mohr, 1955); E. T. Merrill, *Essays in Early Christian History* (London: Macmillan, 1924), pp. 267-333.

[50] On June 26, 1968, Pope Paul VI announced that bones found in excavating had been convincingly identified as those of Peter. See O'Connor (note 48 above), pp. 135ff., 201, 205-9; but also the review of O'Connor by T. D. Barnes, *Journal of Theological Studies* 21 (1970),

Having made these general remarks of an introductory nature, we are now prepared to examine the evidence of the individual books of the New Testament for their evidence pertaining to Peter.

pp. 175-79. A good survey of the whole problem is offered by G. F. Snyder, "Survey and 'New' Thesis on the Bones of Peter," *Biblical Archaeologist* 32 (1969), pp. 2-24.

CHAPTER THREE:
PETER IN THE
PAULINE LETTERS[51]

A rapid review of Galatians and I Corinthians suggests that Peter held a place of importance for Paul. This assertion is supported by the following observations:

—Peter is the first-named *witness* in the list of those who have seen the risen Jesus (I Cor 15:5).

—Peter served Paul as a *source of tradition about Jesus*. This depends on our understanding Gal 1:18 to mean that after three years Paul went up to Jerusalem "to get information [about Jesus] from Cephas."[52] Yet this does not necessarily

---

[51] The discussion for this chapter was led by K. P. Donfried and J. A. Fitzmyer. Four sessions of the task force (November 1971 through February 1972) were devoted to the Pauline evidence, although, since this was the first material we treated, the sessions included a broad consideration of New Testament data and some questions of method.

[52] The problem is centered on the translation of the Greek verb *historēsai;* see G. D. Kilpatrick, "Galatians 1:18: *Historēsai Kēphan,*" *New Testament Essays,* ed. A. J. B. Higgins (*Festschrift* T. W. Manson; Manchester University, 1959), pp. 144-49; W. Bauer, W. Arndt, and F. Gingrich, *A Greek-English Lexicon of the New Testament* (Chicago University, 1957), p. 383. The verb can mean: "to visit, to get to know, to inquire about, to gather information (from someone)." There are reasons for thinking that the last meaning is appropriate in Gal 1:18: namely, that it was on this occasion that Paul gained some of his detailed knowledge about Jesus, e.g., perhaps the tradition that the risen Jesus had appeared to Cephas. Nevertheless, it may be too strong to state that getting information from Cephas was the *purpose* of Paul's first journey to Jerusalem after his conversion. Is it possible that a combined or

imply that Paul's authority as an apostle or his authorization for the gospel which he preached among the Gentiles (Gal 2:2) were dependent on Peter or on any information he had received from Peter.

—Peter was a *leader in Jerusalem* at the time of Paul's first visit as a Christian (Gal 1:18) and continued to be important during Paul's second visit (Gal 2:1ff.).[53]

—Peter had a role in the *apostolate to the circumcised,* alongside Paul's apostolate to the uncircumcised *(apostolē:* Gal 2:8).

With these general observations, let us now consider the letters separately.

A. Galatians

For our purposes, in a study of the letter to the Galatians, it is crucial to ask why Paul found it necessary to discuss with them his relationship to Cephas.[54] There are several options: (1) Judaizers were causing the trouble in Galatia; Cephas had

---

double meaning of *historēsai* best expresses Paul's compressed meaning: he went up to Jerusalem *to visit* Cephas (along with those others who were apostles before Paul—1:17) and in the course of this visit he *got information* about Jesus from Cephas?

[53] For the question as to whether there was a shift in Peter's position at Jerusalem between the two visits, see notes 69-71 below.

[54] For Paul's preference for the name "Cephas," see note 18 above. We have not thought worthy of serious consideration the claim that the "Cephas" of Gal 2:11ff. is to be distinguished from the disciple and apostle Simon Peter, as argued by G. La Piana, "The Tombs of Peter and Paul ad Catacumbas"; K. Lake, "Simon, Cephas, Peter," *Harvard Theological Review* 14 (1921), pp. 53-94, 95-97; and D. W. Riddle, "The Cephas-Peter Problem and a Possible Solution," *Journal of Biblical Literature* 59 (1940), pp. 169-80. See also C. M. Henze, "Cephas seu Kephas non est Simon Petrus," *Divus Thomas* (Piacenza) 61 (1958), pp. 63-67; J. Herrera, "Cephas seu Kephas est Simon Petrus," *ibid.,* pp. 481-84—two Roman Catholic authors with differing views on this problem. Nevertheless, the observation that Paul is talking about only one person, whom he calls Cephas or Peter, need not exclude the possibility that the usage of "Cephas" in Gal 1:18; 2:9, 11, 14, interrupted by the sudden switch to "Peter" in 2:7-8, indicates the use of a source by Paul in these two verses. See E. Dinkler, "Die Petrus-Rom-Frage," *Theologische Rundschau* 25 (1959), p. 198.

been involved in two of Paul's previous confrontations with Judaizers (at Jerusalem in Gal 2:1-10, and at Antioch in Gal 2:11ff.); and Paul mentioned Cephas simply as part of this past history; (2) Cephas himself was causing the trouble in Galatia by preaching "a different gospel" (1:6), and Paul was counter-acting this influence by pointing out that he had trouble with Cephas previously; (3) while Cephas may not have ever been in Galatia himself, the troublemakers in Galatia were, correctly or incorrectly, associating their gospel with the name of Cephas and were thus citing "tradition" against Paul. In our judgment the evidence favors this last option (without excluding all ele-ment of truth in the first), and more specifically the likelihood that Paul's opponents in Galatia were citing Cephas incorrectly and his true views had not reached Galatia.

In this discussion there is no need for us to solve the problem of whether Paul's opponents in Galatia were strictly "Judaizers," i.e., whether their only error was to insist on cir-cumcision for the Gentiles and on the observance of other Jewish legal or cultic laws. (Another suggestion is that they were Gnostics or syncretizers, whose thought involved several "errors,"[55] including that of insisting on Jewish practices.) We recognize the problem of reconstructing their position, espe-cially since Paul had little direct knowledge of them. But what seems clear is that their "different gospel" (1:6) did include Jewish practices, such as circumcision (5:2ff.) and the cele-bration of feasts according to the Jewish calendar (4:10). We are working with the hypothesis that they appealed to Cephas as a support for their position, and that those "who were men of repute" at Jerusalem *(hoi dokountes:* 2:2) were important authorities for them.

Paul sought to counteract them by telling the Galatian

---

[55] See, for example, F. R. Crownfield, "The Singular Problem of the Dual Galatians," *Journal of Biblical Literature* 64 (1945), pp. 491-500; and R. Jewett, "The Agitators and the Galatian Congregation," *New Testament Studies* 17 (1970-71), pp. 198-212. Does Gal 4:3 suggest that the opponents paid homage to the "elemental spirits [*stoicheia*] of the universe"? If so, is this homage related to Jewish calendrical observances (the movements of the heavenly bodies, and the relation of angels to those bodies), or is it of non-Jewish origins?

Christians about earlier events at Jerusalem (2:1-10) and at Antioch (2:11ff.) in which he had confronted demands to impose Jewish practices.[56] In describing his opponents on those earlier occasions, Paul mentions several groups. *In connection with Jerusalem* he speaks of "false brethren *(pseudadelphoi)* secretly brought in, who slipped in, to spy out our freedom" (2:4)—these were Jewish Christians who insisted on the circumcision of Gentile converts. They were defeated on this circumcision issue when James, Cephas, and John, "the pillars" in Jerusalem (2:9), agreed with Paul. *In connection with Antioch* Paul speaks of certain men who "came from James" and of "the circumcision party" (2:12). Now, while James may have shared some emphases with the "false brethren" mentioned in the Jerusalem incident (2:4), it is probable that the men who "came from James" to Antioch (2:12) were different from the "false brethren." As implied by the reference to eating in 2:12,[57] the main emphasis of the men from James concerned, not circumcision, but the imposition on Gentile converts of other aspects of the Mosaic Law, especially the food regulations.[58] The

---

[56] Here we shall confine ourselves to the picture of these events that Paul gives *in Galatians*. Later we shall discuss Acts 15 and try to reconstruct a larger picture of the whole situation in Jerusalem and Antioch concerning the observance of circumcision and the Jewish Law.

[57] If this eating involved eucharistic meals or agape meals, the divisions at Antioch between Jewish Christians and Gentile Christians would have been intolerable for Paul (see I Cor 11:17ff.). However, it is not clear that we can import the later Corinthian problem into the much earlier Antiochene scene. At Antioch, in insisting that the Jewish Christians should not eat with the Gentile Christians, were the men who "came from James" echoing the concept of two separate missions, one to the circumcised and one to the uncircumcised (Gal 2:7-8), while Paul himself advocated one local church integrating Jews and Gentiles?

[58] We suggest that the main emphasis was not circumcision because James had consented that there was no necessity to circumcise Gentile converts (Gal 2:9). But then who constituted "the circumcision party" of whom Cephas was afraid—the party mentioned in the same verse as the men who "came from James" (2:12)? Are these two phrases coextensive, describing the same group of men? Was the "circumcision party" the same as the "false brethren" of 2:4 who had earlier been defeated in Jerusalem on the circumcision question but who continued to press their views on other issues of the Mosaic Law and who would have made common cause with the followers of James on the point now in dispute at Antioch? Were those of the circumcision party whom Cephas feared located in Jerusalem or in Antioch or in both? We can

opponents in Galatia also were advocates of Jewish practices; and all three groups who opposed Paul (at Jerusalem, at Antioch, and in Galatia) shared a legalistic mentality. That is why in writing to the Galatian Christians Paul found it appropriate to recall his previous dealings with Judaizers at Jerusalem and Antioch.

Having discussed the relationship between the various opponents, we are now prepared to return to what is for us the fundamental question, viz., how did the Galatian Christians and Paul regard Cephas? The first part of this question (about the Galatian Christians) can be answered with dispatch: the mention of Cephas in Gal 1:18 would indicate that he was known to the Galatian community as an authority in Jerusalem.[59] They may have gained this knowledge of Cephas from Paul, from the false teachers, or from a third source.

To describe Paul's view of Cephas is a more complex task. Crucial to the discussion is how one interprets Paul's threefold dealings with Cephas: his initial Jerusalem visit with Cephas (1:18); his second visit to Jerusalem on the circumcision question (2:1-10); and his rebuke of Cephas at Antioch (2:11ff.). We have already commented on the initial visit to Jerusalem where Cephas seems to have served Paul as a source of tradition about Jesus.[60]

An attempt to understand the interrelationships involved in the second visit of Paul to Jerusalem (2:1-10) must take into account the meaning of Gal 2:2. Why, in going up to Jerusalem and laying out his gospel privately before "those who were of repute" *(hoi dokountes),* was Paul concerned "lest somehow I

---

only guess at many answers, and we cannot exclude the possibility that "the circumcision party" represents still another faction different from both the "false brethren" of 2:4 and the men who "came from James" (2:12), e.g., they may even have been unconverted Jews rather than Jewish Christians.

[59] It would be difficult to discern how much of this authority was attributed to Peter because of his personal apostolate and how much was attributed to Jerusalem, the most ancient and principal Christian community (see Chapter Four, Section C, below). Perhaps even the Galatians could not have answered such a question because of the close association of Peter with Jerusalem in their minds.

[60] See note 52 above.

should be running or had run in vain"? Was this an implicit acknowledgment by Paul that he was inferior to the Jerusalem authorities of repute (including Cephas,)[61] in the sense that he feared he might be doctrinally "running in vain" if Jerusalem did not approve the solution he had adopted in not circumcising Gentile converts?[62] Or, without recognizing any inferiority on his own part (and superiority on the part of the Jerusalem authorities), did Paul have fears more on the level of practical church politics? Was he concerned that his building of the Gentile churches might be nullified because of Judaizing intrigues against him in Antioch and Jerusalem? If so, Paul would have gone to Jerusalem to set forth his gospel (which involved non-circumcision) and would have brought along the uncircumcised convert, Titus, as a test case to demonstrate what was involved.[63] In the context of this interpretation, some would even go as far as to say that it was Paul's intention to ask whether "those of repute" *would dare* to say that he had "run in vain,"[64] i.e., had built the Gentile churches and made such converts in vain. Paul would not have been concerned that he might "fail the test" of

---

[61] The same type of problem we referred to in note 59 above would have to be considered here. For Paul there was some distinction between Cephas as a personal authority and the authority of the Jerusalem church, but how much?

[62] In accepting Gentiles without circumcision, Paul had taken a bold theological step in loyalty to his understanding of the gospel that had come to him "through a revelation of Jesus Christ" (Gal 1:12). But at the period of his second visit to Jerusalem, some years before he wrote to the Galatians, was he so certain of his interpretation of that revelation that he did not have to fear a rejection of it by men who had known Jesus personally? Was it their confirmation of his interpretation at Jerusalem that enabled Paul to affirm years later to the Galatians that no one, not even an angel from heaven, could contradict his gospel (1:8)? Many interpreters of Paul would deny that even at an earlier period he could have shown such docility toward the Jerusalem leaders.

[63] We are assuming that what Paul says of Titus in Gal 2:3, namely, that he "was not compelled to be circumcised," implies that in fact Titus was not circumcised—he did not submit to circumcision voluntarily for the sake of harmony. Contrast Luke's story of Paul's treatment of Timothy in Acts 16:3.

[64] It may be questioned whether the *mē pōs* ("lest somehow") of Gal 2:2 can carry the connotation of "lest they somehow dare"—the other instances of this usage in Paul refer to a real possibility (I Cor 9:27; II Cor 2:7; 9:4; 11:3; 12:20; Gal 4:11; I Thess 3:5).

Jerusalem's approbation but would have wanted to get to the center of the intrigues against his policy. Moreover, he may have been concerned about the unity among Christian communities—he would not have changed his policy if it had been rejected, and the churches would have been split.

The several possible ways of interpreting Paul's fear of having "run in vain" allow different answers to the question of the degree of authority attributed by Paul to Cephas and the Jerusalem leaders (often hinging on speculation about what Paul would have done had his interpretation of the gospel been rejected). But, at least, it may be said that Paul took these leaders seriously, whether or not he would have ever taken orders from them. The Galatians addressed in Paul's letter, with or without Paul's agreement, recognized "those who were of repute" *(hoi dokountes)* as pillars of the church, and so it helped Paul's argument that they had extended to him and Barnabas the right hand of fellowship. In a similar way, Paul could recognize Cephas as a church authority, but this need not have meant Cephas' ecclesiastical superiority over Paul.[65]

Turning to the third instance cited in Galatians of Paul's dealing with Cephas (2:11ff.), the incident at Antioch, we find that the relationship between Paul and Cephas can be understood in at least two different ways: (1) in the question of compulsory Jewish observances Paul opposed *even* Cephas ("I opposed him to his face"), so that all three Galatian references to Cephas or Peter (1:18; 2:7-9; 2:11ff.) imply a position of superiority or respect for Peter on the part of Paul, no matter how grudging Paul's attitude may have been; (2) Paul's ability to oppose Cephas face to face indicates Paul's increasing importance in relation to Cephas, so that the three Galatian references describe a change of relationship—in 1:18 Paul is inferior to Cephas upon whom he must depend for historical information about Jesus; in 2:7-8 Paul and Peter are on an equal level, entrusted respectively with the gospel and the mission *(apostolē)*

---

[65] The authority of Cephas for Paul may have been based on factors other than ecclesiastical structure or relationships, e.g., on the fact that according to tradition Cephas was the first to have seen the risen Jesus (I Cor 15:5), while Paul was the "last of all" (15:8).

to the uncircumcised and to the circumcised;[66] and in 2:11ff. Paul is superior to Cephas and can directly confront him.

In any case, Paul's primary opposition to Cephas at Antioch seems to have centered, not on Cephas as a person claiming undue authority but on Cephas as acting without principle. What was at issue in 2:11-14 was a matter of "the truth of the gospel" (2:14). Whoever failed to act according to that truth deserved to be reprimanded, and Cephas' importance made his failure all the more grave. Hence from Paul's viewpoint Peter could and should be challenged when he thus erred by not "walking straight in accordance with the truth of the gospel" and not drawing the right consequences from the one (and only) gospel (2:14; 1:7).[67]

This Antioch incident (especially 2:12) raises a further question about Peter that is important for our investigation: What was the relation between Peter and James, at least as implied in chapters 1 and 2 of Galatians? Does the Galatian evidence suggest that some shift in power from Peter to James took place in the church at Jerusalem? Some have found this implication in the changed order of names that we find when we compare 1:18-19 ("I went up to Jerusalem to get information [about Jesus] from *Cephas* . . . I saw none of the other apostles except *James,* the Lord's brother")[68] with 2:9 *("James,* and

[66] Notice that this interpretation concentrates on the mention of "Peter" in 2:7-8, not on the mention of "Cephas" in 2:9. For the possibility that two different traditions are involved in these verses see notes 54 above and 71 below.

[67] We are describing this from Paul's point of view in Galatians. As we shall see, Acts 15 gives a different view of the procedures, according to which, *prima facie,* the Jerusalem authorities in the presence of Paul commanded an observance by the Gentile converts of certain Jewish regulations and thus adopted Peter's position at Antioch, not Paul's. We must face the possibility that what Paul saw as cowardice and failure to act according to principle was interpreted by Peter as intelligent compromise over non-essentials—a spirit not unlike that advocated by Paul (but applied by him in a very different way) in I Cor 8:9; 10:23-24; and Rom 14:1—15:3.

[68] The translation of *ei mē* in the sense of "except" after a negative verb is the common interpretation of Gal 1:19 and implies that James, the Lord's brother, was one of the apostles. However, *ei mē* can also have the meaning of *alla,* "but"; cf. Bauer-Arndt-Gingrich (note 52 above), p. 219; M. Zerwick, *Biblical Greek* (Rome: Pontifical Biblical

Cephas, and John")[69] Presumably, Cephas was the most important Christian in Jerusalem at the time of Paul's first visit (1:18)—at least, for the purpose of obtaining information about Jesus.[70] By the time of Paul's second visit, or, at any rate, by the time Paul wrote Galatians, Paul would think of James first when he was naming the Jerusalem men of repute or pillars of the church.[71] The emergence of James as a major figure in

---

Institute, 1963), ##468-70. The translation "but (only) James" would not necessarily imply that, for Paul, James was an apostle. This question should be kept distinct from the question of whether James, the Lord's brother, is to be identified with one of the several Jameses who appear in lists of the Twelve. Most scholars do not think that James, the Lord's brother, was a member of the Twelve since Acts 1:13-14 distinguishes between the Twelve and the brothers of the Lord (cf. John 6:67-71 and 7:5). For a survey of this problem, see R. E. Brown, *Jerome Biblical Commentary* (note 16 above), article 78, ##167-68.

[69] We accept this as the best textual reading of the verse. Variants include: "James and John" (Alexandrinus); "James, Peter, and John" (Papyrus 46); and significantly *"Peter, James,* and John" (Western witnesses, including D, G, Old Latin, Marcion, Ambrosiaster), a reversed order that reflects "the desire of maintaining the precedence of St Peter" (J. B. Lightfoot, *Galatians* [10th ed.; London: Macmillan, 1890], p. 109). It is worth noting that the best attested order, "James, Cephas, and John," is the order in which the "Catholic Epistles" now appear in the canon: James, I-II Peter, I-II-III John.

[70] The fact that in comparing 1:18-19 with 2:9 one is dealing with two Pauline visits to Jerusalem which had very different purposes affects the import of the order in which Cephas and James are named. One cannot say with certitude that because Paul mentions Cephas prominently in 1:18-19, and James only in passing, Cephas outranked James in the government of the Jerusalem church at the time of Paul's first visit. Nevertheless, the order *may* serve as an implicit indication of Paul's estimate of their importance at that time.

[71] For the view that James is mentioned first in Gal 2:9, not because he had precedence but because he represented the strong Jewish-Christian tendency (i.e., even James agreed!), see H. Conzelmann, *History of Primitive Christianity* (Nashville: Abingdon, 1973; German 1971), p. 55. The import of the order (James, Cephas) in 2:9 is somewhat modified by the prominence given to Peter's gospel and mission to the circumcised in 2:7-8—when Paul looks for a paradigm for his own gospel and mission, he turns to Peter, not to James. However, the impact of the modification may be lessened if in 7-8 (and perhaps 9b-10a) Paul is citing a special source, such as the minutes or protocol of the Jerusalem meeting; for then 9a which gives prominence to James would represent Paul's own comment. (The suggestion of a special, non-Pauline source in 7-8 is prompted by the appearance of the name "Peter" for the only time in all the Pauline writings—see note 18 above.) For the interpretation of the Galatian passages in terms of a shift of power from Peter

Jerusalem offers the interpreter several possible models of church leadership, a problem that we shall discuss when we turn to the role of Peter in the Book of Acts.

B. I Corinthians

As we turn to I Corinthians where Cephas is mentioned by name in four passages (1:12; 3:22; 9:5; 15:5), a different set of problems is encountered.

First, there arises the question of whether Cephas was ever in Corinth. It is clear from other passages in the New Testament that Peter did engage in missionary activity,[72] but did his travels bring him to Corinth, a church founded by Paul? That they did is suggested by I Cor 9:5 where, in arguing for his own rights, Paul calls upon the example of Cephas: "Do we not have the right to be accompanied by a wife, as the other apostles and the brothers of the Lord *and Cephas*?" Since others are mentioned besides Cephas, the passage is not conclusive; but it gains strength when we look at two earlier passages in the letter which refer to various parties or divisions among the Corinthians,[73]

---

to James, see G. Klein, "Galater 2, 6-9 und die Geschichte der Jerusalemer Urgemeinde," *Zeitschrift für Theologie und Kirche* 57 (1960), pp. 275-95, reprinted with an additional note in *Rekonstruktion und Interpretation* (Beiträge zur Evangelischen Theologie, 50; Munich: Kaiser, 1969), pp. 99-128; and Ferdinand Hahn, *Mission in the New Testament* (Studies in Biblical Theology, 47; London: SCM, 1965), pp. 77-86, especially p. 80, note 1.

[72] In Gal 2:7-8 Paul specifies that Peter had a mission or apostolate to the circumcised; Acts 1—12 gives Peter a very active role, not only in Jerusalem, but also in Samaria, Lydda, Joppa, and Caesarea (where he receives the *un*circumcised Cornelius into Christianity); Gal 2:11 brings Cephas further afield by situating him at Antioch; I Peter 1:1 has him address the Christians of a large area in Asia Minor; and finally there is the tradition that he went to Rome (cf. I Peter 5:13 where "Babylon" probably means Rome).

[73] It is difficult to be certain whether three or four parties are represented. At first glance, 1:12 seems to give voice to adherents of four parties: those who are of Paul, of Apollos, of Cephas, and of Christ. But since 3:22 mentions only three (Paul, Apollos, and Cephas), it is possible, for example, that the person in 1:12 who says: "I am of Christ," is Paul himself, by way of crushing response to those who are claiming to be "of Paul," "of Apollos," or "of Cephas." In any case,

one of them bearing Cephas' name. A plausible explanation for such a party is that it consisted of those who were converted by Cephas when he preached at Corinth, but other explanations are possible.[74] However, beyond suggesting the probability of Cephas' presence at Corinth, these passages do not tell us much about his peculiar influence there. The Cephas-party among the Corinthians was presumably Jewish Christian in outlook; it is mentioned in chapters 1-4, but we are not able to connect it with any of the specific ethical or disciplinary problems treated in chapters 5-8. Nor, as we shall see, is there any convincing reason to suppose that the party accurately reflected the theological position of Cephas himself, any more than the Paul-party accurately reflected the position of Paul; for Paul shows no more favor to those who said they were "of Paul" than he does to those who said they were "of Apollos" or "of Cephas."

Next, the reference to Cephas in I Cor 15:5 raises a number of issues about the place of Peter in the churches.[75] An analysis of the list of the six persons or groups (15:5-8) to whom the risen Christ appeared shows a careful structure:

---

in reference to the three names, Paul, Apollos, and Cephas, two facts should be noted: *first,* both Paul and Apollos had preached at Corinth (see also Acts 19:1), and so analogy suggests that Cephas too had been there; *second,* in both 1:12 and 3:22 Cephas is mentioned last in the triad—is this because he had come to Corinth last, or because he was held in special veneration? The fact that Cephas' name does not appear in 3:5-9, where Paul mentions Apollos and himself, is of uncertain significance for the questions we are raising here, especially that of Cephas' presence at Corinth—it may mean no more than that it served Paul's purpose to use *two* men as illustrative examples.

[74] For instance, those who said, "I am of Cephas," may have been Corinthians who were disgusted with the bickering between the parties who had grouped themselves around the two local preachers of Corinthian history, Paul and Apollos, and were appealing to a higher authority (at Jerusalem), namely, the famous Cephas. (One must understand the appeal to Christ somewhat in this manner, whether it was made by a Corinthian party or by Paul.) Or the Cephas-party may have consisted of persons baptized by Cephas in Palestine who had migrated to Corinth —and indeed may have engaged in missionary activity there, increasing the number of those spiritually descended from Cephas.

[75] There would be, of course, many other issues more pertinent to a discussion of the nature and sequence of resurrection appearances, e.g., did the risen Lord appear to Cephas three times: to him alone, to him as part of the Twelve, and to him as part of "all the apostles"? Interesting though these may be, they are not really pertinent to our study.

[5]And that he appeared:
> [1] to Cephas,
> [2] then to the Twelve;
> [6][3] and then he appeared to more than 500 brethren at one
> time, . . .

[7]And then he appeared:
> [4] to James,
> [5] then to all the apostles;
> [8][6] last of all, as to one irregularly born, he appeared also to
> me.

The verses immediately preceding the list of names are generally thought to have been handed down to Paul as an existing formula or parts of a formula ("that Christ *died* for our sins according to the Scriptures; and that he *was buried;* and that he *was raised* on the third day according to the Scriptures; and that he *appeared*").[76] But scholars are not in agreement as to where the pre-Pauline formula ended and where Paul himself began to add: for instance, did Paul himself add the fact that Jesus *appeared?* If that fact was in the pre-Pauline formula, did Paul add all the names, or were some of them already included (e.g., Cephas and the Twelve)? In any case, even if Paul himself added all the names, he was dependent on previous tradition for information about those to whom Jesus appeared.

It is the balanced structure of the list that has given rise to speculation that is of interest to us. Although the appearance to Cephas was probably by tradition the *first* appearance of the risen Jesus to one of those who had been his intimate followers during the ministry (cf. Luke 24:34), and the appearance to Paul was by his own statement the "last of all" (I Cor 15:8), few scholars would maintain that the whole list follows a chronological arrangement. The two groupings of three have attracted attention, and it has been suggested that the first three appearances (Cephas, the Twelve, more than 500 brethren) were to those who had followed Jesus during his lifetime, while the second group of three appearances (James, all the apostles, Paul) were directed to new followers of Jesus. But that would imply that

---

76 A detailed discussion of this question and abundant references to literature can be found in R. H. Fuller, *The Formation of the Resurrection Narratives* (New York: Macmillan, 1971), pp. 9-49.

Paul did not count Cephas among "all the apostles"—a difficulty in light of Gal 2:7-8.[77] Another explanation (that can be complementary) is that the first group of three appearances were "church-founding" appearances, while the second group of appearances were "mission-inaugurating." This suggestion would help us to see the kind of distinction that Christians (and Paul himself) may have drawn between the role of Cephas and the role of Paul, but it is not without difficulty.[78] Another suggestion is that the groupings reflect the joining of rival lists, especially visible in the parallel structure that exists between appearances 1-2 and 4-5 ("to Cephas, then to the Twelve"—"to James, then to all the apostles").[79] This suggestion has implications consonant with the possible shift in power from

---

[77] A possible answer to this objection is that "the Twelve" and "the apostles" are groupings based on *two different callings,* one pre-Easter, the other post-Easter. There can be overlapping between the two groupings, and the obvious example is Peter. The post-resurrection origin of apostleship, therefore, would not exclude Peter from the ranks of the apostles, in Paul's listing.

[78] This suggestion has been defended chiefly by Fuller, pp. 34-38. In order to make the appearance to "more than 500 brethren at one time" a church-founding appearance, Fuller has to identify it with the Pentecost episode, despite the fact that Luke himself does not regard Pentecost as an appearance of the risen Jesus (who had ascended to heaven) and that the number of people whom Luke mentions in the context of the Pentecost scene is "about a hundred and twenty" (Acts 1:15). In order to make the appearance to James a mission-inaugurating appearance, Fuller thinks of James as "the chairman of the central board of missions," inaugurating the mission outside Jerusalem—a role that is not clear in Acts.

[79] A. von Harnack thought of rival reports circulated by the followers of Peter and James respectively. E. Bammel has suggested the possibility of duplicate reports of the same appearances, with James substituted for Cephas, and "all the apostles" substituted for the Twelve. In evaluating these suggestions we must remember that after his conversion Paul had encountered at Jerusalem both Cephas and James (Gal 1:18-19) and thus may have had accurate knowledge of whether there was a tradition of appearances to both. An appearance to Peter has independent support in the New Testament (Luke 24:34); an appearance to James would plausibly account for the fact that a disbelieving brother of the Lord (cf. John 7:5) had become a leading Christian. An appearance to James is reported in fragment 7 of *The Gospel of the Hebrews,* an early second-century Jewish Christian composition. For bibliography on the rival-report approach to I Cor 15:5-8, see Fuller, pp. 11ff. and C. F. Evans, *Resurrection and the New Testament* (Studies in Biblical Theology, second series, 12; London: SCM, 1970), pp. 43ff.

Peter to James that we discussed above in relation to Galatians,[80] but obviously it is highly speculative. As interesting as all these suggestions are, we must face the possibility that the arrangement in the Pauline list may be accidental and/or without functional significance, and that it was simply so inherited by Paul.

More important, because it is not so speculative, is the attitude that Paul expresses after listing those who had seen the risen Jesus. He states that he is the least of the apostles although through the grace of God he has worked harder than any of them (15:9-10). When Paul says, "Whether then it was I or they, so we preach [kēryssomen] and so you believed" (15:11), he makes it clear that the Corinthians had also heard the kerygma from other apostolic preachers—a message that the Corinthians had received in faith (15:1) at the time of their conversion. Besides Paul, the most likely example of such an apostolic preacher is Cephas. Moreover, unlike Galatians (where we had to raise the possibility that Cephas himself was preaching "a different gospel" in Galatia and where Paul accused Cephas of not having been straightforward at Antioch about the truth of the gospel [2:14]), Paul in writing to the Corinthians affirms *the harmony* of the apostolic preaching. Therefore, what divided the Corinthian parties mentioned earlier in the letter (those belonging to Paul, to Apollos, and to Cephas) was not a question of a difference in the kerygma they had received or proclaimed, but seemingly a difference in the interpretation of the ethical implications of the kerygma. Paul's enthusiastic reference to the common preaching of those who had been apostles to the Corinthians makes it dubious that he attributed to the men named by the parties as their leaders even this difference.

C. II Corinthians

Paul does not mention Cephas (Peter) by name in this (perhaps composite) letter written shortly after I Corinthians,

---

[80] See also note 41 above.

but some scholars have argued that there are indirect references to him.[81] If this were true, it would be of importance for our study, since most of the passages in question are of a sharply hostile tone. For instance, in 10:7 Paul polemicizes: "If someone is confident that he is Christ's, let him remind himself that we are Christ's as much as he is." Again in 11:4-5: "If someone comes who proclaims [*kēryssei*] another Jesus, not the Jesus whom we proclaimed, . . . you submit to it readily enough. But I think that I am not in the least inferior to these superlative apostles." In the view under discussion, Cephas is identified as the "someone" who has caused the difficulties at Corinth to which Paul is now addressing himself.[82] C. K. Barrett argues that, though Peter's heart was in the right place, he was easily frightened and was used by "ecclesiastical politicians." Barrett says, "Peter, in the hands of those who made use of him, was on the way to ruining Paul's work at Corinth."[83]

In general, we have not accepted this interpretation. It depends almost entirely on a very speculative identification of vague references in II Corinthians. Even though an attempt has been made by its supporters to tie it in with I Corinthians,[84] it really runs against the (at least) neutral or favorable attitude toward Cephas evinced by Paul in I Corinthians. Indeed, if we have correctly understood the implications of I Cor 15:11 (see the last paragraph of our treatment of I Corinthians), Paul, in

---

[81] T. W. Manson, "The Corinthian Correspondence (1)," *Bulletin of the John Rylands Library* 26 (1941), pp. 101-20, reprinted in *Studies in the Gospels and Epistles,* ed. M. Black (Philadelphia: Westminster, 1962), pp. 190-209. C. K. Barrett, "Cephas and Corinth," *Abraham Unser Vater,* ed. O. Betz *et al. (Festschrift* Otto Michel; Leiden: Brill, 1963), pp. 1-12; and *The Signs of an Apostle* (Philadelphia: Fortress, 1970), especially the Introduction by J. Reumann, pp. 11-14. E. Meyer, *Ursprung und Anfänge des Christentums,* III (Stuttgart: Cotta, 1923), pp. 432-59.

[82] Cf. also II Cor 2:17; 3:1; 5:12; 10:10-18; 11:5; 11:19-20. If one accepts the theory, one may speculate why Paul does not mention Cephas by name, since he mentions him in I Corinthians and does not hesitate to criticize Cephas' actions in Galatians? Is Peter now more powerful? Does Paul not want to antagonize Jerusalem?

[83] *Abraham Unser Vater* (note 81 above), p. 12.

[84] In particular, with an interpretation of I Cor 3:10 where Cephas is identified with the "other man" who builds on the foundation laid by Paul.

addressing the same community a few months before he wrote
II Corinthians, had joined himself to Cephas as a fellow apostolic preacher of the same kerygma.[85] How then could he now
be saying that Cephas' kerygma was the proclamation of "another Jesus"?

[85] Note that the same verb (*kēryssein*, related to the noun *kērygma*)
is used in I Cor 15:11 and II Cor 11:4.

CHAPTER FOUR:
PETER IN THE
BOOK OF ACTS[86]

If the Pauline letters give us an insight (sometimes with a polemic coloring) into the way Peter was viewed by Paul and by certain church factions in the mid-50's, the Book of Acts gives us a Christian view of Peter some thirty years later.[87] And it is precisely on Acts as a work produced toward the end of the century, reflecting the genius of Luke as a theologian of history, that we shall place our primary emphasis. True, it is generally agreed that, in writing Acts, Luke made use of earlier written and/or oral sources,[88] the composition of which would be chron-

---

[86] The discussion for this chapter was led by G. Krodel. A session and a half of the task force (April and May 1972) were devoted to the evidence of Acts, although some of the material in Acts had entered into our discussions of the Pauline material.

[87] A rigidly chronological approach to the New Testament would have inclined us to treat the Gospel of Mark after the Pauline letters and to put Acts with the Gospel of Luke. For the reasons why we have made this one exception to chronological sequence and have chosen to treat Acts here, see Chapter Two, B, 2. It is there also that we caution the reader that Acts cannot be treated as straight history.

[88] J. Dupont, *The Sources of Acts: The Present Position* (London: Darton, Longman and Todd, 1964); E. Haenchen, *The Acts of the Apostles: A Commentary* (Philadelphia: Westminster, 1971), pp. 81-90. Of interest for our purposes is the suggestion of J. Jervell, *Luke and the People of God* (Minneapolis: Augsburg, 1972), pp. 19-39, that some reports of missionary successes of the Twelve were passed down as traditions. This is in contradiction to the thesis of Dibelius and Haenchen (see note 92 below) that Luke lacked prior traditions of importance in relation to the apostles.

ologically closer to the Pauline letters. But it is often impossible for us to assess the view of Peter in these pre-Lucan sources, since the detection of the source material is problematical. It is still more difficult to move back beyond both Lucan redaction and pre-Lucan sources to the historical level. Yet some attempt must be made to do so, and to compare the historical picture of Peter's role detected behind Acts and its sources with the historical picture we have detected behind the writings of Paul.[89]

A. The General Picture of Peter in the First Half of Acts

It has often been observed that Peter dominates the story of the spread of Christianity narrated in the first half of Acts (he is not mentioned after Acts 15), while Paul dominates the story in the second half. Before we begin to discuss the most difficult scenes involving Peter, we shall imitate our procedure at the beginning of the chapter on the Pauline letters and give a rapid review of fairly straightforward items that highlight Peter's prominence:

—In Acts 1:13 Peter is named *first in the post-resurrectional list*[90] *of the Eleven*. This brings to mind Luke 24:34 where apparently Simon is the first of the Eleven to have seen the risen Jesus.

—Peter plays a significant role in the *election of Matthias* to fill the place (or office: *episcopē*, in the Scripture citation in Acts 1:20) left vacant by Judas.[91] He urges that a suc-

---

[89] An immense literature has been devoted to the relative reliability of Luke as compared to Paul (see Haenchen, pp. 110-12), and it would lie beyond the scope of our study to become entangled in the details of the question. Obviously Paul was closer to some of the events concerning Peter than was Luke, but we remind the reader that at times the apologetic character of Paul's letters may have lent a subjective coloring to Paul's report of what happened.

[90] This agrees with Luke 6:14 where the first in the list is "Simon whom he named Peter." In general Luke shows a marked preference for the name "Peter," using "Simon" in Acts only in 10:5, 18, 32, and "Cephas" not at all (see notes 119 and 244 below).

[91] The scene described in Acts 1:15-26 raises the question of why Judas had to be replaced, since there is no mention of subsequent efforts

cessor be selected and suggests the criteria which should be used for the process. This scene illustrates the difficulty in distinguishing between Lucan redaction and pre-Lucan sources. While Peter's role may belong to a pre-Lucan source, a number of factors, including the use of the Greek Scriptures in Peter's speech (1:20), indicate that Peter's address to the "brethren" is a Lucan construction.[92]

—Peter is *a preacher* in the Jerusalem church, a missionary preacher to outsiders, and a spokesman for the Christian community.[93]

—Peter is *a miracle worker* and some of his miracles resemble those of Jesus in the Gospel accounts. But it is important to note that this aspect of Peter's career is not unique in Acts, for Paul too is a miracle worker and some of his miracles resemble those of Jesus.[94]

---

to replace other members of the Twelve whose places were vacated by death (e.g. James, the brother of John, whose death is recorded in Acts 12:2). The problem with Judas is that in dying he has gone "to his own place" (1:25, i.e., Hades), whereas the ultimate destiny of the Twelve is to sit on thrones in the kingdom judging the tribes of Israel (Luke 22:30). Consequently there is no need to replace members of the Twelve when they die a good death, for they have gone to the kingdom to play their eschatological role. Moreover, for Luke, it was necessary to fill Judas' place *before Pentecost,* so that the apostolic college would be complete when the Spirit came.

[92] As a sample of scholarly disagreement, compare the conservative approach to this scene by K. H. Rengstorf in *Current Issues in New Testament Interpretation,* ed. W. Klassen and G. F. Snyder *(Festschrift* O. Piper; New York: Harper & Row, 1962), pp. 178-92, with that of Haenchen (note 88 above), pp. 157-65, especially p. 164, who speaks of "the comparatively meager material" that Luke possessed from tradition. See also note 120 below on the use of the Greek Scriptures.

[93] Acts 2:14-36; 3:12-26; 4:8-12; 5:29-32; 10:34-43; 15:7-11. But it is interesting to note that Peter can be sent to Samaria by the apostles at Jerusalem (8:14) and that on occasion he has to justify his actions to them (11:1-18).

[94] References to Peter's miracles are found in Acts 3:1-10; 5:1-11; 5:15; 9:32-35; and 9:36-42. For parallels to incidents in Paul's career, compare 5:15 with 19:12; 3:1-10 with 14:8-18; and 9:36-42 with 20:7-12. A close resemblance between a miracle of Peter and a miracle of Jesus is detected by comparing Acts 9:40 with Mark 5:41 (cf. Luke 8:54). Similarly, a resemblance between a miracle of Paul and a miracle of Jesus is detected by comparing Acts 28:7-10 with Mark 1:30-31 (Luke 4:38-39). Thus, the resemblance between Peter in Acts and Jesus in the Gospels cannot be used facilely in arguing for Peter as the "vicar of

—Peter is *the object of miraculous divine care,* and he receives heavenly guidance. Once again there are parallels in Paul's career.[95]

How many of the above items reflect not merely Luke's view or that of the pre-Lucan tradition, but also can be considered seriously as evidence for the historical career of Peter and his prominence? As we have indicated, the problem of Lucan redaction in the Matthias report severely limits our ability to reconstruct the historical scene. The other items allow more certainty. Peter is named first in the Marcan (3:16) and Matthean (10:2) lists of the Twelve as well.[96] That Peter had a prominent role in the Jerusalem church and that he was a missionary and a spokesman are at least partially supported by the Pauline letters, as we have seen. That Peter worked miracles and that he was the object of miraculous care are harder to verify as history, but we note that Paul associates "signs, wonders, and mighty works" with apostleship.[97]

Christ." Such resemblances are a Lucan trait: recall how Luke (Acts 7:60) depicts the death of Stephen as similar to the death of Jesus (Luke 23:34).

[95] Peter is rescued miraculously in Acts 5:17-21 and 12:6-11 (note the Pauline parallel in 16:25-31) and he receives heavenly or visionary guidance in 10:9-48 (note the Pauline parallels in 9:3-19; 16:10; 18:9; 20:22-23; 21:10-11; 26:19; 27:23-24).

[96] There is a minority opinion that the Twelve did not exist as a unit in Jesus' lifetime and came into existence only after the resurrection. A still more radical opinion is that the notion of the Twelve apostles is altogether a literary construct. For a further discussion of this matter, see G. Klein, *Die zwölf Apostel* (Göttingen: Vandenhoeck, 1961) and the literature cited by R. E. Brown, *Jerome Biblical Commentary* (note 16 above), article 78, #160.

[97] II Cor 12:12; Rom 15:18-19; see also the reference to Christian "miracle workers" in I Cor 12:28-29. It has been suggested that the portrait of Peter and Paul as miracle workers has been influenced by a "divine man" (*theios anēr*) perspective that was current in the Hellenistic world. For a review of this matter, see H. D. Betz, "Jesus as a Divine Man," *Jesus and the Historian,* ed. F. T. Trotter (*Festschrift* E. C. Colwell; Philadelphia: Westminster, 1968), pp. 114-133; also R. H. Fuller, *The Foundations of New Testament Christology* (New York: Scribner's, 1965), pp. 68-72, 227-29. For possible Old Testament background for the miracle worker, see R. E. Brown, "Jesus and Elisha," *Perspective* 12 (1971), pp. 85-104. See also the work of D. L. Tiede cited in note 169 below.

B. Peter and the Conversion of the Gentiles (Acts 10:1–11:18)

We turn now to Peter's conversion of the Roman centurion Cornelius at Caesarea Maritima and his subsequent justification at Jerusalem of his action. From this Lucan scene one gets the impression that Peter took precedence in the mission to the Gentiles and was, indeed, its inaugurator. Is this historically correct, especially in the light of Gal 2:7-8, where Paul claims to have been entrusted with the gospel to the uncircumcised (Gentiles), "just as Peter had been entrusted with the gospel to the circumcised"?[98]

To some extent the Lucan picture of the Petrine inauguration of the Gentile mission is modified by the fact that earlier in Acts the author records conversions outside the narrow confines of Judaism, e.g., the conversions effected by the Hellenist Philip among the Samaritans and the baptism of an Ethiopian (Jew or Gentile?) eunuch (Acts 8). Moreover, Luke emphasizes that Cornelius was a "God-fearer" (10:2), i.e., one who was favorable to Judaism and already observant of many Jewish practices. Thus, Luke does not portray Peter's role in relation to the Gentiles in exactly the same sense in which we normally speak of Paul as the apostle to the Gentiles, i.e., the first one to convert mass numbers of Gentiles who had no previous connection with Judaism. Nevertheless, Luke does describe the

---

[98] Paul's words stand in strong contrast to Peter's statement in Acts 15:7: "God made choice among you that by my mouth the Gentiles should hear the word of the gospel and believe." The contrast is somewhat modified if we hold (note 71 above) that Gal 2:7-8 constitutes a pre-Pauline formulation, and that Paul's own mind is better expressed by 2:9 where his mission is not contrasted with Peter's on a one-to-one basis—rather, we are told, James, Cephas, and John gave the hand of fellowship to Paul and Barnabas. The mention of several figures on each side suggests a more complicated picture; and, in fact, there were probably missionaries to the Gentiles before either Peter or Paul (see Acts 8:1b, 4). The dispute at Antioch described in Gal 2:11ff. implies the existence of a Gentile Christian community at Antioch for whose origins we have little information. Acts 11:19-26 connects the Antioch mission with the Hellenist dispersion from Jerusalem. However, the evidence for a mission to "the Greeks" (*Hellēnes,* i.e., Gentiles) at Antioch is complicated by the variant reading in 11:20, "the Hellenists" (*Hellēnistai,* i.e., perhaps, Greek-speaking Jews).

conversion of Cornelius in such a dramatic way that he gives the impression that through this inspired action of Peter it was first revealed to the church that God intended Christian salvation to extend to the Gentiles (11:18). In harmony with this, he describes Paul's first missionary activity as taking place only *after* Peter's decisive action.

One possible explanation of the picture in Acts 10—11 is that Luke is giving us *history,* even though it be dramatized history. The hypothesis can be advanced that Peter did make such a convert,[99] and that this conversion was recalled later at Jerusalem as a precedent when the problem raised by Paul's massive conversions of Gentiles was discussed.[100] Another possibility, favored by many scholars today, is that we have here a creation of Lucan *theology.* According to Luke's conception such a major step as the mission to the Gentiles had to be the work of the Twelve;[101] and so, one of the Twelve, indeed the most prominent, is described as converting a Gentile[102] under divine guidance. This action then serves as the legitimation or legal basis for the decision in chapter 15 (see verses 7-8) to

[99] Haenchen (note 88 above), pp. 355-63, lists the many disputants in the arguments over (a) whether the basic story of Cornelius' conversion came to Luke from a pre-Lucan source—so Dibelius; and (b) whether the story had a historical kernel.

[100] This hypothesis, in positing a historical core, need not imply that Peter was more important than Paul in the Gentile mission. It need mean no more than that an action by Peter carried weight with many Christians—perhaps more weight as a precedent than an action by Paul. Some scholars have argued that Peter remained active in the Gentile mission (see note 72 above), and we have discussed the thesis that Peter's missionary activity caused much of the strife and division at Corinth (notes 81-84 above).

[101] We are assuming the common scholarly view about the importance that Luke attached to the Twelve, so that for him they were *the* apostles of the church. For a recent detailed discussion of the different notions of apostleship in the primitive church see R. Schnackenburg, "Apostolicity: The Present Position of Studies," *One in Christ* 6 (1970), pp. 243-73; also "Apostles Before and During Paul's Time," *Apostolic History and the Gospel,* ed. W. W. Gasque and R. M. Martin (*Festschrift* F. F. Bruce; Grand Rapids: Eerdmans, 1970), pp. 287-303.

[102] And not only a Gentile—a Roman! This is important for Luke's *heilsgeschichtlich* approach to the spread of Christianity. As we shall see, Rome replaces Jerusalem at the end of Acts as the center stage of Christian endeavor.

accept the Gentiles without imposing circumcision. As Haenchen remarks, "It was in other words no 'freelance' who began the mission to the Gentiles, but the legitimate, apostolic Church."[103] While we cannot solve the question as to the extent of the interplay here between historicity and theology, all must admit that Acts 10—11 are chapters heavily marked by Luke's editorial hand and theological spirit.

C. Peter's Relation to Jerusalem and the Jerusalem Authorities

The question of whether Peter had a major role in the decision to accept Gentiles into Christianity is closely related to the problem of who supervised the spread of Christianity and had authority over the various Christian congregations. In Acts (8:14; 9:32; 15:6-7, 22-23) we find both the Jerusalem apostles and Peter mentioned at important moments affecting the Christian missionary endeavor, and we may ask whether we should speak of a Petrine supervision or of a Jerusalem supervision. If the latter, who holds authority in Jerusalem? Perhaps it is appropriate at this time to focus on the picture given in Acts of the interrelationship of Jerusalem, Peter, and James ("the brother of the Lord"—Gal 1:19).[104]

We may suspect that the authority of Jerusalem in early Christianity rested on several bases:

—Jerusalem had served as the holy city of God for Israel, both in history and in eschatological expectation (Isa 2:2-3). This gave Jerusalem importance for the early (Jewish) Christians as well.

—Jerusalem was the city where Jesus had been crucified and raised from the dead.[105]

---

[103] Haenchen (note 88 above), p. 360.

[104] For a recent Roman Catholic attempt to situate Peter within a wider spectrum of early church authority, see R. Schnackenburg, "The Petrine Office: Peter's Relationship to the Other Apostles," *Theology Digest* 20 (1972), pp. 148-52 (a digest of a longer German article in *Wort und Wahrheit* 26 [1971], pp. 206-15).

[105] Indeed, the Fourth Gospel would have Jesus spending a good part of his public ministry in Jerusalem. See also Rev 11:8.

—According to Luke-Acts (and John 20) the appearances of the risen Jesus all took place in Jerusalem and its environs.

—If Acts 2 is correct, Jerusalem was the place of the first public manifestation of the Spirit in Christian preaching (Pentecost).

—According to Acts, the Twelve apostles (especially Peter and John) functioned at Jerusalem in the early days.

—The first major Christian community was at Jerusalem.[106]

With all of this background, it is no surprise that, as the early Christian movement spread geographically, in the new communities there was a certain loyalty toward and respect or concern for Jerusalem. This attitude is attested not only in Acts but also in Paul; yet it is not always easy to determine which of the above reasons gave rise to it.[107]

Although Peter and the Twelve functioned in Jerusalem in the early days (the evidence of Acts is partially confirmed by the reference to apostles and Peter at Jerusalem in Gal 1:17-18), it is not clear whether he or they functioned as local church leaders in the ordinary sense of that term. If the picture in Acts is historical, the Twelve probably had such a leadership when there was a very small community of Christians in Jerusalem. But when the Jerusalem Christians became a fairly large local community, did Peter and the Twelve act as its local leaders or caretakers? Is their statement in Acts 6:2 ("It is not right that we should give up preaching the word of God to serve tables") an indication that they did not want such a task?[108]

---

[106] Some have argued for the existence and even priority of Galilean Christianity, but details remain speculative and the exact phenomenon problematic. See E. Lohmeyer, *Galiläa und Jerusalem* (Göttingen: Vandenhoeck, 1935); L. E. Elliott-Binns, *Galilean Christianity* (Studies in Biblical Theology, 16; London: SCM, 1956).

[107] For instance, notice the earliest Pauline passage pertinent to the subject (I Thess 2:14): "You, brethren, became imitators of the churches of God ... which are in Judea." Here and in Gal 1:22 Paul does not confine the reference only to the church in Jerusalem.

[108] It may well be that the daily distribution of food (and money?) and waiting on tables—the subjects of dispute in Acts 6:1-6—constituted only one aspect of the larger question of pastoral care. Thus, the decision in Acts 6 *may* be interpreted as the beginning of local leadership in the proper sense, with James and the elders (presbyters) ministering to the

It is implied in Acts (cf. 21:18) that James ultimately became the local leader in Jerusalem.[109] Was James the main mover behind the letter directed "to the brethren who are of the Gentiles in Antioch, Syria, and Cilicia" (15:23)?[110] If so, his area of concern may have been wider than Jerusalem. Are we to think of something like a "province" in which the leader of the Jerusalem church had influence, e.g., churches founded directly from Jerusalem? Does the interference of "those from James" at Antioch (Gal 2:12) also imply this?

Indeed, we may wonder whether James had a role in the universal church beyond his local leadership in Jerusalem (and even in its "province")?[111] Paul could presume that the name of James was known to the Galatians (Gal 1:18; 2:9, 12) and to the Corinthians (I Cor 15:7). Even after Peter seemingly disappeared from the Jerusalem scene (he is never mentioned there after Acts 15 and Gal 2:9), Jerusalem remained important to Paul—witness his zeal for the collection for the saints at Jerusalem[112] and his determination to go up to Jerusalem even

---

Hebrew Christians of Jerusalem, and the seven leaders mentioned in 6:5 ministering to the Hellenist Christians. Although the Seven are traditionally (and mistakenly) regarded as deacons, A. Farrer is closer to the historical situation when he describes them as forerunners of presbyters in the church ("The Ministry in the New Testament," *The Apostolic Ministry,* ed. K. E. Kirk [London: Hodder and Stoughton, 1946], pp. 113-82, especially p. 138).

[109] Subsequent church tradition identified other "brothers of the Lord" with names on the list of early "bishops" of Jerusalem, for instance, Simeon, and later Jude (cf. the names in Mark 6:3). This identification and other reports about the important role of "relatives of the Lord" in the early church (see Eusebius, III, 11, 20, and 32) have given rise to the idea that the leadership of the Jerusalem church was a type of "caliphate," i.e., that it was passed on to the blood relatives of the prophet. See H. Chadwick and H. von Campenhausen, *Jerusalem and Rome* (Facet Books, Historical Series, 4; Philadelphia: Fortress, 1966).

[110] The letter is actually sent in the name of "the apostles and the elders" at Jerusalem, but the solution that it imposes (15:28-29) is the solution that James proposed (15:19-20).

[111] Above (note 78) we mentioned Fuller's thesis that James inaugurated and guided the mission outside Jerusalem. We note that I Cor 15:7 allots to James an appearance of the risen Lord, a tradition that might give him apostolic authority. It is interesting that in seeking a comparison for his own rights as an apostle, Paul compares himself to "the brothers of the Lord" (I Cor 9:5).

[112] Rom 15:25-28, 31; II Cor 8:1—9:15.

at cost of his life.[113] Many factors could explain this, but was one of them the importance of James' role in the universal church? When he did get to Jerusalem, did Paul "check in" with James (Acts 21:17-18) simply because James ran the local church?

We cannot answer these questions with any certainty, but obviously they are related to the theory, already discussed in relation to Galatians (notes 41, 70, 71), that there was a shift in power at Jerusalem, and that Peter was succeeded by James in the leading role. We noted that the hints in Galatians were tenuous; but, as we shall see below, some would find confirmation in Acts 15 where, although Peter speaks first (verses 7-11), James seems to have the final word and to carry the day (12-31).

All in all, the evidence leaves itself open to several interpretations, and among them we find the following possible models for early church leadership, as it involved Jerusalem:

—Peter and the other members of the Twelve were concerned with a Christian mission far more extensive than just Jerusalem. They were never really local church leaders, once Jerusalem became big enough to require such caretakers. James was the first leader of the local church at Jerusalem (at least for the Hebrew Christians) and remained there after Peter and the other members of the Twelve left the scene, whether through death or on travels. James had authority only in Jerusalem (and its "province"), but his name was known more widely because he was a blood relative of Jesus. Paul's loyalty was to the "mother church" or community of the saints in Jerusalem. His respect for James was a respect for the local leader of that church.

—Peter was a local leader at Jerusalem (even though he was known more widely because he had been a close follower of Jesus during the ministry). James took Peter's place as the local Jerusalem leader (when Peter left Jerusalem[114] or even

---

[113] Acts 20:22-24; 21:10-14.

[114] According to Acts 12:17 Peter left Jerusalem when he escaped from prison. (A later church tradition would maintain that it was then that he went to Rome and, indeed, founded the church in Rome—there is no scientific support for this tradition, and it does not deserve serious discussion.) It has been theorized that Peter's departure supplied the

earlier). Neither of them had a role as leader in the universal church; for, in fact, there was no single leader in the universal church.

—Peter was a universal leader, operating from Jerusalem as the center of Christianity, and was succeeded by James.[115] In other words, the position of universal influence that Peter had at Jerusalem (except his apostleship) was transferred to James when Peter left Jerusalem or even earlier.

Whichever option one selects as best meeting the evidence, one should remember that Peter still had a position that James did not have—Peter was one of and, indeed, ranked first among the Twelve. But James had a position that Peter did not have—James was "the brother of the Lord."

D. Peter at the "Council" of Jerusalem (Acts 15) [116]

With this overview of the possible interrelationships of Peter, James, and Jerusalem, we now turn our attention to Acts 15 which describes a crucial decision made at Jerusalem concerning the admission of Gentiles to Christianity. What role in this decision does Luke give to Peter by having him speak first (15:7-11)? Is James portrayed as overshadowing Peter, since it is James who makes the second and decisive speech (15:13-21; cf. 22ff.)? In asking who plays the decisive role in the Lucan picture of the council, it is well to remember that Paul and Barnabas, Peter and James, and the apostles and the elders of Jerusalem all play significant roles. A decisive role is given

occasion for James to take over the leadership in the Jerusalem church. Indeed the wording of 12:17 may suggest this: "Tell this to James and to the brethren." But Peter is pictured back at Jerusalem for the "council" in Acts 15. He is not mentioned after that in the Book of Acts. Presumably Luke would have us think that Peter left Jerusalem again after the council. For the possible importance of James in the development of the episcopal office, see W. Telfer, *The Office of a Bishop* (London: Darton, Longman and Todd, 1962), pp. 1-23.

[115] Cullmann, *Peter* (note 45 above), pp. 41ff.

[116] We shall occasionally use this terminology of "council," although we are aware that it has given rise to the almost unconscious abuse of thinking of this meeting on the analogy of the ecumenical councils that began in the fourth century.

to Peter in that he cites as a precedent for the admission of the Gentiles his own conversion of Cornelius—an act of God "giving the Holy Spirit to them just as He did to us" (15:8). A decisive role is given *to James* who enunciates his "judgment" (15:19-20) that, while the Gentiles should not be troubled over circumcision, they should be bound by four regulations. A decisive role is given *to the apostles and the elders* who send the letter imposing James' judgment upon the Gentiles in Antioch, Syria, and Cilicia (15:23). Peter provides the decisive witness; James provides the decisive judgment or decision; the apostles and elders provide the sentence or the enforcement of the decision.

Conceived in this manner, the overriding theme in the chapter, as elsewhere in Acts, is found in the term *homothymadon,* "one-mindedness" (15:25).[117] In harmony with the previous actions of Paul and Barnabas, the leaders at Jerusalem (Peter, James, the apostles and the elders) took the same stand for freedom, opposing those who argued that Gentile Christians must be subject to circumcision and the whole Law (15:5). Peter urged no circumcision or Law (15:10), and James set forth only a few regulations to be observed by the Gentile Christians, seemingly lest they scandalize the followers of Moses who lived alongside of them (15:21). When the apostles and the elders wrote to the Gentile Christians, they stressed the positive side: "It has seemed good to the Holy Spirit and to us to lay upon you no greater burden than these necessary things" (15:28). It is true that, if we read carefully, we discover that James has apparently conceded less than the full freedom from the burden of the Law that Peter proposed, and the apostles and the elders have followed James. Nevertheless, on the level of his own theological interpretation, Luke stresses the "one-mindedness" rather than a division between the positions of Peter and James.

---

[117] Note that the Revised Standard Version translates *homothymadon* here as "in assembly." Occurring as a key word in Acts at 1:14; 2:1 (some mss.); 2:46; 4:24; 5:12; 7:57; 8:6; 12:20; 18:12; and 19:29, it covers a wide range and can be used for the unity of a mob as well as the unity of the church.

Most scholars who probe behind the Lucan editing of the chapter suspect that the "one-mindedness" is, in part at least, a creation of Luke. Since the position taken in Acts 15:7-11 by Peter (no circumcision or Law) is similar to that of Paul (Gal 2:9-10), the problem centers around the more restrictive four regulations proposed in Acts 15:20 by James and imposed by the apostles and elders in 15:29—abstaining from the pollution of idols, from unchastity *(porneia),* from what is strangled, and from blood. In Paul's own account of his Jerusalem encounters he never mentions any such restrictive regulations. From Gal 2:9-10 one would get the impression that at the decisive second visit to Jerusalem the Pauline argument for freedom had triumphed completely, under the one condition that "they would have us remember the poor, the very thing I was eager to do." Indeed, Paul's subsequent argument with Peter at Antioch was over Peter's rethinking the advisability of eating with Gentiles, since apparently the Gentile Christians at Antioch were not observing the Jewish dietary laws. How could such an argument have arisen if the Jerusalem apostles and elders had promulgated James' four regulations (which included the Gentile observance of some dietary laws) and sent them to Antioch with Paul and Barnabas (Acts 15:22-29)? If one accepts the picture in Acts and reflects upon Gal 2:11ff., the men who "came from James" and the circumcision party would have been correct in forcing Peter back into obeying the apostolic letter, and Paul would have been in open defiance! Moreover, Paul's subsequent attitude on the permissibility of eating food dedicated to idols (I Cor 8:13; 10:14-30) would be very difficult to justify if he had accepted regulations from Jerusalem to the contrary. Having to choose, then, between the Pauline indications and the account of the four regulations in Acts, most scholars suspect the historicity of the Lucan picture.[118]

Let us press further, therefore, into this question of the four

---

[118] A contrary view is that of J. Hurd, *The Origin of I Corinthians* (New York: Seabury, 1965) who maintains that at Corinth, while Paul at first imprudently allowed complete freedom to the Gentile Christians on these matters, he later repented his "enthusiasm" and tried to introduce the Jerusalem decrees, thus arousing the opposition to which he addressed himself in the Corinthian correspondence.

regulations. Originally such regulations were part of the Israelite law governing the behavior of the foreigner *(gēr)* resident in Israel. The Gentile residents had to abstain from these impurities so that Israelites could associate with them without contamination (Lev 17:8-12; 18:6ff.). Was such a Jewish attitude more or less automatically carried over into the Jewish Christian communities in reference to Gentile converts, and did Luke create a legal basis for this attitude by attributing it to a Jerusalem decision? Is the letter, supposedly sent by the Jerusalem apostles and elders (Acts 15:22-29), a Lucan construction, or did it come to Luke from a source? Certainly there seem to be elements of Lucan style present in the letter.[119] In the Scripture citation used in his speech (15:16-18) James seems to follow the Greek Bible rather than the Masoretic Hebrew,[120] and this leads to the suspicion that his speech is not a historical report but a Lucan construction. Peter's speech centers on the Cornelius episode (cf. 15:7-9); and since, as mentioned above, many scholars question the historicity of that episode, doubt has been cast on the historical value of the entire Lucan account.[121] Indeed, it may be the dominant view in current critical

[119] An example would be *homothymadon* in 15:25. Others have pointed to the expression "the apostles and the elders" in 15:23 (cf. 15:2, 4, 6, 22; 16:4). However, since this expression occurs only in chapters 15 and 16 of Acts, one might question whether it can be described as a "Lucanism." If one posits a pre-Lucan source for the letter, Luke may have drawn this phrase from the letter in writing his description of the council. In the broader question of Lucan style throughout chapter 15, one interesting non-Lucan item should be noted, i.e., the name "Simeon" *(Symeōn)* in 15:14. Clearly Luke understands Simeon to be Peter; yet he never uses that spelling of "Simon" elsewhere in Luke-Acts (see note 90 above). Was Luke using a source where "Simeon" occurred? In that source did the name refer to Peter, or perhaps to someone else, like Simeon Niger (Acts 13:1)?—so S. Giet, "L'assemblée apostolique et le décret de Jérusalem: Qui était Siméon?" *Recherches de Science Religieuse* 39 (1951), pp. 203-20.

[120] A rough count indicates that the Acts quotation uses 34 of the 53 terms found in the Septuagint Greek version of Amos 9:11-12. It is not impossible that Acts follows a Greek version independent of the Septuagint—a Greek version that, in turn, translates a Hebrew recension different from the Masoretic Hebrew. This Amos text circulated at Qumran; see J. A. Fitzmyer, *Essays on the Semitic Background of the New Testament* (London: Chapman, 1971), pp. 51, 86-87.

[121] Haenchen (note 88 above), p. 464, states: "Luke's version of the

scholarship that Luke composed the scene from only two basic living traditions or memories: first, that at Jerusalem leaders such as Paul, Peter, and James had come to an agreement that Gentiles could be admitted to Christianity without being circumcised (a tradition confirmed for us by Paul in Galatians); and second, that in some mixed Christian communities, by custom going back to apostolic times, Gentiles had to observe certain Jewish regulations concerning impurity in order to permit fellowship with Jewish Christians.

As prominent as this minimal view of historicity is in modern scholarship, there are many other approaches that would seek to reconcile the Lucan and Pauline information in terms of varying combinations of the data.[122] For the sake of balance, it may be worthwhile to present to the reader one such view which acknowledges that Acts 15 in its present form is not a straight historical report of the "council of Jerusalem," but proposes that underlying Luke's modifications there is a considerable body of historical data. It has been suggested that Acts 15 is a conflation of two Jerusalem meetings. The *first* ended with Peter's speech in Acts 15:11 (or 12) and was the same meeting described in Gal 2:1-10—a meeting vindicating Paul's position on freedom from circumcision. In this first meeting Peter's siding with Paul was the decisive factor in the outcome. The *second* meeting took place later, and was perhaps provoked by arguments involving meals shared by Jewish and Gentile Christians, such as the argument over this subject

---

Apostolic Council—in this Dibelius is correct—does not possess historical value."

[122] We shall make no attempt to be exhaustive, but the following hypotheses exhibit some styles of approach: (1) Gal 2:1-10 and Acts 15 are concerned with the same Pauline visit to Jerusalem, but Galatians describes a private meeting between Paul and the Jerusalem authorities, while Acts describes the later, public meeting. (2) Gal 2:1-10 does not describe the same Pauline visit to Jerusalem of which Acts 15 speaks— the visit (and meeting) mentioned in Galatians is to be identified with the visit in Acts 11:27-30 (the famine visit) or with 18:22 or with a visit not mentioned in Acts. (3) Gal 2:1-5 and 6-11 represent separate Pauline visits to Jerusalem, which are then identified with any of the three to five visits to Jerusalem by Paul mentioned in Acts. Haenchen (note 88 above), p. 455, speaks of "the jungle of problems" in Acts 15; with equal appropriateness one may speak of the jungle of solutions.

between Paul and Peter at Antioch in Gal 2:11ff.[123] Jerusalem
(and James) decreed the four regulations for the Gentile
Christians of Antioch, Syria, and Cilicia (Acts 15:23). In this
hypothesis, Paul was not present at the second meeting; and he
never enforced its decree, perhaps because he did not know of
it (see Acts 21:25 where James and the Jerusalem elders in-
form him of it), and/or perhaps because his churches were
outside the area addressed by the decree.[124] This hypothesis
also casts light on the understanding of the role of James: he
was the decisive factor at the second meeting, precisely because
it concerned a problem that affected the "province" of Jerusalem of which he was the local leader.

Faced with such diverse hypotheses which make it very
difficult to delineate the borderline between history and theology
in Acts 15, we are hampered in making any firm decision about
the historical role that Peter played at the Jerusalem "council."
He was there; his voice was heard; his consent was important;
but it is not clear that his voice was supremely authoritative so
that one could speak of his primacy at the council. And indeed,
even if we bypass questions of pre-Lucan sources and of histor-

[123] By placing the Antioch controversy *before* the second meeting,
this hypothesis avoids some of the contradictions that we mentioned in
comparing Galatians and Acts 15. In evaluating the historicity of Acts
15:13ff. (the "James section") two correspondences with Gal 2:11ff.
should be noted: in both accounts *the name of James* is associated with
a strict position concerning the obligation of keeping the Jewish dietary
laws, and the discussion of this matter involves emissaries from James
or Jerusalem *to Antioch*. These correspondences offer an obstacle to the
thesis of complete fiction in the Acts section. We should note, however,
that the geographical designations of Acts 15:23 (Antioch, Syria, Cilicia
—see also Antioch in 15:30) are not repeated in the reference to the
letter in Acts 21:25 which speaks simply of "the Gentiles who have believed." One may theorize that the latter was the more original tradition,
and that Luke supplied "Antioch, Syria, and Cilicia" because that was
the region for which he was writing—unless again Luke was citing the
letter in mentioning the three places.

[124] In this hypothesis, when Acts 16:4 tells us that Paul and Timothy
communicated to cities like Derbe and Lystra the decisions reached by
the Jerusalem apostles and elders, the reference would be solely to the
decision reached in Acts 15:1-11 (12), the decision that circumcision
was not to be imposed on Gentile converts. Further detail on and bibliography for this hypothesis may be found in J. A. Fitzmyer, *Jerome
Biblical Commentary* (note 16 above), article 45, ##72-77.

icity, and return to the level of Luke's redaction of the scene, it is not clear that Luke presents Peter as the supreme voice in Acts 15. For Luke, as we have seen, Peter was an important part of the "one-mindedness" *(homothymadon)* voiced by the other major Jerusalem figures (James, the apostles and the elders).

After chapter 15 Peter disappears from the scene in Acts,[125] leaving Paul to dominate the subsequent narrative. This convenient disappearance warns us that Luke's primary interest was not to give a description of authoritative structure in the early church, but to substantiate a *heilsgeschichtlich* claim that would establish a connection between the churches of late first-century Christians (in which Luke lived) and the Jesus of Palestine through the medium of apostles and missionaries.[126] In order to do this, Luke begins the narrative of the Book of Acts in Jerusalem with "the (Twelve) apostles" (Acts 2:37), especially Peter and John. Then Luke passes on to "the apostles and the elders" (chapter 15 and 16:4), and finally to "James and all the elders" (21:18). This sequence in terminology may reflect a sequence of authority in the Jerusalem church, but it is not the main thrust of Lucan thought. The overall plan of Acts passes from Jerusalem and from Peter (Acts 1—15) to the Gentile churches of Asia Minor/Greece/Rome and to Paul (Acts 16—28). It is clear that for Luke Peter played an important role in the foundation period of the early church in Jerusalem, and for purposes of Lucan *Heilsgeschichte* Paul was his successor—an observation that makes it impossible to gain

---

[125] After 16:4 the apostles also are never mentioned in Acts.

[126] The connection would be historical if, as traditionally held, Luke was a companion of Paul—if he was part of the "we" in Acts 16:10-17; 20:5-15; 21:1-18; and 27:1—28:16. Yet the connection is not necessarily lost if the "we" of Acts represents a redactional literary device. In the "we" *Luke* could be expressing modestly his fictitious presence with *Paul,* who in turn was the connecting link with the genuine apostolic period represented by *Peter,* who was a companion of *Jesus.* Thus Luke would be underlining the continuity of the tradition and of normative apostolic preaching. For a different argumentation, see E. Haenchen, " 'We' in Acts and the Itinerary," *The Bultmann School of Biblical Interpretation: New Directions?* ed. J. M. Robinson *et al.* (New York: Harper, 1965), pp. 65-99.

from Acts any information about the role Peter played in the church after the council of Jerusalem or about a historical succession to some of Peter's tasks. Perhaps of significance for the Petrine question is the Lucan interest in Rome which seems at the end of Acts to replace Jerusalem as the center stage of *Heilsgeschichte*.

CHAPTER FIVE:
PETER IN THE
GOSPEL OF MARK[127]

As we turn from the Pauline letters and Acts to the Gospels, we begin to study Peter in a different perspective. An older biblical exegesis might have phrased the distinction thus: in Paul and in Acts one sees Peter's career in the history of the church; in the Gospels one sees Peter's career in the ministry of Jesus. The very fact that we treated Paul and Acts before treating the Gospels illustrates that we do not accept this type of distinction; for, as we insisted in Chapter Two (B, 3), the formation of the Gospels reflects early church history. Consequently, when we study Peter in the Gospels, we study both Peter's career in the ministry of Jesus and Peter's career in the history of the nascent church. Nevertheless, the light that the Gospels throw on how various Christian communities and theologians throughout the first century came to evaluate Peter is much more indirect than the light cast by Paul and Acts. Perhaps the Gospels can help to fill in the picture we have already seen, but we warn the reader that much of what one discovers depends on inference.

We shall treat the Gospel of Mark as the first of the Gospels

---

[127] The discussion for this chapter was led by P. Achtemeier. One session of the task force (December 1972) was devoted to the evidence of Mark, although some of the Marcan material had entered our discussions of Matthew and Luke.

(written in the 60's?). The portrait of Peter that it paints is to be dated intermediate between the Pauline portrait (50's) and that of Acts (latter part of the century).[128]

A. The General Picture of Peter in Mark

Simon or Peter[129] figures prominently in Mark; indeed it may be said that Mark gives us the basic outlines of the Gospel portrait of Peter familiar to most Christians. Let us begin by listing the passages or details in Mark that concern Peter.

(1)   Simon and his brother Andrew were fishermen on the Sea of Galilee (1:16).

(2)   Jesus called them (as the first of his disciples) to follow him and become fishers of men (1:17-18).

(3)   At the house of Simon and Andrew in Capernaum,[130] Jesus healed Simon's mother-in-law (1:29-31).

(4)   When Jesus was praying after a day of healing in Caper-

---

[128] For our general suppositions about the Gospel of Mark, see Chapter Two (B, 4). While it is useful to fit Mark chronologically between Paul and Acts, we remind the reader that chronological succession can be deceptive, especially in a study like this. We have little knowledge of the interrelationships among the Pauline churches, the Marcan church(es), and the Lucan church(es), or even among the various authors (except that Luke used the Gospel of Mark). Therefore, we cannot assume a linear chronological development in ideas about Peter. If the material comes from different places, later material may have a less developed view of Peter than earlier material, simply because some churches may have had little contact with Peter.

[129] In 3:16 Mark refers to "Simon whom he surnamed Peter." Before that (in 1:16, 29, 30, and 36) only the name "Simon" appears. After that there are eighteen references to "Peter" and only one to "Simon" (14:37). Does this almost consistent pattern of usage mean that Mark thought that it was on the occasion of appointing the Twelve (3:14) that Jesus gave the name "Peter" to Simon? (The fact that the verbs in 3:14 and 3:16, "appointed" and "surnamed," are both in the aorist tense may suggest this.)

[130] John 1:44 describes Bethsaida as the town of Andrew and Peter. Both Capernaum and Bethsaida were at the north end of the lake. Harmonization has been attempted, e.g., by the suggestion that, while Peter had been born at Bethsaida, he had moved to Capernaum where he had a house at the time he encountered Jesus; or Peter was from Bethsaida, but his mother-in-law's house was in Capernaum.

naum, Simon and others searched him out to report that people were seeking him; but Jesus wished to go on to the next towns (1:35-38).

(5)   Jesus appointed Twelve to be with him, to be sent out to preach, and to cast out demons; and the first of these, in the list of their names, is Simon "whom he surnamed Peter" (3:14-16).

(6)   When Jesus entered the ruler's house to revive his daughter, he allowed no one to follow him except Peter, James, and John. This is the first of the traditional three scenes involving an "inner group" of three disciples among the Twelve (5:37).[131]

(7)   On the way to Caesarea Philippi, in response to Jesus' question to his disciples, "Who do you say that I am?," Peter answered, "You are the Messiah." Jesus charged them to tell no one this, and taught the disciples about the suffering, death, and resurrection of the Son of Man. When Peter rebuked Jesus, Jesus in turn rebuked Peter, calling him "Satan" (8:27-33).

(8)   Jesus took Peter, James, and John up a high mountain and was transfigured before them. Peter offered to make three booths (for Jesus, Moses, and Elijah), "for he did not know what to say, and they were exceedingly afraid." A heavenly voice spoke to them, "This is my beloved Son; listen to him." As they came down from the mountain, Jesus spoke to them concerning the Son of Man and Elijah. This is the second of the three traditional "inner group" scenes (9:2-13).

(9)   Peter said to Jesus, "We have left everything and followed you." Jesus promised that those who had left family or possessions to follow him would receive a hundredfold in this life (with persecutions) and eternal life in the age to come (10:28-30).

---

[131] Yet, as we shall see in #11, the scene in Mark 13:3 has a group of four disciples (these three, plus Andrew), a grouping also found at the beginning of lists of the Twelve (cf. Matt 10:2; Luke 6:14; Acts 1:13). Apparently there was some flexibility about the composition of the "inner group." See also note 174 below.

(10) The day after Jesus had cursed the fig tree (11:12-14), when Jesus and his disciples were passing by the spot, Peter remembered and called attention to the withered tree. Jesus told them to have faith in God (11:20-22).

(11) When Jesus was sitting on the Mount of Olives, after he had predicted the destruction of the temple buildings, Peter, James, John, and Andrew[132] asked him privately when this would be, and thus gave occasion to Jesus' apocalyptic discourse (13:3ff.).

(12) At the Last Supper Jesus predicted that they would all fall away when he was struck, but that he would be raised up and go before them to Galilee (14:27-28). Peter said, "Even though they will all fall away, I will not." Jesus predicted that Peter would deny him three times that very night, but Peter insisted, "If I must die with you, I will not deny you." And they all said the same (14:29-31).

(13) In Gethsemane the other disciples were told to sit while Jesus prayed; but he took Peter, James, and John with him and told them of his distress of soul. They were instructed to remain and watch while he went farther on and prayed. Jesus returned to them three times, each time to find them sleeping. At the first return he spoke to Peter, "Simon, are you asleep? Could you not watch one hour?" This is the third of the three traditional "inner group" scenes (14:32-42).

(14) When Jesus was arrested and taken to the high priest and the Sanhedrin, Peter followed him at a distance into the courtyard of the high priest (14:54). Subsequently, he denied Jesus three times, swearing and cursing. At the second cockcrow Peter remembered that Jesus had predicted this, and he broke down and wept (14:66-72).

(15) The young man dressed in white (an angel?) said to the women who came to the empty tomb: "Go, tell his dis-

---

[132] Note the presence of Andrew here, alongside the "threesome" of Peter, James, and John. The call of these four men to be disciples is narrated together by Mark in 1:16-20, and their names are given as the first four among the Twelve in 3:16-19.

ciples and Peter that he is going before you to Galilee. There you will see him as he told you" (16:7—see #12 above).

Even if Mark had not told us that Peter (along with Andrew) was called to discipleship first and had not named Peter first in the list of the Twelve, these passages would make it clear that, for Mark, Peter was the most prominent among the Twelve in the Gospel picture of Jesus' ministry. In ## 4, 7, 9, 10, 12, and 15, while other disciples or members of the Twelve are mentioned or are on the scene, special attention is focused on Peter. Indeed, in ## 7, 8, 9, and 10 Peter serves as a kind of spokesman for others. If there are three scenes where he appears with James and John as constituting an "inner group" (## 6, 8, 13), in two of these Peter is singled out for special mention. And the scene in #14 is built entirely around Peter.

Yet the Marcan picture of Peter has its dark side too. Precisely because he is portrayed as prominent, on those occasions when the disciples of Jesus do *not* live up to their call, Peter is often the embodiment of their failure. In #4 those who seek Jesus out have not diagnosed his purpose, but only Simon is identified in this group.[133] We shall discuss in detail the scene at Caesarea Philippi (#7), where only Peter is identified as making a confession that is apparently inadequate. In #8 Peter speaks for James and John as well as himself, and Mark tells us that he did not know what to say. In #13 Peter's sleeping is focused upon and he is chastised by name. And, if all the disciples forsake Jesus and flee (14:50), only Peter's denial is singled out and dramatized (##12, 14). The vigorous brush with which Mark paints Peter's weaknesses is seen especially in two verses: in 14:71, if one understands that verse to mean that Peter invoked a curse on Jesus;[134] and in 8:33 where Jesus

---

[133] We regard as less likely the interpretation of #6 (Mark 5:37-40) which would have Peter and his two companions included among those who "laughed Jesus to scorn" and who were expelled from the room where the raising of Jairus' daughter took place.

[134] For a justification for translating 14:71 to mean "he began to invoke a curse on Jesus" rather than "a curse on himself," see H. Merkel, "Peter's Curse," *The Trial of Jesus,* ed. E. Bammel (*Cambridge Studies*

says to Peter: "Get behind me, Satan! For you are not on the side of God, but of men."

How do we account for this mixed Marcan picture of Peter? Is Mark simply describing the past: Peter was very important in the ministry of Jesus but exhibited weakness and impetuosity (which he eventually overcame)? Is Mark emphasizing the prominence of Peter in order to rehabilitate his memory and offset attacks on his reputation in contemporary Christian quarters? Or is Mark hostile to the memory of Peter, and does he seek to remind the reader of Peter's failings?[135] As we indicated in Chapter Two (B, 4), we have to ask the question whether Mark is pro-Petrine, anti-Petrine, or both, or neither.

In even beginning to deal with these questions, one must keep in mind that Peter may have representative value for Mark, so that he is not to be considered only as an individual. For instance, Mark may think of Peter as a representative of the disciple or of discipleship, both in his generosity and in his failings. As a disciple he is called to be a fisher of men, and he and his brother set an example in immediately leaving their nets and following Jesus (1:16-18), so that he can speak for the group when he says, "We have left everything and followed you" (10:28). Yet in his falling away at the time of the passion, he is also typical of the group (14:29-31). Moreover, if Peter is a typical disciple, since the disciples of Jesus are meant to serve as lessons for the readers of the Gospel, Peter may also be the lesson *par excellence* for Christians as to the demands of discipleship upon them.

The way one answers the question of Mark's attitude toward Peter will depend in part on one's analysis of Mark's theological outlook and his purpose in writing the Gospel. Different scholars can go through the above-listed references to Peter and fit them into very different schemes of Gospel understanding. In T. J.

in honour of C. F. D. Moule; Studies in Biblical Theology, second series, 13; London: SCM, 1970), pp. 66-71.

[135] Of course, this is a possibility only if the testimony of Papias that Mark was Peter's interpreter is totally rejected (see notes 22-24 above). For an interesting emphasis on the positive and negative aspects of Peter, see O. Cullmann, "L'apôtre Pierre, instrument du diable et instrument de Dieu," *New Testament Essays* (note 52 above), pp. 94-105.

Weeden's hypothesis,[136] which sees the Gospel as an effort to counteract a *theios anēr* christology in Mark's community (see note 97 above), the disciples are presented by Mark as holding the view that Jesus was a wonder-worker. Mark has Jesus correct them by insisting on a theology of suffering and the cross. In particular, for Weeden,[137] Peter is presented by Mark as the spokesman of an erroneous christology; and this interpretation affects the evaluation of many Petrine scenes. For instance, Peter's offer to build three booths on the occasion of the Transfiguration is seen to reflect a divine man christology; and Mark counteracts it in 9:6 by indicating that Peter was a "dunce."[138]

Another example of how the scenes in Mark pertinent to Peter are interpreted in light of a larger view of early Christianity is G. Klein's study of Peter's denials.[139] Klein thinks that the idea that Peter followed Jesus to the courtyard of the high priest after the arrest (14:54) is a patent contradiction of 14:27 and 50 which indicate that all the disciples fled and forsook Jesus. He finds in Luke 22:31-32a[140] an older tradition whereby, through Jesus' prayers, Peter did not fail by denying him. For Klein, the invention of the story of Peter's denials is part of a larger anti-Petrine movement which even led to suppressing from the Gospel tradition the story of the risen Jesus' appearance to Peter (I Cor 15:5).[141]

---

[136] T. J. Weeden, "The Heresy That Necessitated Mark's Gospel," *Zeitschrift für die neutestamentliche Wissenschaft* 59 (1968), pp. 145-58. Also *Mark—Traditions in Conflict* (Philadelphia: Fortress, 1971).

[137] *Mark—Traditions*, p. 56.

[138] *Ibid.*, p. 123. See note 157 below.

[139] "Die Verleugnung des Petrus. Eine traditionsgeschichtliche Untersuchung," *Zeitschrift für Theologie und Kirche* 58 (1961), pp. 285-328, reprinted with an additional note in *Rekonstruktion* (note 71 above), pp. 49-98. His thesis has been attacked by E. Linnemann, "Die Verleugnung des Petrus," in the same journal 63 (1966), pp. 1-32; and he has responded in the *Zeitschrift für die neutestamentliche Wissenschaft* 58 (1967), pp. 39-44. Linnemann does not believe in the historicity of Peter's denials either, but she thinks that the story about Peter is simply a concretizing of the general denial of all the disciples.

[140] Klein assumes that the phrase in 32b "when you have turned" is a gloss to make the original prediction that Peter would not fail conform to the later and contradictory idea that Peter denied Jesus.

[141] See note 41 above.

We have not attempted to evaluate these suggestions about every Petrine passage in Mark, for we were of differing opinions as to their respective merits. But it is worth our while to examine in detail two scenes to show how the evaluation of Peter is affected by general attitudes toward Mark and his sources.

B. Peter's Confession of Jesus as Messiah (Mark 8:27-33)

As we indicated in Chapter Two (B, 3), we are assuming the need of studying such a passage on at least three levels of Gospel formation. In the passage under discussion, the discernment of the three levels will have to be applied to five separate items in the scene. Since the other two Synoptic Gospels are at least partially dependent on Mark for this scene, they are not of great help to us in detecting pre-Marcan material.[142] Of more importance is John's account which many think to be independent of Mark (Chapter Two, B, 7).

(1) The question as to who men say that Jesus is (8:27-28). The Marcan passage is set in the context of a journey of Jesus and his disciples to the villages of Caesarea Philippi. Although John 6:66-71 does not have this place name,[143] it is of significance for our discussion to note a general parallel of sequence between Mark and John, a sequence that may be based on tradition.[144] It is difficult to pass judgment on the historicity

---

[142] We have not accepted the thesis of Rudolf Bultmann (note 26 above), which would see behind Mark an older Aramaic tradition now found only in Matt 16:17-19. For Bultmann, Mark omitted the part favorable to Peter, and this omission came from an anti-Petrine motif.

[143] Since this place name appears nowhere else in the Gospels and the locality belongs to a largely Gentile region, it is often looked upon as a guarantee of the story's historicity, because there would be no apparent reason for inventing such a setting. See K. L. Schmidt, *Der Rahmen der Geschichte Jesu* (Berlin, 1919), pp. 215-17.

[144] Notice the following pattern:

Multiplication for 5000	Mark 6:30-44	John 6:1-15
Walking on the sea	Mark 6:45-54	John 6:16-24
(Then skipping to the end of Mark's second multiplication account which is found in Mark 8:1-10)		
Request for a sign	Mark 8:11-13	John 6:25-34
Remarks on bread	Mark 8:14-21	John 6:35-59
Confession of Peter	Mark 8:27-30	John 6:60-69
Passion theme; Satan/devil	Mark 8:31-33	John 6:70-71

of the question that Jesus directs to the disciples ("Who do men say that I am?") and of the report about the various answers that are in circulation (John the Baptist, Elijah, one of the prophets). There is no exact parallel in John, but in John 6:67 Jesus directs a different question to the Twelve ("Will you also go away?"). The fact that a similar attempt to identify Jesus (John the Baptist, Elijah, one of the prophets of old) is reported earlier in Mark 6:14-16 suggests the *possibility* that a "floating" pre-Marcan tradition to this effect has been adapted by Mark to serve as an introduction to what follows.[145]

(2) Peter's confession of Jesus as the Messiah (8:29). Did Peter actually make such a confession of Jesus? If so, did he do it during Jesus' ministry or after his resurrection, e.g., when Jesus appeared to Peter? In dealing with the question of historicity we shall assume that the term "Messiah" in question here bears a meaning that would be consonant with the aspirations of intertestamental Judaism, e.g., the anointed king of the House of David expected to come and deliver Israel from its enemies and to establish a world empire, marked with justice and peace.[146] We are therefore not giving to the term the Christian coloration that developed when the concept of messiahship was tailored to fit Jesus, e.g., suffering Messiah, divine Messiah. Nor, in asking whether Peter confessed Jesus as the Messiah, are we asking about Jesus' view of himself—whether or not he thought he was the Messiah. Overall, the likelihood that some of those who followed Jesus during his lifetime would have thought that he was the Messiah and have expected him to play a regal role is suggested by the fact that Jesus was crucified as

---

[145] E. Dinkler, "Peter's Confession and the 'Satan' Saying: The Problem of Jesus' Messiahship," *The Future of Our Religious Past*, ed. J. M. Robinson (Essays in Honour of Rudolf Bultmann; New York: Harper & Row, 1971), p. 178: "The question in Mark 8.27b, therefore, could be original, if one accepts the view that here the evangelist has completely reworked the tradition he received and introduced into his christological theme, by the insertion and omission of material, something important and well-known to the community."

[146] The literature on the Jewish concept of the Messiah is enormous. For a brief sketch of the development of the concept, see J. L. McKenzie, *Jerome Biblical Commentary* (note 16 above), article 77, ##152-63.

a would-be Messiah king.[147] That Peter made a dramatic confession in a scene where Jesus had addressed himself to the Twelve is a tradition echoed in John 6:67-69.[148] This Johannine parallel does not solve the historicity issue but favors the existence of, at least, a pre-Marcan tradition.[149]

(3) Jesus' charge to the disciples to tell no one about him (8:30). This is an instance of the famous "Messianic secret," which since the beginning of the century has been the keystone of the thesis that the Gospels (including Mark) are not simple history but have been elaborated in the light of later theology. W. Wrede[150] advanced the theory that the secrecy imposed by Jesus on those who glimpsed his identity or experienced his divine power was a device employed by Mark to explain why people did not recognize Jesus to be the Messiah during his lifetime. Most scholars, then, would regard 8:30 as stemming from the Marcan redaction of the scene.

(4) The prediction that the Son of Man must suffer, be killed, and after three days be raised again (8:31). This is the

---

[147] N. A. Dahl, "Der gekreuzigte Messias," *Der historische Jesus und der kerygmatische Christus,* ed. H. Ristow and K. Matthiae (Berlin: Evangelische Verlagsanstalt, 1961), pp. 149-69.

[148] The Johannine form of Peter's confession is "You are the Holy One of God." (A number of lesser textual witnesses have attempted to conform it to the Synoptic form of the confession, particularly the Matthean—a harmonization showing that ancient scribes saw the connection between the two traditions.) Even though we do not know of the "Holy One of God" as a messianic title, the difference from "Messiah" should not be pressed. A comparison of the demonic recognitions of Jesus in Mark 1:24 and 3:11 suggests that "Holy One of God" and "Son of God" are interchangeable, and the latter designation stands in apposition to Messiah (or Christ) in the better textual witnesses of Mark 1:1 and in 14:61.

[149] Perhaps another Johannine passage that favors the existence of a pre-Marcan tradition is 1:41 where *Andrew's* announcement "We have found the Messiah" is associated with the call of Simon Peter. While it is not Peter who makes the confession, can it be accidental that the recognition of the Messiah is associated with a story about him?

[150] *The Messianic Secret* (Greenwood, S.C.: Attic, 1972; German ed. 1901), especially pp. 62, 67-68, 119, 140-41. Wrede does not claim that Mark invented the idea, but it was Mark who inserted it into the Gospel tradition. V. Taylor (note 23 above), pp. 12-24, argues that the Marcan secret "is the reflection of historical reality." The passages that exemplify the secret include Mark 1:25, 34, 44; 3:11-12; 5:43; 7:36; 8:26; and 9:9.

first of three passion predictions (cf. 9:31; 10:33-34). In the abundant recent literature on these predictions,[151] the more common opinion is that, while Mark has drawn on earlier tradition concerning the passion of Jesus,[152] it was the evangelist himself who shaped the predictions into their present form. Thus, the majority of scholarship would attribute the final wording of Mark 8:31 and its placement here to the redactional level.

(5) Peter's refusal to accept the suffering of the Son of Man, and Jesus' rebuke of Peter (8:32-33). If the prediction of the suffering of the Son of Man stems from Mark in its present wording and localization, then the wording of Peter's unfavorable reaction (to the point of rebuking Jesus) stems from Mark as well. But this judgment need not affect the rebuke to Peter by Jesus in 8:33, "Get behind me, Satan! For you are not on the side of God, but of men." This may have been a traditional saying[153] for which Mark has supplied an introduction. Indeed, unless one posits the creation of such a saying by an anti-Petrine group, there is a real possibility that we may be dealing with a historical reminiscence.[154] Certainly

---

[151] For instance, H. J. Tödt, *The Son of Man in the Synoptic Tradition* (Philadelphia: Westminster, 1965), pp. 141ff.; G. Strecker, "The Passion and Resurrection Predictions in Mark's Gospel," *Interpretation* 22 (1968), pp. 421-42; R. H. Fuller, *Foundations* (note 97 above), pp. 118-19, 151-54; J. Jeremias, *New Testament Theology* (note 41 above), pp. 277ff.

[152] N. Perrin, "Towards an Interpretation of the Gospel of Mark," *Christology and a Modern Pilgrimage*, ed. H. D. Betz (Claremont, 1971), p. 13: "... suggests that the original pre-Markan tradition was of a Petrine confession and that the addition of the prediction unit is by Mark himself." The possibility of a pre-Marcan pattern of *three* predictions is raised by the fact that John has three statements of Jesus concerning the "lifting up" of the Son of Man (3:14; 8:28; 12:32-34). See Brown, *John* (note 31 above), I, pp. 145-46, 477-79. While it is not impossible that Jesus spoke of his coming death and God-given victory, critical scholarship is virtually unanimous in rejecting the historicity of an exact prediction by Jesus of the details of his passion, death, and resurrection.

[153] It is of importance that in the Johannine parallel (John 6:69-70) Peter's confession of Jesus is followed immediately by Jesus' reference to a devil among the Twelve. Only, for John, it is not Peter but Judas who plays the role of Satan (cf. 13:2, 27).

[154] Dinkler (note 145 above), p. 174: "In the case of a saying that rebukes Peter as sharply as this one does, one must deal as thoroughly

those circles in which Peter had influence or was respected never invented such a saying!

Thus the study of the five separate items leaves us with a good likelihood of pre-Marcan tradition for at least (2) Peter's confession of Jesus and (5) Jesus' rebuke of Peter. Such scholars as Hahn, Fuller, and Dinkler are inclined to see (either on the level of history or of pre-Marcan tradition) a direct union of the confession and the rebuke[155]—Jesus sharply rejected Peter's confession of him as the Messiah because he was no religious-national king, which is what Peter meant. If this be true, then in its earlier form the scene was not one of praise for Peter. Historically or for the earlier tradition, his confession may have been another instance of his somewhat bungling enthusiasm.

When we move to the redactoral level of Mark's intent, based on the full scene with Mark's insertions included, there is a dispute. We have already mentioned Weeden's thesis that for Mark, Peter is the spokesman of an erroneous christology.[156] However, the Marcan insertions that now separate the confession in 8:29 from the rebuke in 8:33 can be interpreted quite differently. The command to secrecy in 8:30 is not a rejection of Peter's confession but a temporary suppression of it until after the death and resurrection of Jesus when his messiahship can be proclaimed to all.[157] Mark does not object to the

as possible with the probability of historical authenticity before minimizing the difficulty by assuming a relocation of the saying during the period of rivalries within the church."

[155] F. Hahn, *The Titles of Jesus in Christology* (London: Lutterworth, 1969), pp. 223-25, argues for an original biographical apophthegm consisting of Mark 8:27a . . . 29b, 33. Fuller, *Foundations* (note 97 above), p. 109, speaks of a pronouncement story in three parts: a setting (8:27-28); an action (Peter's confession in vs. 29); and the pronouncement by Jesus (vs. 33). Dinkler (note 145 above), p. 188, confines the original fragment to Peter's confession and Jesus' rebuke.

[156] See note 137 above. In Mark 13:21-22 Mark warns against the man who will proclaim, "Here is the Messiah," and Peter is such a man.

[157] We have mentioned Weeden's interpretation of the Transfiguration as an anti-Petrine scene (note 138 above); but others would see the Transfiguration as a confirmation of Peter's confession. The heavenly voice that identifies Jesus as His Son agrees with Peter's insight. Only once again the notion of suffering is introduced as a modifier (Mark 9:9). Cf. C. Masson, "La transfiguration de Jésus (Marc 9:2-13),"

confession of Jesus as Messiah since his Gospel is the Good News of Jesus *Christ* (1:1) and in the Marcan trial scene before the high priest Jesus acknowledges that he is the Messiah (14:62).[158]

In this interpretation the function of the Son of Man saying introduced by Mark in 8:31 is not a rejection of Peter's confession but a corrective to it by the addition of a note of suffering. Peter's confession is inadequate because he does not see that suffering is part of the career of the Messiah.[159] It is only when Peter rejects this note of suffering that Mark (8:33) has Jesus rebuke him sharply by calling him Satan. The Satanic work of Peter is not in his confession of Jesus as Messiah but in his tempting Jesus toward a notion of messiahship that does not recognize the divinely ordained suffering and death of Jesus (see 1:13 for Satan the tempter).[160]

Thus, Mark does not present Peter as the first to understand completely who Jesus is (and in this Mark differs from Matthew, as we shall see), but he may still allow some credit to Peter as the first of the Twelve to recognize that Jesus is the Messiah.

C. A Post-Resurrectional Message to Peter (Mark 16:7)

At the empty tomb of Jesus a young man dressed in a white

Revue de Théologie et de Philosophie 97 (1964), pp. 1-14; M. E. Thrall, "Elijah and Moses in Mark's Account of the Transfiguration," *New Testament Studies* 16 (1969-70), pp. 305-17; J. A. Ziesler, "The Transfiguration Story and the Markan Soteriology," *Expository Times* 81 (1970), pp. 263-68. See also note 168 below.

[158] Another possible sign of the positive importance that Mark attributes to Peter's confession of Jesus as the Messiah is the thesis that this confession is the turning point of the Gospel, a confession coming roughly at the middle of the Gospel and one that begins to point toward Jesus' death. It would be matched by a confession at the end of the Gospel—the centurion's proclamation: "This man was (the) Son of God" (15:39).

[159] Another way of phrasing the Marcan attitude toward the confession of Jesus as the Messiah is that it is a correct confession when accompanied by the companion insight that Jesus is the (suffering) Son of Man (8:29, 31; 14:61-62) or Son of God (the best text of 1:1; also a comparison of 8:29 and 15:39).

[160] See O. Cullmann, *The Christology of the New Testament* (rev. ed.; Philadelphia: Westminster, 1963), pp. 122-23.

robe tells the women, "Go, tell his disciples and Peter that he is going before you to Galilee. There you will see him as he told you." Although the other Synoptic Gospels have a parallel to this (closer in Matt 28:7 than in Luke 24:6), only Mark mentions Peter.

Because of the post-resurrectional setting where a messenger (thought by most scholars to be an angel) communicates a revelatory interpretation of the significance of the empty tomb, the problem of studying the scene on a historical level is formidable. There are scholars today who question the historicity of the existence of an empty tomb. And even for many of those who do accept the historical fact of the empty tomb, the interpretative angelic dialogue is to be regarded as Christian reflection on the significance of that fact—a later reflection made possible only after the appearances of the risen Jesus. Once Jesus had appeared, his followers came to understand why the tomb was empty, viz., the body had not been stolen, but Jesus had been raised from the dead. In order to make this clear, when they narrated the discovery of the empty tomb, they used the figure of the revealing angel of the Lord to give voice to their understanding of what had happened.[161]

Be this as it may, when we move from the level of historicity to that of pre-Gospel sources, a question has been raised as to whether Mark 16:7 belonged to an earlier form of the angelic dialogue that interpreted the empty tomb. The presence of verse 7 in Mark 16 is very awkward[162] since the subsequent verse almost contradicts it: the women are told in verse 7 to go to the disciples and Peter with an important message, but in verse 8 it is reported that they said nothing to anyone. If 16:7 is re-

---

[161] This view has found expression in recent books on the resurrection: P. Benoit, *The Passion and Resurrection of Jesus Christ* (New York: Herder & Herder, 1969), p. 260; R. H. Fuller, *Formation* (note 76 above), p. 56; R. E. Brown, *The Virginal Conception and Bodily Resurrection of Jesus* (New York: Paulist, 1973), pp. 117-23.

[162] Mark 16:7 is intimately associated with 14:28 ("But after I am raised up, I will go before you to Galilee") which is also intrusive in its context, for it breaks the continuity between verses 27 and 29. Fuller, *Formation,* p. 60, states: "There is no question that verse 28 is not an authentic logion of Jesus, for it contains an obvious *vaticinium ex eventu.*" On pp. 57-64 he gives a full discussion of 16:7.

garded as a later insertion by the evangelist, the sequence between verses 6 and 8 is improved.

Why would such a message have been inserted? One explanation is that Mark 16:7 represents a half-way step toward associating a narrative of the appearance(s) of the risen Jesus with the narrative of the discovery of the empty tomb.[163] Mark is a Gospel that has no account of the appearances of the risen Jesus,[164] while the other (later) Gospels do have such accounts. But perhaps when Mark was being completed, the evangelist's community was already familiar with a narrative of how Jesus had appeared to Peter and to the Twelve. The insertion of 16:7 makes allowance for such a narrative, for it indicates that the disciples and Peter will see the risen Jesus in Galilee. Indeed, many scholars have concluded from this verse that Mark was aware of the tradition that Jesus had appeared first to Peter.[165]

Such an interpretation would enhance the picture of Peter in the Gospel of Mark. Having narrated the story of Peter's denials, Mark is reminding his readers that Peter was restored

---

[163] We assume here the common position of critical scholarship that these are two different types of narratives that were not originally joined. Documentation may be found in the books listed in note 161 above.

[164] Again here we make an assumption that is nigh universal in modern scholarship, namely, that the various endings of Mark found in some Greek manuscripts after 16:8 are not authentically Marcan. The contention that the long ending (Mark 16:9-20) is not from Mark's hand does not necessarily mean that it is not canonical Scripture. (It continues to be used liturgically in many churches; and for Roman Catholics it comes under the decision of the fourth session of the Council of Trent which declared canonical the books of Scripture *and their parts* as they are in the ancient Latin Vulgate.) Much more difficult than the question of the non-Marcan authorship of the various supplied endings is the question whether Mark's Gospel originally ended with 16:8 or whether there were additional Marcan verses that were lost. The interpretation of the function of Mark 16:7 that we have given above implies that 16:8 was the original ending of the Gospel. See the literature cited by P. W. van der Horst, "Can a Book End with *gar?* A Note on Mark xvi. 8," *Journal of Theological Studies* 23 (1972), pp. 121-24.

[165] I Cor 15:5 and Luke 24:34 suggest that the appearance to Peter (Cephas, Simon) was the first appearance of the risen Jesus to a member of the Twelve. Why does Mark mention the disciples before Peter? Does Mark mean, "Tell the disciples, *especially* Peter," so that the basis of the order of names is not one of chronology but one of emphasis— Peter had denied Jesus but he too is to be assured that he will see the risen Jesus?

to favor by the risen Jesus who accorded to him an appearance. Peter would have been known to the Marcan community as one of the most important witnesses of the risen Jesus, the only one mentioned by name among those who saw him. If we combine this with the information in Mark 3:16, namely, that it was Jesus who gave the name "Peter" ("rock") to Simon,[166] Mark may be giving implicit testimony to the tradition that, by the will of Jesus, Peter had real importance for the church.

But here again another and quite different interpretation of Mark 16:7 has been advanced. It has been argued that the words about seeing Jesus in Galilee do not refer to a post-resurrectional appearance but to the parousia—in Galilee they will see him come back as the Son of Man.[167] Weeden has interpreted the absence of resurrection appearances in Mark as a sign of Marcan dislike for such phenomena, since they belonged to the *theios anēr* christology that Mark opposed. Mark tried to counteract the traditions of resurrection appearances by an emphasis on the parousia.[168] Those inclined to such a view could interpret the reference to Peter in 16:7 as an attempt to discredit the tradition that Jesus had appeared to him—Go and tell the disciples, *even* Peter (who is supposed to have seen the

---

[166] Of course, we know nothing of how Mark interpreted the significance or symbolism of this name.

[167] E. Lohmeyer (note 106 above) suggested this in the mid-1930's, and it is a theory adopted by such scholars as R. H. Lightfoot, W. Michaelis, W. Marxsen, and T. J. Weeden. Recently N. Perrin (note 152 above), p. 38, has stated that it is *inconceivable* that Mark 16:7 refers to a resurrection appearance and not to the parousia.

[168] Weeden's views on Mark 16:7 are found in *Mark—Traditions* (note 136 above), pp. 11-13. For Weeden, pp. 121-24, the Transfiguration was originally a resurrection appearance; but Mark retrojected it into the ministry and interpreted it as a proleptic experience of the parousia. For arguments and literature against the interpretation of the Transfiguration as a resurrection appearance, see Fuller, *Formation* (note 76 above), pp. 165-66; also C. H. Dodd, "The Appearances of the Risen Christ: An Essay in Form-Criticism of the Gospels," *Studies in the Gospels,* ed. D. E. Nineham *(Festschrift* R. H. Lightfoot; Oxford University, 1955), pp. 9-35—reprinted in *More New Testament Studies* (Grand Rapids: Eerdmans, 1968), pp. 102-33; H. C. Kee, "The Transfiguration in Mark: Epiphany or Apocalyptic Vision?" *Understanding the Sacred Text,* ed. J. Reumann (Valley Forge, Pa.: Judson, 1972), pp. 135-52. See note 157 above for additional bibliography on the Transfiguration.

risen Lord) that you Christians will really see Jesus in Galilee when the parousia occurs.

We have presented this second interpretation of the scene, not because the task force has judged it highly persuasive,[169] but as an example, lastly, of how much the assessment of Peter's role in the Marcan Gospel is influenced by one's overall view of Mark's theology. The fact that at the moment a great deal of scholarly attention is being focused on Marcan theology, resulting in some very different interpretations, has complicated our task.

---

[169] For a challenge to Weeden's hypothesis, see D. L. Tiede, *The Charismatic Figure as Miracle Worker* (SBL Dissertation Series, 1; Missoula, Mont., 1972), pp. 257-60.

CHAPTER SIX:
PETER IN THE
GOSPEL OF MATTHEW[170]

When we turn to the Gospel of Matthew, we see a Christian portrait of Peter drawn toward the end of the century, some twenty or more years after Mark wrote. We have made no specific judgment about the make-up of the community addressed by "Matthew" (by which name we shall refer to the evangelist), but it is a common opinion among scholars that at least part of Matthew's community was more familiar with Judaism than was Mark's community.[171] This opinion should be remembered; for, as we saw in Chapter Three in dealing with Paul, it has been argued that Peter's backing in the early church came from Jewish Christian circles, while Paul's came from Gentile Christian circles. The very favorable view of Peter in Matthew may possibly be related to the Jewish Christian background of the Matthean community.

---

[170] The discussion for this chapter was led by J. Burgess. Two sessions of the task force (in March 1972—one of them longer than usual) were devoted to the evidence of Matthew, and special studies of Matthean passages were subsequently done by J. A. Fitzmyer and M. M. Bourke.

[171] Kümmel (note 24 above), pp. 80-83, cites the literature and the usual arguments on the subject of whether Matthew's Gospel reflects a Gentile Christian or a Jewish Christian background. He opts for the thesis that Matthew has rewritten the Marcan tradition from a Jewish Christian standpoint—a Jewish Christianity, however, very open to the admission of Gentiles.

A. The General Picture of Peter in Matthew

We have agreed on the working hypothesis that Matthew drew upon Mark (Chapter Two, B, 5). And so it is not surprising to find that most of the Petrine scenes or sayings in Mark also appear in Matthew. If the reader turns to the list of Petrine passages in Mark given at the beginning of the previous chapter, he will discover that in the two Gospels there is no significantly different treatment of Peter[172] in ##1, 2, 3, 5, 8, 9, 12, 13, and 14.[173] Thus, one may say that in the common material Matthew has taken over the broad outlines of the Marcan highlighting of Peter.

The five incidents (##4, 6, 10, 11, 15) where Matthew has omitted the Marcan reference to Peter betray no significant difference in theological outlook. For instance, Matthew just does not report the incident in #4 where Mark has "Simon and those who were with him" search out Jesus to report that people are seeking him. In the first of the three "inner group" scenes involving Peter, James, and John (Mark #6),[174] as well

[172] Matthew's use of the names "Simon" and "Peter" is somewhat different from Mark's (note 129 above). *If* it was Mark's idea (3:16) that Jesus conferred the name "Peter" upon Simon at the moment when Jesus appointed the Twelve, that is not Matthew's idea. Not only does Matthew have a special scene in 16:18 where Jesus says to Simon Bar-Jonah, "You are Peter"; but also in the parallel to Mark 3:16 (namely Matt 10:2) Matthew simply mentions that Simon was commonly known by the name "Peter" ("Simon who is called Peter"), an item of information that is also supplied at the time when Simon appears for the first time in the Gospel (Matt 4:18). The usage of "Peter" is about five times as frequent as the usage of "Simon" in Matthew, and indeed antedates the giving or explaining of the name "Peter" in 16:18 (see note 210 below). For example, while Mark (1:29-31) speaks of Simon's house and mother-in-law, Matthew (8:14-15) refers to Peter's house and mother-in-law. The combination "Simon Peter" occurs in Matt 16:16.

[173] In the Gethsemane scene (#13), however, Peter is more benevolently treated in Matthew. Mark 14:37 has Jesus say to Peter, "Simon, are you asleep? Could you [singular] not watch one hour?" Matt 26:40 has Jesus say to Peter, "So you [plural] could not watch one hour with me?"

[174] As for #6, the resuscitation of the ruler's daughter, Matthew's account of the whole scene (9:18-26) is very different from Mark's (5:21-43); and it is not impossible that here Matthew has drawn upon a non-Marcan form of the story that did not mention Peter, James, and John. (See also note 131 above.) The more common view is probably

as in the scene involving Peter, James, John, and Andrew on the Mount of Olives (Mark #11), Matthew gives no personal names and, in the latter instance, prefers the ambiguity of "the disciples."[175] In the remark concerning the fig tree (Mark #10) "the disciples," rather than Peter, speak in Matthew's account. Somewhat more important is Matthew's omission of "and Peter" (Mark #15) from the angelic message to the women at the empty tomb. But, as we saw in the last chapter, Mark's special mention of Peter in this scene may be related to his omission of post-resurrectional appearances. Matthew (28:16-20) does have a narrative of the appearance of the risen Lord to *the Eleven* on a mountain in Galilee, and that may partially explain why Matthew (28:7) does not have the angel make a distinction between Peter and the disciples when he speaks to the women about who will see Jesus in Galilee.[176]

If a few of the omissions of Marcan scenes just discussed might lessen slightly the impression of Peter as a spokesman for the disciples, that lessening is compensated for by Matthew's introduction of Peter into two other minor incidents (15:15; 18:21-22) for which there are, respectively, Marcan and Lucan parallels. Both Matthew and Mark have a scene where the

---

that of G. D. Kilpatrick, *The Origins of the Gospel According to St. Matthew* (Oxford: Clarendon, 1946), p. 73, namely, that occasionally Matthew reduces Mark's fullness of detail.

[175] P. Minear, "The Apostolic Structure of the Church," *Andover Newton Quarterly* 6 (1966), pp. 15-37, especially 26ff.; and E. R. Martinez, "The Interpretation of *Hoi Mathētai* in Matthew 18," *Catholic Biblical Quarterly* 23 (1961), pp. 281-92, argue that in Matthew's Gospel "the disciples" usually means the Twelve.

[176] If in the tradition there were accounts of appearances both to the (Eleven) disciples and to Peter (I Cor 15:5), and if Matthew (or the pre-Matthean tradition) had retrojected elements of the appearance to Peter back into the ministry, then both Mark's form of the angel's directive and Matthew's correction of it would be intelligible (see note 196 below). Another explanation is offered by J. Jeremias, *New Testament Theology*, p. 307, who thinks that Matthew omitted the phrase "and to Peter" from Mark 16:7 because he had at his disposal no account of an appearance to Peter—it had already been suppressed (see note 41 above). Jeremias observes that Matthew both reports "overwhelming praise of Peter" (16:17-19) and deletes favorable references to him (like Mark 16:7) or tells us of his wavering faith (14:28-33). Jeremias judges this "unconcerned juxtaposition of conflicting traditions" to be almost characteristic of Matthew.

Pharisees and scribes challenge Jesus on the non-observance of Jewish tradition by his disciples, in response to which Jesus says that what defiles a man is not what goes into him but what comes out of him (Matt 15:11; Mark 7:15). But, while in Mark 7:17 *the disciples* ask Jesus to explain this parabolic saying, in Matt 15:15 it is *Peter* who says, "Explain the parable to us." The other instance is the "Q" saying of Jesus (Matt 18:22; Luke 17:4) concerning how frequently one must forgive one's brother (seven or seventy times seven). Matthew alone (18:21) introduces this saying by having *Peter* ask a question, "Lord, how often shall my brother sin against me, and I forgive him?" If Luke agreed with Matthew, this would be an important instance of Peter's appearing in the "Q" tradition (see note 27 above); but the insertion of the name is probably to be attributed to Matthean redaction, in harmony with the general picture of Peter's serving as a spokesman.

If the material thus far considered adds little new to the Marcan picture of Peter, it is in three passages for which there are neither Marcan or Lucan parallels that Matthew makes his principal contribution to the New Testament data on Peter. These are (a) the incident of Peter's walking on the water, sinking, and being rescued by Jesus (14:28-31); (b) Peter's confession of Jesus not only as the Messiah (Mark #7) but also as the Son of the living God; and Jesus' answer consisting in a blessing and a promise to Peter concerning the rock on which the church would be built and the keys of the kingdom (16:16b-19); (c) the question about paying the Temple tax, and Jesus' telling Peter to catch a fish in whose mouth there would be a shekel to pay the tax for Jesus and Peter (17:24-27).

Before we begin to treat these three scenes separately, it would be in order to make a few general remarks about their possible pre-Matthean origins and their present place in Matthew's Gospel. They resemble each other in involving a close interchange between Jesus and Peter. The first and last suppose an extraordinary miracle done on Peter's behalf—Bultmann [177]

---

[177] *History* (note 26 above), p. 353. There are other instances of the legendary in Matthew's passion and resurrection accounts, e.g., 27:19, 52-53; 28:2.

characterizes them as the only two examples of the legendary introduced into the peculiarly Matthean account of the ministry of Jesus. Thus the possibility suggests itself that Matthew drew upon a collection of Petrine materials for the three scenes. In fact, the first two (involving Peter's walking on the water, and Jesus' saving him when he showed signs of little faith; then, Peter's confession of Jesus as the Son of the living God, and Jesus' promise that he would be the rock on which the church would be built) have been thought to stem from a now-lost narrative of the post-resurrectional appearance of Jesus to Peter, especially since the incidents mentioned have a certain resemblance to the account in John 21 of the risen Jesus' appearance to Simon Peter and others at the Sea of Tiberias.[178] Nevertheless, the amount of Matthean language that appears in these scenes shows, at least, heavy editing; and many scholars tend to think of a pre-Matthean *oral* tradition of diversified character, rather than of a Petrine source.[179] We shall have to analyze each scene separately and in detail on this question.

The three passages under consideration appear in what is often called the Fourth "Book" of the Matthean Gospel (13:53—18:35), a section of the Gospel that betrays Matthew's ecclesiastical concerns.[180] For instance, it is in this Fourth "Book" that there occur the only two instances of the word *ekklēsia* ("church, community") to be found in the four Gospels (Matt 16:18; 18:17). And much of chapter 18 concerns relationships within the Christian community. Therefore, the setting of the three Petrine passages has direct reference to the question that most interests us: the role of Peter in the first-century church.

---

[178] Brown, *John* (note 31 above), II, pp. 1085-92.

[179] Kilpatrick (note 174 above), pp. 38-44, points out in detail the Matthean features in these three passages (along with Matt 15:15 and 18:21, which we discussed separately) and concludes that they were not taken from a written source and are of various derivation (p. 44). Cullmann, *Peter* (note 45 above), p. 184, states concerning Matt 16:17-19 that, in whole or in part, Matthew found these words "in an ancient oral tradition."

[180] See W. D. Davies, *The Setting of the Sermon on the Mount* (Cambridge University, 1964), pp. 337-38.

B. Jesus Saves Peter as He Sinks While Walking on the Water (Matt 14:28-31)

The first of the three Petrine scenes has been woven into an already existing Marcan scene.[181] In Mark 6:45-52, after the multiplication of the loaves, Jesus made his disciples enter a boat and cross over to the other side of the lake while he dismissed the crowd and went into the hills to pray. At evening he saw the boat in the midst of the sea and the disciples having a hard time rowing against the wind. And so he came walking upon the sea and "meant to pass by them"; but when they all saw him walking, they thought it was a ghost and were terrified. Jesus told them, "It is I; have no fear." The scene concludes with Jesus getting into the boat, the wind ceasing, and the disciples utterly amazed; "for they did not understand about the loaves, but their hearts were hardened."[182]

Matthew changes the tone of Mark's misunderstood epiphany by inserting the Petrine material (14:28-31) between the saying of Jesus, "It is I; have no fear," and the Marcan conclusion. (Matthew prepared for this insertion earlier by omitting any reference to Jesus' intention of passing them by; cf. Matt 14:25 with Mark 6:48.) According to Matthew, in response to the saying of Jesus, Peter answers, "Lord, if it is you, bid me to come to you on the water." Jesus invites him to come; and so Peter gets out of the boat, walks on the water, and comes to Jesus. But when he sees the wind (sic), he becomes afraid and begins to sink. In response to his plea, "Lord, save me," Jesus reaches out his hand and catches Peter, saying, "O man of little faith [oligopistos], why did you doubt?" The conclusion of the story then changes: Both Jesus and Peter get into the boat, the wind ceases; and those in the boat worship Jesus saying, "Truly, you are (the) Son of God" (see note 188 below).

---

[181] Luke offers no basis for comparison, for the great Lucan omission of Marcan material (i.e., of Mark 6:45—8:26) begins precisely with this scene. However, John 6:15-21 offers a parallel that agrees substantially with Mark and shows no awareness of the Matthean scene concerning Peter.

[182] Bultmann, History (note 26 above), p. 216, classifies this as one of the nature miracle stories and suggests that even in Mark it is a confla-

The basic story in which Jesus works a miracle for Peter, almost as a proof (vs. 28), is quite unusual.[183] Since Matthew is our only authority for the scene, decisions about the historical level and about the pre-Matthean source level are very difficult. A partial parallel is the scene in John 21:7-8 where the risen Jesus stands on the shore of the Sea of Tiberias and Simon Peter (having been told by the Beloved Disciple, "It is the Lord") springs from the boat into the sea to go toward him. Of course, in John 21 there is no miraculous walking on the water (a modesty that might be more original); but there is the same basic action of leaving the boat to go to Jesus in a context of hesitation as to whether or not it is Jesus. Note also the parallel references to Jesus as "Lord." The recognition and the "Lord" motifs are quite characteristic of resurrection scenes, and the theme of Peter as a man of little faith who sinks and has to be saved by Jesus would fit very well into an appearance of the risen Jesus to Peter after Peter had denied him.[184] However, we can only guess at such a pre-Matthean post-resurrectional setting, and it is best to concentrate on the import that Matthew himself gives to the Petrine incident.

Is Matthew's picture unfavorable to Peter? At the worst, is Peter painted as a man who confounds pretentious enthusiasm with faith, and who consequently fails and needs Jesus' salvation? This interpretation stresses the designation of Peter as *oligopistos* ("of little faith") in vs. 31. It would have Peter

---

tion, for the stilling of the storm seems to have little to do with the miracle of Jesus' walking on the water.

[183] Kilpatrick (note 174 above), pp. 40-41, speaks of it as "standing quite unparalleled in whole or in part to the rest of the gospel material"; but the amount of Matthean Greek suggests to him: "either that the evangelist is the first to put the story into writing, or else that, if he had a written source before him, he has completely rewritten it in his own style. The way in which the story wholly depends on the Marcan context favors the former alternative."

[184] In his analysis of scenes which are now found in the context of Jesus' ministry but which originally may have been post-resurrectional, Dodd, "Appearances" (note 168 above) is quite conservative about conceding such a possibility. However, in relation to the whole scene of Jesus' coming to the disciples on the water, he acknowledges (pp. 23-24) the presence of many features which are appropriate to the literary form of a post-resurrectional appearance narrative.

speaking and acting much as he did in the matter of denying Jesus, promising "Even if I must die with you, I will not deny you" (Matt 26:35), and yet failing miserably. Or in a more favorable interpretation, is Peter painted as a typical disciple both *in his real love* for Jesus, as he desires to go to him, and *in his insufficiency of faith* during Jesus' ministry? Bonnard [185] hovers between the two interpretations, while Bultmann and Held[186] stress more the element of typical discipleship. Certainly Jesus' invitation to Peter to come to him (vs. 29) and his giving Peter the power to do what he himself has just done (walking on the water) echo a pattern found in other scenes of discipleship (e.g., Matt 4:19; 10:1).

But are there not still more favorable indications about Matthew's conception of Peter in this scene? Does the scene illustrate Peter's prominence or even preeminence among the disciples?[187] We note the contrast with Mark where none of the disciples speak; here Peter reacts to Jesus' walking on the water by calling him "Lord" (vs. 28; cf. vs. 30; but also 8:25 where all the disciples use this title). Does this indicate that while he may have had little or insufficient faith, Peter had at least the first glimmerings of faith? This would heighten the parallel to the second Matthean Petrine scene (Peter's confession of Jesus as the Son of the living God) that we shall discuss next. That such a parallel may be Matthew's intention is suggested by his changing the conclusion of the scene. No longer are the disciples simply "utterly astonished" because of a lack of understanding and a hardness of heart, as in Mark 6:51-52; but they worship

185 P. Bonnard, *L'Évangile selon saint Matthieu* (Commentaire du Nouveau Testament; 2nd ed.; Neuchâtel: Delachaux et Niestlé, 1970), p. 223.

186 Bultmann, *History* (note 26 above), p. 216; G. Bornkamm, G. Barth, and H. J. Held, *Tradition and Interpretation in Matthew* (Philadelphia: Westminster, 1963), pp. 204-6.

187 P. Benoit in the *Matthieu* of the fascicle publication of the *"Bible de Jérusalem"* (Paris: Cerf, 1961), p. 10, sees this as a scene that illustrates the primacy of Peter. Subsequent church interpretation often carried the scene in that direction, e.g., by making the boat the "bark of Peter" in which the other disciples came to faith by worshiping and confessing Jesus. Without any tendency to go that far, H. J. Held in Bornkamm, *Tradition* (note 186 above), p. 272, thinks there is an ecclesiastical nuance.

Jesus and confess him as "Son of God" (Matt 14:33)—virtually the same confession[188] that Peter will make in Matt 16:16b and which Jesus will praise as the gift of divine revelation. This favorable interpretation catches both the strength and weakness of Peter: he begins to see, and yet remains a weak and impulsive man who needs Jesus. In both his strength and his weakness he is a lesson for Christian disciples. In addition, it is important for Matthew's community to know that Jesus saves Peter when he begins to sink, because, as Matthew will later narrate, Peter is the rock on which the church is to be built. Such an interpretation would match the general Matthean setting of the incident, namely in the Fourth or ecclesiastical "Book" of the Gospel, as explained above.

With such diverse interpretations of the scene it would be unwise to draw any conclusions without discussing the other two Petrine scenes.

C. Peter's Confession and Jesus'
Promise to Him (Matt 16:16b-19)

We now come to the passage that more than any other has figured in controversies about the role of Peter in the New Testament and the implications for the subsequent church. In recent centuries it has become *the* text cited by the Roman Catholic Church as scriptural basis for the authority of the papacy,[189] even to the point that "Tu es Petrus et super hanc petram aedificabo ecclesiam meam" is painted in huge gilt letters inside the cupola of St. Peter's Basilica in Rome, a church that may liter-

---

[188] In Matt 14:33 the confession is anarthrous, i.e., there is no article in the Greek before "Son of God," while in Matt 16:16b, there is an article before "Son of the living God." It is difficult to assess the importance of this difference.

[189] In the exegesis of the Church Fathers and, indeed, even of the medieval theologians (including Thomas Aquinas) surprisingly little attention was focused on this text for establishing the authority of the Roman church. See J. Ludwig, *Die Primatworte Mt. XVI, 18-19 in der altkirchlichen Exegese* (Neutestamentliche Abhandlungen, XIV, 4; Münster: Aschendorf, 1952); K. Froehlich, *Formen der Auslegung von Mt 16, 13-18 im lateinischen Mittelalter* (Tübingen: Präzis, 1963). Also note 4 above.

ally have been built on Peter, if the bones in the crypt beneath the altar really are his, as Pope Paul VI has asserted (note 50 above). However, it was a contribution of the Protestant scholar Oscar Cullmann, much of whose book on Peter is devoted to a study of Matt 16:17-19,[190] to attempt a study of the text without seeing it through the optic either of Protestant polemic or of Roman Catholic counter-polemic. And so, in this vein, we shall approach Matt 16:16b-19 just as we have approached other texts—not primarily from the aspect of what it came to mean in the later church,[191] but from the historical, pre-Matthean, and Matthean levels of significance.

As with the previous Petrine scene, we are facing a peculiarly Matthean passage woven into the midst of an episode that Matthew shares with Mark. We analyzed Mark 8:27-33 in the previous chapter, dissecting it into five elements: (1) The question as to who men say that Jesus is (Mark 8:27-28); (2) Peter's confession of Jesus as the Messiah (8:29); (3) Jesus' charge to the disciples to tell no one about him (8:30); (4) The prediction that the Son of Man must suffer, be killed, and after three days rise again (8:31); (5) Peter's refusal to accept the suffering of the Son of Man, and Jesus' rebuke to Peter as Satan (8:32-33). Matthew has preserved all the five Marcan elements, but he has expanded Mark's element 2 by having Peter confess Jesus not only as the Messiah but also as "the Son of the living God" (Matt 16:16b). And between Mark's element 2 and element 3 Matthew has inserted three verses (16:17-19) in which Jesus blesses Simon, calls him Peter, the rock on which the church is to be built, promises to give him the keys of the kingdom of heaven, and tells him that whatever he binds or looses on earth will be bound or loosed in heaven. Finally, Matthew expands the rebuke of Peter in Mark's element 5, "Get behind me, Satan!", by adding: "You are a stumbling-block [*skandalon*] for me" (16:23).

---

190 *Peter* (note 45 above), pp. 161-242.

191 Of course, we do not ignore the significance of our study for that problem—we have indicated that we undertook this study with an ecumenical interest—but we have not let later disputes establish the state of the exegetical question.

We have spoken of Matthew's expanding Mark by insertion,[192] and in this instance our general assumption of Marcan priority is supported by the absence of the Matthean material in the parallel passages of Luke 9:18-22 and John 6:66-71. To argue that Matthew's version was the earliest would require an explanation of the absence of the Matthean material in the other traditions (with at least Mark and John seemingly independent of each other).[193] Moreover, John has elements parallel to the Matthean material scattered through the Fourth Gospel (see John 1:42; 20:23), a fact that suggests that Matthew may have gathered and inserted here material that once belonged to another setting or other settings.[194]

In his study of this problem, Cullmann was inclined to relate the special Matthean material in this scene to Luke 22:31-32, a passage at the Last Supper where Jesus prays for Simon that his faith may not fail, and that, when Simon has "turned again," he will strengthen his brethren. From this relation Cullmann concludes: "The saying in Matthew 16:17ff. most probably belongs to the Passion story; it was originally transmitted in connection with the prediction of Peter's denial, but was placed by Matthew in another setting."[195] Cullmann has not had much following in this hypothesis; and there is greater support for the thesis that the pre-Matthean setting, in whole or in part, was post-resurrectional.[196]

---

[192] In times past, as part of the polemic surrounding this passage, there were attempts to dismiss these verses as later tendentious addenda and therefore not an authentic part of the Gospel. Today we can reach virtual unanimity in declaring that there are no significant textual problems in them and that they are not later interpolations.

[193] Yet we remind the reader of Bultmann's thesis (note 26 above) that the Matthean form of the scene is older than the Marcan form, for Mark has omitted material favorable to Peter.

[194] It is possible, of course, that it was not Matthew but a pre-Matthean composer who gathered the material together, and that 16:16b-19 came to Matthew already, in substance, a unit. Cullmann, *Peter* (note 45 above), p. 184 thinks this of 16:17-18 and perhaps 19a.

[195] *Ibid.*, p. 191. See also his article cited in note 135 above.

[196] The arguments are well marshaled by R. H. Fuller, "The 'Thou art Peter' Pericope and the Easter Appearances," *McCormick Quarterly* 20 (1967), pp. 309-15. Weeden, *Mark* (note 136 above), pp. 64-69, has argued that even Mark's account of Peter's confession of Jesus as the Messiah may have been post-resurrectional (a corollary of Weeden's

Let us go through the Matthean material verse by verse to investigate the possibilities of such a post-resurrectional setting, to ask ourselves what the relation would be between a saying of the risen Jesus and a reflective development of the pre-Matthean community,[197] and finally to determine what the whole scene meant to Matthew.

(1) *Peter's confession of Jesus as "the Son of the living God"* (16:16b). Whatever doubt there may be as to whether for Mark Peter's confession of Jesus as the Messiah is wrong or only incomplete, there can be no doubt that for Matthew Peter's confession is to be considered true and perceptive, since Jesus himself praises it in the following verse as the product of divine revelation. "Son of God" is one of the most exalted New Testament titles for Jesus, and at times it seems to have been yoked to "Messiah" in order to correct any inadequacy in the understanding of messiahship and to introduce a divine element.[198] Thus John 20:31, coming after Thomas' confession of the risen Jesus as "My Lord and My God," states the purpose of the Fourth Gospel: "That you may believe that Jesus is *the Messiah, the Son of God,* and believing, you may have life in his name." The very context in John suggests that "Son of God" is a confession which belongs more to post-resurrectional faith than to the faith or trust in Jesus that developed during the historical ministry. Indeed, it might be theorized that Matthew has combined two Petrine confessions, the confession attested in Mark "You are the Messiah," which belonged to Jesus' ministry, and the more exalted confession "You are the Son of (the living) God," which belonged to the first appearance of the

thesis that the confession reflects a *theios anēr* christology, as do post-resurrectional appearances) and that Mark retrojected it into the ministry as part of his polemic against post-resurrectional appearances. The fact that the Johannine parallel to Peter's confession (John 6:66-71) is situated in the ministry in a sequence roughly the same as Mark's (note 144 above) creates a difficulty for Weeden's theory.

[197] In dealing with this post-resurrectional material, we shall find that the dividing line between the "historical" level and the pre-Matthean level tends to get blurred.

[198] See note 159 above for the Marcan tendency to unite "Son of God" and "Messiah."

risen Jesus after his resurrection, the appearance to Peter.[199] While this remains highly speculative, the appearance of a confession of Jesus as "Son of God" in Matt 14:33, the first of the three Matthean Petrine scenes, is worthy of notice in this connection, precisely because we saw some possibilities that that scene was also post-resurrectional in origin.

The Matthean addition of "the Son of the living God" to the Marcan Petrine confession of "the Messiah" effects some changes in the way we have to consider this confession in Matthew. In Mark Peter was the spokesman of the disciples when he made his confession. Although Matthew has the same introduction to the confession that Mark has, pointing in the direction of Peter as a spokesman, the addition involved in the Matthean confession evokes from Jesus the exclamation that Peter got his insight through no human means ("flesh and blood"). The revelation expressed in his confession was a personal gift of God to Peter, and so he was not just the spokesman of a common faith.[200] Moreover, Peter's confession is no longer the turning point of the Gospel, a function that seemingly it had in Mark (note 158 above). In Matthew it is not really the first confession of Jesus by those who accept him: his messianic origins have already been the subject of discussion and proclamation ("Son of David" in 9:27; 12:23; 15:22), and all the disciples have confessed him as Son of God (14:33).[201]

---

[199] In the form-criticism of post-resurrectional appearance narratives (see Dodd's article in note 168 above), the recognition of the risen Jesus, sometimes through hailing him as "Lord," is an important element. In John 20:28, as mentioned above, Thomas combines "Lord" and "God" in his recognition-confession of Jesus. See E. F. Sutcliffe, "St. Peter's Double Confession in Mt 16:16-19," *Heythrop Journal* 3 (1962), pp. 31-41.

[200] E. Haenchen, *Der Weg Jesu* (Berlin: Töpelmann, 1966), p. 301, states that in Matthew "Peter is here no longer the spokesman of the disciples, who expresses in words their common faith; but he is the receiver of a revelation, lifted up to a place that no other disciple can share with him." There remains the problem of how this insight can be reconciled with the fact that all the disciples make almost the same confession as Peter in 14:33.

[201] The existence of previous confessions (yet see note 188 above) betrays the fact that the exuberant expression of Jesus' enthusiasm for Peter's confession is scarcely in its original sequence.

(2) *"And Jesus answered him, 'Blessed are you, Simon Bar-Jonah! For flesh and blood has not revealed (this) to you, but my Father who is in heaven'"* (16:17). How much of this verse stems from Matthean redaction, and how much may be pre-Matthean material? That there are Matthean redactional elements is clear.[202] The beatitude or macarism, absent from Mark, is a favored Matthean style of expression (thirteen times); but it is also frequent in Luke and so may represent a "Q" pattern. It occurs twice in John, once (20:29), interestingly, as part of a post-resurrectional episode. Indeed, the frequency of the beatitude in the many traditions may indicate that it stems from Jesus himself. "Father who is in heaven" is more clearly Matthean, being found in Matthew's version of the Lord's Prayer (Matt 6:9), as contrasted with Luke's almost certainly more original "Father" (Luke 11:2).

On the other hand, the information that Simon's father was named Jonah[203] is a bit of pre-Matthean tradition, confirmed partially by John 1:42 where Peter is addressed as "Simon son of John" (in a context similar to that in Matthew, namely, on the occasion of his being told that he would be called Cephas or Peter). Another and more serious argument against treating vs. 17 as entirely the product of Matthean redaction lies in the

---

[202] The case for Matthean redaction has been argued strongly by the Catholic scholar A. Vögtle, "Messiasbekenntnis und Petrusverheissung. Zur Komposition Mt 16, 13-23 par.," *Biblische Zeitschrift* 1 (1957), pp. 252-72; and 2 (1958), pp. 85-103; reprinted in *Das Evangelium und die Evangelien: Beiträge zur Evangelienforschung* (Kommentare und Beiträge zum Alten und Neuen Testament; Düsseldorf: Patmos, 1971), pp. 137-70. An argument for seeing pre-Matthean material in vs. 17 is that the verb "has . . . revealed" (*apokalyptein*) lacks a direct object in Greek, as it does in 11:27 where Matthew draws upon "Q" (cf. Luke 10:22). Presumably if Matthew were composing the verse on his own, he would have phrased it more clearly and smoothly.

[203] We deem unlikely the suggestion that *bar iōna* is derived from an Akkadian loan-word in Aramaic, meaning "terrorist," and designates Simon as a political terrorist or zealot—a thesis mentioned with hesitation by Cullmann, *Peter* (note 45 above), pp. 23-24; *The State in the New Testament* (New York: Scribner's, 1956), pp. 8-23; *Jesus and the Revolutionaries* (New York: Harper & Row, 1970), p. 9, note 13. See the comments of M. Hengel, *Was Jesus a Revolutionist?* (Facet Books, Biblical Series, 28; Philadelphia: Fortress, 1971), pp. xiii, 9-10, 11-12 (note 29).

clause, "Flesh and blood has not revealed [*apokalyptein*] this to you," a clause that may also offer evidence for the originally post-resurrectional context of Jesus' words to Peter. In Gal 1:16, where Paul describes his experience of the risen Jesus, he says that when God "was pleased to reveal [*apokalyptein*] his Son to me, . . . I did not confer with *flesh and blood*."[204] In both Matthew and Galatians there is a contrast between a revelation from God and a communication from "flesh and blood."[205] It is unlikely that a borrowing, one from the other, explains this harmony between Matthew and Paul;[206] more probably, both appropriated language from a traditional way of describing the post-resurrectional appearances of the glorified Jesus.[207]

We conclude, then, that in 16:17 Matthew has redactionally brought together elements that came to him from an earlier tradition. In so doing he has produced a verse that gives Peter a special distinction: he is the only disciple in the Gospels who is the named recipient of a dominical blessing, and his insight about Jesus is confirmed as being a revelation from Jesus' Father.

(3) *"And I tell you, you are Peter; and on this rock I will build my church, and the gates of Hades shall not prevail against*

---

[204] Note also the use of the noun *apokalypsis* in 1:12 where Paul describes how the gospel came to him "through a *revelation* of Jesus Christ."

[205] It is noteworthy that Matthew uses a verb form in the singular (*apekalypsen*) with the plural subject "flesh and blood." Of course, "flesh and blood" is also a standard rabbinic circumlocution for man in his weakness; see R. Meyer, *"Sarx," Theological Dictionary* (note 20 above), vol. 7, p. 116.

[206] This is against the thesis of A.-M. Denis, "L'élection et la vocation de Paul, faveurs célestes," *Revue Thomiste* 57 (1957), pp. 405-28; and "L'investiture de la fonction apostolique par 'Apocalypse': Etude thématique de Gal. I, 16," *Revue Biblique* 64 (1957), pp. 335-62, 492-515.

[207] See Fuller, "Peter" (note 196 above), pp. 311-13. He suggests that this tradition of using *apokalyptein* may have arisen at a very early period when the first appearance of the risen Jesus (to Peter) was looked upon "as an advance disclosure of Jesus as he was to be revealed in the end, viz., as the Son of Man, exactly as in Rev. 1:1." It is possible that, if the language was associated in an earlier tradition with an appearance to Peter, part of Paul's reason for using it was to show that the appearance of which he was a witness was on a level with that to Peter.

it" (16:18).[208] Once again we must ask the question whether and to what extent the verse is redactional. Kilpatrick,[209] who consistently leans toward assuming Matthean redaction, says that the first part of the verse could be a conversion into direct speech of Mark 3:16, which reads literally, "And he put the name Peter on Simon." However, there remains the difficulty that in John 1:41-42, after Andrew's announcement, "We have found *the Messiah,*" there is a parallel both to verses 17a and 18a in Matthew; for the Johannine Jesus says, "You are *Simon son of John;* you will be called *Cephas* (which is translated *Peter*)." If John is independent of Mark, the parallelism between John and Matthew is better interpreted as representing an earlier tradition about the giving of the name Cephas/Peter [210] of which Mark 3:16 is only a summary notice.

Again Kilpatrick argues that "on this rock I will build my church" resembles Matt 7:24 which speaks of "a wise man who built his house on the rock," a passage that may reflect Matthean redactional language since the Lucan form (Luke 6:48) of the "Q" saying is quite different. Yet this argument is somewhat offset by the recognition of an Aramaic substratum underlying Matthew's Greek in 16:18. The play on the name in Greek is not perfect since it involves slightly different nominal forms: "You are *Petros* and upon this *petra* I will build."[211] In

---

[208] We take as commonly agreed that the "it" in "shall not prevail against it" refers to the church and not to the rock, although the feminine Greek pronoun *autēs* would allow either reference. The Revised Standard Version correctly interprets the "gates of Hades" *(pylai Hadou)* as the "powers of death." The image demands a metaphorical (synecdochical) reading of *pylai,* "gates," as "gatekeepers" or "powers," while *Hadēs* can refer to the place of death where the forces of evil are at work.

[209] *Matthew* (note 174 above), p. 39.

[210] We are assuming here that the scene in Matthew is a name-giving scene. It is not impossible that (in Matthew's mind) Simon already bore the name "Peter," and Jesus is simply offering an explanation of why that name was appropriate. But, to the best of our knowledge, the name "Rock" was not an ordinary personal name in either Hebrew/Aramaic or in Greek. It would be more comparable to the American nickname "Rocky" and therefore would have to be explained, e.g., the one who bears it has a rough or "tough" character, etc. Compare the appellation *maqqāb(āy),* "hammer(like)," given to Judas Maccabeus.

[211] This difference has led some to suggest that all we have in Greek

Aramaic there is identity: "You are *Kephā'* and upon this *kephā'* I will build." Another Semitism, "gates of Hades" for "powers of death" (note 208 above), plus the Semitisms "flesh and blood" in the preceding verse and "bind and loose" in the following verse (also the presence of Semitic parallelism—see vs. 19 below), constitute impressive evidence for proposing that these verses originated in a setting where Aramaic was a native tongue, and this supports the thesis of a pre-Matthean origin of the basic material.[212]

The reference to building *a church* fits in with the thesis of a post-resurrectional setting for the words of Jesus, for there are difficulties in assuming that the Jesus of the ministry planned for a church. But we must proceed with care here. Whether the Jesus of the ministry expected the end within the immediate future is still an unresolved question.[213] If he did not, he could

---

is a play on words and no suggested identity between *petra,* "rock," and *Petros,* "Peter" (a view that is challenged by the demonstrative pronoun "on *this* rock," which suggests identity). See H. Burton, "The Stone and the Rock. St. Matthew 16, 13-19," *The Expositor,* 2nd series, 6 (1883), p. 434; W. C. Allen, *A Critical and Exegetical Commentary on the Gospel According to St. Matthew* (International Critical Commentary; 3rd ed.; Edinburgh: Clark, 1912), p. 176; W. A. Wordsworth, "The Rock and the Stones," *The Evangelical Quarterly* 20 (1948), pp. 9-12; F. Stagg, *Matthew* (Broadman Bible Commentary, 8; Nashville: Broadman, 1969), pp. 172ff.

[212] Matthew's own Greek elsewhere is not so heavily Semiticized as the material in these verses. Aramaic-speaking origin is not necessarily equivalent to origin from the historical Jesus or even origin in the Jerusalem Christian community. There would, of course, be scholars who think that the Jesus of the ministry did speak these words, e.g., K. L. Schmidt, "*Ekklēsia,*" *Theological Dictionary* (note 20 above), vol. 3 (English 1965; German 1942), pp. 518-26. We have pointed out the possibility of post-resurrectional origins; but, as mentioned (note 197 above), that possibility has to be combined with a theory of subsequent *community* influence on the development of the scene. Many have thought that a more likely Jewish Christian community than that of Jerusalem would be that of Antioch or some Palestinian-Syrian community (depending on one's theory about the geographical situation of the Matthean community—see note 171 above). Bultmann, *History* (note 26 above), pp. 138-40, asserts with characteristic confidence that it is "quite impossible to take Matt. 16:18-19 as a genuine saying of Jesus," and that it stems "from the Palestinian Church."

[213] Compare the differing treatments in W. G. Kümmel, *Promise and Fulfillment: The Eschatological Message of Jesus* (Studies in Biblical Theology, 23; London: SCM, 1961); and N. Perrin, *Rediscovering the*

have planned for a church. But even if he did have this expectation of the end (and the majority of scholarship favors that assumption), while it may exclude his having planned for a church of extended or indefinite continuity, does it necessarily exclude his having planned for a renewal of the people of Israel within a structured community? The theology of the Qumran (Dead Sea Scroll) group was marked by apocalypticism. Its members expected the end soon; but still they developed a structured community with rules for admitting and disciplining members. Thus, they could be thought of as a *qāhāl* ("assembly, community"—one of the Hebrew words often proposed as background for *ekklēsia*) [214] with the power of binding and loosing. We cannot say with certainty that the Jesus of the ministry could not have thought of building a church in a similar sense of organizing a people preparing themselves for the imminent end. Nevertheless, having made this important allowance, we would have to judge that vs. 18, with its reference to the "gates of Hades" ("powers of death") that shall not prevail over the church, seems to imply a permanence of expectation that would go beyond the foresight of the Jesus of the ministry. It would be more appropriate in the context of a post-resurrectional appearance of Jesus, especially if we agree that some of these appearances were "church-founding" appearances (note 78 above) which provided for preaching, baptizing, forgiving sins and other means of beginning, enlarging, and continuing the Christian community.

Thus far we have been discussing the pre-Matthean origins of vs. 18, pointing to the possibility of its stemming from a post-resurrectional appearance of Jesus and its being preserved and perhaps developed in an Aramaic-speaking community. On that level, precisely because of the Aramaic identity of *Kephā'*/ *kephā'*, there can be no doubt that the rock on which the church was to be built was Peter. Is this true also for Matthew in whose

_____

Teachings of Jesus (New York: Harper & Row, 1967), especially pp. 154-206.

[214] On one of the banners to be prepared for the eschatological war (1QM 4:10), the Qumran group refers to itself as "the assembly of God" (*qᵉhal 'El*).

Greek there is the slight difference *Petros/petra*? Probably the most common view would be that it is.[215] Other interpretations, however, are possible. For instance, the *petra* might not be *Petros* (Peter) himself, but Peter's confession—or, more precisely, Peter when he confesses and "thinks the things of God" (16:23).[216] A possible implication of this view would be that when Peter "thinks the things of men," he can become a stone of stumbling (*skandalon*) for Jesus (16:23).

This brings us to the question of the relation (on the level of the evangelist's intention) between Peter the rock on which the church is to be founded (16:18) and Peter the stumbling-block for Jesus (16:23). It is significant that, despite the way Matthew has magnified Peter in the special material he has inserted into the Marcan scene of Peter's confession, he has also kept and indeed heightened the rebuke of Peter at the end of the scene (Matt 16:23=Mark 9:33). It is true that to some extent this ending is now dissociated from the confession and blessing of 16:16b-19 by the fresh start that Matthew has introduced in 16:21 (cf. Mark 9:31). The prediction of the passion, which is the subject of Jesus' rebuke to Peter, is now introduced by: "From that time forth." Nevertheless, the Matthean form of the rebuke, with its added clause, "You are a stumbling-block [*skandalon*] for me," has, intentionally or not, created a kind of triple parallelism:

---

[215] It would be pointless to list all the commentaries holding this view, but it is found in two popular one-volume commentaries, Protestant and Catholic respectively: K. Stendahl in *Peake's Commentary on the Bible* (2nd rev. ed.; London: Nelson, 1962), p. 787; J. L. McKenzie, *Jerome Biblical Commentary* (note 16 above), article 43, #114.

[216] This is an ancient view attested in many Church Fathers (Origen, Eusebius, Ambrose, Theodore of Mopsuestia, Chrysostom, etc.). An example of a modern proponent is A. H. McNeile, *The Gospel According to St. Matthew* (London: Macmillan, 1915), p. 241. Also ancient (Origen, Augustine, and later) and still encountered occasionally in contemporary exegesis is the contention that the rock is Christ (an identification found elsewhere in the New Testament, e.g., I Cor 10:4). See O. J. F. Seitz, "Upon This Rock: A Critical Re-examination of Matt. 16:17-19," *Journal of Biblical Literature* 69 (1950), pp. 329-40, and *One Body and One Spirit: A Study of the Church in the New Testament* (Greenwich, Conn.: Seabury, 1960), pp. 78-83; G. A. F. Knight, "Thou Art Peter," *Theology Today* 17 (1960), pp. 168-80. For more detail on the Patristic exegesis, see the books cited in note 189 above.

16:16: *sy ei ho Christos* ... ("You are the Messiah ...");
16:18: *sy ei Petros* ... ("You are Peter ...");
16:23: *skandalon ei emou*
    ("You are a stumbling-block for me.")

The second and third members of this parallelism are found in Matthew alone, and the key to the contrast between them may lie in the difference between the present and future roles of Simon. In response to his confession, he is given a name to signify his future role as the rock on which the church will be built, a role that (in Matthew's mind) Peter would play after the resurrection. In response to his misunderstanding the necessity of the suffering of the Son of Man, he is called a stumbling-block for Jesus, a tempter doing the work of Satan, setting up man's values instead of God's values. He is showing the kind of weakness that will lead him to deny Jesus in the face of suffering,[217] a denial from which Jesus will have to reconstitute or save him so that he will be able to play the role of the foundation rock (cf. earlier Petrine scene in 14:28-31). Others, however, take Matthew to mean that, besides having been a *skandalon* by his failure to accept the necessity of suffering, Peter, who has become a man of faith after the resurrection, is still capable of being a *skandalon*,[218] e.g., as he was

---

[217] Yet when Matthew speaks of *skandalizein* in relation to Peter's denials of Jesus, it is not Peter but Jesus who becomes a stumbling-block: "You will all fall away ["stumble," *skandalizein*] *because of me*" (Matt 26:31; cf. vs. 33).

[218] Does the rock image offer a double possibility—foundation rock (16:18) *or* stone of stumbling (*skandalon*; 16:23)? For instance, Isaiah knows both "a stone for a foundation ... a tested cornerstone of a sure foundation" (28:16) and "a stone of offense ... a rock of stumbling" (8:14). B. Lindars, *New Testament Apologetic: The Doctrinal Significance of the Old Testament Quotations* (Philadelphia: Westminster, 1961), pp. 175-83, argues that the two "stone" images from Isaiah had a rather wide currency in the early church (Rom 9:33; I Peter 2:6) and were "influential in the formation of the Petrine passage of Matt 16:17-19, 23" (p. 181). He calls attention to the fact that an older Roman Catholic scholar, M.-J. Lagrange, *L'Évangile selon saint Matthieu* (Études Bibliques; 8th ed.; Paris: Gabalda, 1948), p. 331, had alluded to the possibility of a Matthean reference to both Isaiah texts but had not followed up on it. As part of his argument, Lindars stresses that in citing the "rock of stumbling" from Isa 8:14, both Rom 9:33 and I Peter 2:8 use the non-Septuagintal phrasing *petra skandalou* (the LXX

for Paul at Antioch (Gal 2:11). But this means broadening the role of *skandalon* beyond 16:23, for it involves Peter's becoming a stumbling-block for others, whereas 16:23 makes him a stumbling-block for Jesus. Moreover, the suggestion that Matthew was emphasizing the possibility of Peter's continuing to be a stumbling-block in the Christian church is hard to reconcile with Peter's being a foundation rock for a church that will prevail against the powers of death.[219]

(4) a. *"I will give to you the keys of the kingdom of heaven.*

　　b. *Whatever you bind on earth shall be bound in heaven;*

　　c. *whatever you loose on earth shall be loosed in heaven"* (16:19).

To facilitate discussion, we have divided this verse into three lines, lettered (a), (b), and (c). This arrangement calls visual attention to the parallelism between (b) and (c). Parallelism is a feature of Semitic poetry and, along with the already noted

---

has *petra ptōmati*); and so the *petra* of Matt 16:18 and the *skandalon* of Matt 16:23 could have been associated by a Christian reader familiar with this tradition. However, it should be noted that in Isa 8:14, Rom 9:33, and I Peter 2:8 it is respectively the Lord or the Gospel or Christ which is the stone of stumbling because of the attitudes taken by men. It would be a violent change in imagery for Peter to become a stone of stumbling (for others) because of his own weakness. For further information, see C. F. D. Moule, "Some Reflections on the 'Stone' Testimonia in Relation to the Name Peter," *New Testament Studies* 2 (1955-56), pp. 56-58; A.-M. Dubarle, "La primauté de Pierre dans Matthieu 16, 17-19. Quelques références à l'Ancien Testament," *Istina* 2 (1955), pp. 335-38; P. Dreyfus, "La primauté de Pierre à la lumière de la théologie biblique du reste d'Israël," *ibid.,* pp. 338-46.

[219] If this suggestion of Peter's continuing to be a stumbling block can be taken seriously as an interpretation of Matthew's intention, it would belong to the context of Peter's being seen as an example of the whole panorama of discipleship, including its negative aspect. We may note that since Origen, but especially since Augustine, the figure of the Peter who was rebuked by Jesus, along with the Peter who denied Jesus and was rebuked by Paul at Antioch, has been exploited as a model for a paradoxical combination of human weakness and divine strength in the believer and in the prelate. See A.-M. La Bonnardière, "Tu es Petrus. La péricope Matthieu XVI, 13-23 dans l'oeuvre de S. Augustin," *Irénikon* 34 (1961), pp. 451-99.

Semitism "bind/loose," points toward the non-Greek origins of the verse. It is true that once again there are signs of Matthean editing, e.g., Matthew's favorite expression "the kingdom of heaven"; but we are on reasonably firm ground in suspecting that the substance of vs. 19 comes from a pre-Matthean tradition. As for whether the saying might be post-resurrectional in origin, it is of note that the closest non-Matthean parallel to lines (b) and (c) is John 20:23, a post-resurrectional saying directed to the disciples: "If you forgive men's sins, their sins are forgiven; if you hold them, they are held fast."[220]

The focus of our discussion in this Matthean verse is its logic. Is line (a) the equivalent of lines (b) and (c), so that the power of the keys to the kingdom of heaven is identical with the power of binding and loosing on earth, which will be ratified in heaven? Or is the power of the keys a generic power of which the power of binding and loosing is only a specification? This question is crucial because the power of the keys is mentioned only in this saying directed to Peter, while the power of binding and loosing is a function given also to the disciples in 18:18.[221] If the two powers are the same, then all the disciples received the power of the keys.

We would be better able to answer the question of the significance of the power of the keys if we knew the exact background of the imagery. One suggestion is that the verse is evocative of Isa 22:15-25 where Shebna, prime minister[222] of King Hezekiah of Judah, is deposed and replaced by Eliakim on whose shoulder God places "the *key* of David; he shall *open*

---

[220] The resemblance is heightened once we recognize that the saying in John is also constructed in parallelism, and that John's passive tenses ("are forgiven"; "are held fast") and Matthew's reference to being bound or loosed "in heaven" are two Semitic circumlocutions for describing the action of God. See Dodd, *Tradition* (note 32 above), pp. 347-49.

[221] The disciples are specified as the audience in 18:1. See note 175 above for the thesis that in Matthew "the disciples" are the Twelve.

[222] The prime minister, more literally "major-domo," was the man called in Hebrew "the one who is over the house," a term borrowed from the Egyptian designation of the chief palace functionary. The bureaucracy of the Hebrew monarchy was adopted from Egyptian models. See R. de Vaux, *Ancient Israel* (New York: McGraw-Hill, 1961), pp. 129-32.

... and he shall *shut*."[223] The power of the key of the Davidic kingdom is the power to open and to shut, i.e., the prime minister's power to allow or refuse entrance to the palace, which involves access to the king. If this were the background of Matthew's "keys of the kingdom," then Peter might be being portrayed as a type of prime minister in the kingdom that Jesus has come to proclaim, and the power of binding and loosing would be a specification of the broader power of allowing or refusing entrance into the kingdom.[224] What else might this broader power of the keys include? It might include one or more of the following: baptismal discipline; post-baptismal or penitential discipline; excommunication; exclusion from the eucharist; the communication or refusal of knowledge; legislative powers; and the power of governing.[225]

But the Isaian scene is only one suggestion for a possible background of vs. 19, and the thesis that the power of binding and loosing is a specification of the power of the keys is only one possible approach. Cullmann[226] calls attention to the expres-

---

[223] This Isa 22:22 passage was known to Christians in reference to Jesus. In Rev 3:7 he is described as the one "who has the key of David, who opens and no one shall shut, who shuts and no one shall open."

[224] We pointed out that the terminology in John 20:23 is one of "forgiving" and "holding" sins, while Matthew 16:19 speaks of "binding" and "loosing." J. A. Emerton, "Binding and Loosing—Forgiving and Retaining," *Journal of Theological Studies* 13 (1962), pp. 325-31, wonders if Jesus' original saying was not modeled on the Isaian imagery: "Whatever you shut will be shut; whatever you open will be opened." In the Matthean tradition the Isaian language would have been conformed to a well-known Jewish legal formula ("open" becoming "loosen"; "shut" becoming "bind"), while the Johannine tradition would have reshaped the saying to apply to sin ("open" becoming "release, forgive"; "shut" becoming "hold fast").

[225] Some of these suggestions are garnered from the assumption that the saying of Jesus originally had a post-resurrectional setting and that the power of the keys should be related to the powers bestowed by the risen Jesus, e.g., the powers of preaching repentance and the forgiveness of sins spoken of in Luke 24:47 and John 20:23. Or else one may assume a parallel between this Petrine scene in Matthew and the Petrine scenes in Luke 22:31-33 and John 21:15-17 and consider the functions envisaged for Peter in those scenes (strengthening the brethren; feeding the sheep of Jesus). Cf. also Luke 11:52: "Woe to you lawyers! for you have taken away *the key of knowledge*, ... and you hindered those who were entering."

[226] *Peter* (note 45 above), pp. 209-10.

sion *"gates* of Hades" in the preceding verse, an imagery that would make the symbolism of keys intelligible—in Rev 1:18 the Son of Man asserts, "I have the *keys* of Death and *Hades."* Moreover, Cullmann draws attention to the relationship between the house of the church (whose building was just mentioned and of which Peter is to be the rock foundation) and the heavenly house of which Peter receives the keys. According to Cullmann, the original meaning was that after the death and resurrection of Jesus, Peter would open the door to the kingdom of heaven by his preaching mission, letting people into the kingdom. In this he would differ from the Pharisees whom Jesus condemned (Matt 23:13) because they closed the door to the kingdom of heaven. The power of binding and loosing, then, would not be so much a specification of a broader power of the keys, but a later pre-Matthean reinterpretation. (Cullmann does not think that 19a was originally joined to 19bc.) A similar thesis of historical reinterpretation would be that the power of the keys originally referred to the power of forgiving sins through baptism (see note 225 above), and that this power was later reformulated in terms of the rabbinic pattern of binding and loosing.

Perhaps this is an appropriate moment to ask what exactly might be covered by the power of binding and loosing. The combination of these two verbs appears in the rabbinic literature most often with the sense of imposing or removing an obligation by an authoritative doctrinal decision. Another, less frequent, meaning of the verbs is centered around imposing or lifting a ban of excommunication. Which meaning best fits the two binding-and-loosing passages in Matthew (16:19 addressed to Peter, and 18:18 addressed to the disciples)? Or do the two passages have different meanings? Much depends on how one envisages the Matthean church situation. Is it a church that has recently emerged from within Judaism and set itself up as a Christian synagogue or group of synagogues against the synagogues of Pharisaic (rabbinic) Judaism?[227] If so, there would be

---

[227] Does the formula "'their synagogues" in Matt 4:23 hint that Matthew's Christians are no longer thinking of the Jewish synagogues as "our synagogues"?

plausibility to Stendahl's argument[228] that it is the power of promulgating an obligation that is appropriately given to Peter in Matt 16:19. (He holds that the other interpretation of binding/loosing, the power of excommunicating, best fits 18:18, since the context there is one of church discipline.) The Jewish Christians in the synagogue(s) of the Matthean community think of Peter in terms of a chief rabbi who can promulgate binding rules and make authoritative decisions about teaching,[229] in contrast to "the teaching of the Pharisees and Sadducees" of which they have been warned to beware (Matt 16:12—note, in the same chapter as 16:19).

Yet it is not clear that such is the Matthean church situation. Had Matthew's community completely broken with Judaism? In Matt 23:2-3 Jesus instructs his disciples to practice and observe whatever is told them by the scribes and Pharisees because they "sit on the chair of Moses"! This does not sound like a complete break, nor does it favor the idea of a chief Christian rabbi. A different church situation could be envisaged that would make the power of excommunication the best explanation of the binding and loosing of Matt 16:19.[230] For instance, Matthew's church seems to be a church into which Gentiles were entering in numbers (Matt 8:11-12), perhaps to the point of overwhelming the Jewish Christian segment (Matt 21:41), so that part of the Gospel's purpose was to explain this phenomenon. We have seen in our study of Galatians and Acts that Peter was more favorable than were the extreme Jewish Christians to the admission of the Gentiles. Does Matthew have

---

[228] K. Stendahl, *The School of St. Matthew* (Philadelphia: Fortress, 1968 reprint), p. 28. For the thesis that Matthew's Gospel was directed against post-A.D. 70 Judaism, see Davies, *Setting* (note 180 above), pp. 256-315.

[229] So Stendahl in *Peake* (note 215 above), p. 787; R. Hummel, *Die Auseinandersetzung zwischen Kirche und Judentum im Matthäusevangelium* (Beiträge zur Evangelischen Theologie, 33; Munich: Kaiser, 1963), p. 63; B. H. Streeter, *The Four Gospels: A Study of Origins* (rev. ed.; London: Macmillan, 1930), p. 515. Also Bornkamm, as cited in note 239 below.

[230] F. Büchsel, *"Deō (Lyō),"* *Theological Dictionary* (note 20 above), vol. 2 (English 1964; German 1935), pp. 60-61, who gives the rabbinic references for the various meanings of binding/loosing, opts for the excommunication meaning.

to remind the Jewish Christians in his own community that the power of admitting to the church and excluding from it (binding/loosing) was given to Peter who stands behind the decision to admit Gentiles?

With all these possibilities the reader will see how difficult it is to decide whether the power of the keys promised to Peter in Matt 16:19 is exactly the same as the power of binding and loosing promised to him in the same verse—and also whether the power of binding and loosing associated with Peter, the rock on whom the church was to be built, is in all aspects the same power to be exercised by the disciples in general according to Matt 18:18, where the context is one of dealing with recalcitrant Christians. Those who think that the same power is involved throughout look on 18:18 as democratizing the power given to Peter in 16:19, so that now it can be exercised in a more collegial fashion. For them, the fact that all the disciples can bind and loose means that in Matthew's church (local or universal?)[231] there is no one ruler playing Peter's part (and thus no succesor to him). Has the antipathy to anyone being called "rabbi" (or "father" or "master")[232] militated against the emergence or preservation of one, supreme earthly teacher (chief rabbi)? Obviously such a suggestion is speculative; for were that injunction taken literally, no one could exercise any power of binding and loosing in the Matthean church (since it

[231] In Matt 16:18, when Jesus speaks of building *his* church, certainly "church" cannot be interpreted to refer simply to the local Matthean community, in isolation from the other Christian communities. (A universalistic outlook in Matthew is attested in 28:18-19 where the disciples are commissioned to go forth to make disciples of all nations and baptize them.) But Matthew also knows of *ekklēsia* applied to the local community (18:17). It is interesting that the binding/loosing power given to the disciples (18:18) is mentioned in the context of the latter, while the binding/loosing power given to Peter is mentioned in the context of the former.

[232] Matt 23:8-12: "You are not to be called rabbi, for you have one teacher, and you are all brethren. And call no man your father. . . . Neither be called masters. . . ." There was some form of authority in the Matthean church, e.g., it had "prophets, wise men, and scribes" (23:34). But those who had authority were not to lord it over others (20:25-28). What Matthew is attacking, then, is not precedence but a style of precedence. The faithful servant of 24:45 is set over the household, even though he has fellow servants (24:49).

is a rabbinical authority), and 18:18 would be just as much affected as 16:19. However, it does illustrate the problem of discerning to what extent 16:19 gives Peter a role that separates him from the other disciples.

We shall sum up our conclusions from this whole treatment after we discuss the last Petrine passage in Matthew.

D. Jesus, Peter, and the Temple Tax (Matt 17:24-27)

This is more of a self-contained unit than the preceding Petrine passages, for Matthew does not weave it intricately into a passage he has borrowed from Mark. Rather, Matthew interrupts the Marcan order and inserts the Petrine scene. According to Mark, *a scene containing Jesus' second passion prediction,* uttered as he and his disciples passed through Galilee (Mark 9:30-32=Matt 17:22-23), is followed by *a scene containing Jesus' question,* asked when they come to Capernaum, as to what the disciples were discussing on the way—a question that results in Jesus' giving them a lesson on becoming like little children (Mark 9:33-37; cf. Matt 18:1-5). In preparing for his intercalation, Matthew has taken over from Mark the Capernaum place setting that belonged to the second scene and used it to introduce the Petrine episode which he has fitted between the two Marcan scenes. It is difficult to see that the immediate context of these two scenes is particularly pertinent to the Petrine episode, although the second Marcan scene which now follows the Petrine passage in Matthew deals with who is greatest in the kingdom of heaven (Matt 18:4). The choice of context was probably determined by geographical considerations: Matthew wanted to insert the Petrine passage which involves a tax-collecting question in a context that mentioned Capernaum, since that town (of Jesus) was previously mentioned in relation to the profession of tax collecting (cf. Matt 9:1, 9-13). See also the mention of Peter's coming "to the house" in 17:25—Peter's house was at Capernaum (Matt 8:5, 14).

In 17:24-27 collectors of the didrachma or half-shekel tax approach Peter and ask, "Does your [plural] teacher not pay the tax?" Peter answers yes; but when he comes to (his) house, Jesus speaks to him first, addressing him as "Simon" and asking him from whom earthly kings collect their toll, from their sons or from others. Peter responds, "From others," and Jesus points out that the sons, then, are free of such tolls. However, in order not to give offense "to them" (tax collectors? authorities?), Peter is to go fishing. The first fish that he catches will have a stater or shekel (= two didrachmas) in its mouth which he is to give "to them" (tax collectors) for Jesus and for himself.

While there are linguistic signs that betray Matthean editing, it is commonly agreed that Matthew used earlier material.[233] In order to discuss this material, we must dissect the scene into its three components: the setting involving Peter and the tax collectors (17:24-25a); the pronouncement of Jesus on the sons' not paying the tax (17:25b-26); the implied miracle of catching the fish with the coin in its mouth (17:27). Let us begin with the last mentioned item, the miracle.[234]

We are not told in 17:27 that Peter actually caught a fish which had in its mouth exactly the amount to pay the tax for two, but that is implied. This miraculous way of providing for the tax really has little to do with the main problem of the preceding verses, namely, whether there is an obligation on Jesus and his disciples to pay. It is the closest thing in all the Gospel tradition to a miracle performed for the convenience of the miracle worker and would be most suspect historically.[235]

---

[233] Kilpatrick, *Matthew* (note 174 above), p. 41, points out the Matthean traits. The following are among those who judge the material as pre-Matthean tradition: W. Trilling, *Das wahre Israel* (3rd ed.; Munich: Kösel, 1964), p. 159, note 68; J. Roloff, *Das Kerygma und der irdische Jesus* (Göttingen: Vandenhoeck, 1970), pp. 117-19; and G. Strecker, *Der Weg der Gerechtigkeit* (3rd ed.; Göttingen: Vandenhoeck, 1971), pp. 200-01. Strecker also points out Matthean features, and suggests Matthew's dependence upon oral tradition.

[234] The fact that Jesus knows Peter's mind before he speaks (17:25: "Jesus spoke to him *first*") may imply miraculous knowledge, but Matthew does not develop this motif.

[235] Of the Matthean Petrine scenes that we have discussed, this is the only one that has no parallel in the post-resurrectional episode involving Simon Peter in John 21. Could vs. 27 represent a complete Matthean recasting of the Lucan/Johannine tale of a miraculous catch of fish? Bultmann, *History* (note 26 above), pp. 34-35, classifies the catch of the fish with a coin in its mouth, along with Peter's walking on the water,

If we leave aside vs. 27, the setting of the passage in vs. 24 involves the problem of whether the Temple tax should be paid. Before the destruction of the Jerusalem Temple in A.D. 70, every male Jew above nineteen years of age paid a half-shekel yearly to the upkeep of the Temple (cf. Neh 10:32; Exod 30:11-16). If that tax is meant, obviously Matthew is reporting a pre-70 tradition. However, we cannot exclude the possibility that what is involved is the poll tax imposed on the Jews after A.D. 70 for the support of the temple of Jupiter Capitolinus, the so-called *fiscus iudaicus*.[236]

Is the role of Peter in 17:24-25a pre-Matthean? We have seen 15:15 and 18:21, instances where Peter was not mentioned in the respective parallel passages in Mark and Luke, but where Matthew introduced Peter to raise a question for Jesus to answer. It is difficult to say whether the same redactional process was at work here.[237] However, the fact that Jesus speaks to Peter as "Simon" (vs. 25) urges caution in judging that Peter's presence was not pre-Matthean. We saw the same usage of "Simon" in a seemingly pre-Matthean passage in 16:17.

The part of the scene that has the best chance of being pre-Matthean and even of going back to the historical Jesus is the pronouncement of Jesus in 17:25b-26.[238] It is a saying not un-

---

as legend. Nevertheless, since such a legendary motif was found in Judaism, its presence does not necessarily imply for Bultmann the origin of the pericope in Hellenistic circles.

[236] Bultmann, *ibid.*, opts for the Jerusalem Temple tax; H. Montefiore, "Jesus and the Temple Tax," *New Testament Studies* 11 (1964-65), pp. 60-71, opts for the *fiscus iudaicus*. (It is noteworthy that Jesus asks about the right of earthly *kings* to tax.) Kilpatrick, *Matthew* (note 174 above), p. 42, points out that the *fiscus iudaicus* was obsolete by the beginning of the second century. This is questioned by J. D. M. Derrett, "Peter's Penny: Fresh Light on Matthew xvii 24-7," *Novum Testamentum* 6 (1963), pp. 1-15.

[237] Kilpatrick, *ibid.*, "A saying now irrecoverable may have been converted into a story by the introduction of the dialogue with Peter. Whether the tax collectors are part of the original setting or were added when Peter was introduced is uncertain."

[238] Bultmann, *ibid.*, classifies the whole incident as basically an apophthegm and thus centered around the saying of Jesus. Roloff (note 233 above) argues for the authenticity of this saying of Jesus, as does Montefiore (note 236 above).

like Jesus' response to the problem of paying the tribute to
Caesar (Matt 22:18-21 and parallels), for it remains ambigu-
ous on the particular course of action to follow, but looks at
the problem from a point of view different from that of the
questioners—God's point of view.

The likelihood that diverse pre-Matthean elements have
been woven together to form 17:24-27 makes any judgment
on the significance that Peter may have had on the pre-
Matthean level impossible. But clearly Peter does have a significance in the final scene that Matthew has given to us. It is
not only that through Peter Jesus confronts the tax problem.
Matthew takes it for granted that those wanting to know about
"the teacher" would approach Peter. Why do they not approach Jesus directly, as happens elsewhere (Matt 9:14 and
parallels)? Bultmann suggests that they approach Peter because
this is a tax problem that historically confronted the Christian
church, which in turn gets its answer from Jesus. (Note that
Jesus knows Peter's mind before Peter asks.) Peter's affirmative
answer to the tax collectors' question means that the (Jewish?)
Christians are paying the tax. But is it right for them to do so?
The divine answer given to Peter is yes—but not because they
have a real obligation to do so. As sons of God, they are free
from such impositions. And the implied miracle may mean that
God will ultimately provide the Christians with the means to
meet the tax.

Whether or not all the details of this explanation of the
story are correct, it seems clear that, for Matthew, Peter will
be able to give the correct answer on this problem and act
correctly because Jesus has told him what to do. Both Trilling
and Bornkamm [239] see the pericope as indicating that Peter
possessed teaching authority exercised in the name of Jesus, an
exemplification of the type of authority ascribed to Peter in
Matt 16:18-19. Since Peter was no longer alive when Matthew
wrote, what does this emphasis on Peter's authoritative teaching

[239] Trilling (note 233 above), p. 159; G. Bornkamm, "The Authority
to 'Bind' and 'Loose' in the Church in Matthew's Gospel," *Jesus and
Man's Hope*, vol. 1 (Pittsburgh Theological Seminary; *Perspective* 11
[1970]), pp. 37-50.

role mean? Bornkamm and Hummel [240] think that Peter's authority still functioned for Matthew's community in terms of a tradition given out under Peter's name, indeed the tradition enshrined in the Gospel of Matthew. Strecker,[241] however, sees Peter only as typical of the disciples in respect to obeying the word of Jesus. Obviously, the question is parallel to that of the interpretation of Matt 16:19—whether or not Peter has an authoritative role that goes beyond that of the other disciples? If all the authority is meant for the body of disciples, why is Peter so often the one singled out by Matthew? *A priori,* was he not a somewhat unlikely choice since he denied the master publicly? Or did that very fact give Peter a special place not only as a type but as a person?

E. Summary Analysis

The Matthean material is so broad that a summary of our discussion is called for. Peter already occupied a position of prominence in the Gospel of Mark. Matthew has taken over this feature and expanded it noticeably.

(1) As in Mark, Peter is one of the first two disciples to be called (Matt 4:18-20), and he is the first named in the list of the Twelve (10:2). Indeed, Matthew adds the word "first" (*prōtos*) before Peter's name, a touch not found in Mark's list. In the overall Matthean picture of Peter it seems that Peter's priority has taken on a special coloring from 16:16b-19; for even this early reference in chapter 4 to "Simon who is called Peter," at the beginning of the list of the Twelve, anticipates the solemn proclamation of Jesus in 16:17-18: "Simon Bar-Jonah. . . . You are Peter." In Matthew's eyes it is only logical that Peter's priority or preeminence carries over from the ministry of Jesus into the church situation to which Matthew speaks.

(2) In this church situation Peter is seen as the rock on whom the church is built. When church problems arise, it is Peter who gets involved. For instance, it is Peter who asks

---

[240] Bornkamm, *ibid.;* Hummel (note 229 above), p. 63.
[241] Strecker (note 233 above), pp. 254-55.

Jesus to explain his remarks on why the disciples are not bound by the Jewish food regulations (15:15). It is Peter who proposes to Jesus a problem troubling the Christian community, namely, the problem of the intensity of the obligation to forgive (18:21-22). Again, the problem as to whether Christians should pay the Temple tax is brought to Peter who, in turn, is instructed by Jesus. This ecclesiastical import of Peter in the Matthean church is not to be explained simply as the result of his own ingenuity or as the survival of the fittest in church politics. It was Jesus who gave Peter the name that foreshadowed the role he would play; it was Jesus who gave him the keys of the kingdom; it was Jesus who saved him when he was sinking.

(3) Matthew does not hint (as some would interpret Mark 16:7 to do) that Peter was the first among the Twelve to see the risen Jesus; and indeed in his account of the appearance of the risen Jesus to the Eleven on the mountain in Galilee (28:16-17), Matthew leaves no room for an earlier appearance to Peter. Nevertheless, much of the Matthean special material about Peter may have had its original locus in a post-resurrectional setting. (The possibilities include: Peter's leaving the boat to go to Jesus and having to be saved by him; Peter's confession of Jesus as "the Son of the living God"; Jesus' promise to Peter that he would be the rock on which the church would be built; the giving of the power of binding and loosing.)

(4) The question of Peter's relationship to the other disciples remains difficult. As in Mark, so in Matthew, Peter is the spokesman of the disciples; and in many ways he is a typical disciple (see note 29 above). Yet in Peter's crucial confession of Jesus as "the Messiah, the Son of the living God," Matthew does not present Peter simply as the spokesman of a common opinion. He is the recipient of a special divine revelation, for which Jesus gives him a unique blessing (16:17). It is true that previously all the disciples have confessed Jesus as "Son of God" (14:33—in response to what Jesus did for Peter), and therefore Peter's confession is not so unique as it is in Mark. Nevertheless, Matthew has chosen not to focus the same attention on the previous confession by all the disciples that he focuses on Peter's confession because he records no laudatory

reaction to the disciples' confession. If Peter's confession in Matthew has lost its chronological priority, it seemingly has gained an ecclesiastical priority in the sense that Jesus responds to it by declaring that Peter is the rock on which the church will be built. We have not been able to settle the question of whether and to what extent Peter's power of binding and loosing is a power shared by all the disciples, since what is said to Peter in 16:19bc is said to the other disciples in 18:18. The fact remains, however, that only to Peter and to none other does Matthew have Jesus say, "I will give to you the keys of the kingdom of heaven." The coin that will be found in the fish's mouth is to pay the tax for Jesus and for Peter (alone, among the disciples). Peter does function in Matthew as a model of discipleship in general, but beyond this Matthew gives him a prominence that the others do not get.

(5) The weaker side of Peter's character that is apparent in Mark is not played down in Matthew. The denials of Jesus by Peter and the reference to Peter as "Satan" are taken over from Mark. And, in fact, even in the special Matthean material which is so favorable to Peter, there are impressive references to his weakness. One may speak of a somewhat disconcerting inconsistency in the Matthean picture of Peter. He who is called a "man of little faith" (14:31) is soon afterwards praised for having expressed a faith so perceptive that it can be explained only as a gift of God (16:17-18). And yet the Peter who is blessed for this (16:17) is within a few lines cursed as "Satan" and a "stumbling-block" for Jesus precisely because he thinks the thoughts of men and *not* the thoughts of God (16:23).

The picture of Peter in Matthew is variegated indeed; but overall one can understand why Matthew has been favored by those Christians who give special theological emphasis to Peter's continued importance in the church.

CHAPTER SEVEN:
PETER IN THE
GOSPEL OF LUKE[242]

Like the Gospel of Matthew, the Gospel of Luke gives us a Christian portrait of Peter drawn toward the end of the first century, some twenty years or more after Mark wrote. While both Matthew and Luke drew upon Mark, it is generally agreed that neither evangelist knew the other's work. This independence suggests that the communities served by Matthew and Luke were in different areas (and makes difficult any attempt at a comparative dating of the two Gospels on the basis of their theological differences). While it is quite likely, as we have seen, that there was a strong Jewish Christian element in Matthew's community, it is generally agreed that Luke's community was more Hellenized, whether through Greek-speaking Jews or through Gentiles. This would fit in with the emphasis on Paul's missions in the second part of Luke's work, the Book of Acts. Indeed, it is not implausible that the Gospel of Luke was written for a church or churches that had been converted or influenced by Paul.[243] Thus, it will be interesting for us to com-

---

[242] The discussion for this chapter was led by M. M. Bourke. One session of the task force (April 1972) was devoted to the evidence of Luke.

[243] Antioch in Syria, or the Pauline churches (in Asia Minor and/or Greece), or Rome have been advocated as possibilities. If one posits Antioch as the place of origin for Luke's Gospel, then Matthew's Gospel (which is often also thought to be of Syrian origin) could be placed in an East Syrian context, or in the Damascus area.

plement our study of Matthew by seeing how Peter was regarded, roughly at the same time, in a somewhat different
Christian context.

A. The General Picture of Peter in Luke

Luke too has taken over the basic Marcan picture of Peter
but has effected more changes than Matthew did. He has done
this by rearrangement (especially at the beginning) and by
omission. The rearrangement appears in the fact that Luke
places the call of Simon after the healing of his mother-in-law;
and so the Lucan order of the incidents that we listed at the
beginning of our chapter on Mark would be ##3, 4, 1, and 2.

There is no significant difference from Mark in Luke's
report of the healing of Peter's mother-in-law (#3). Unlike
Matthew, Luke 4:42-43 reproduces the scene in Mark (#4)
where, after a day's ministry in Capernaum, Jesus withdraws
to a lonely place. But, instead of having "Simon and those who
were with him" (Mark 1:36) come to Jesus to tell him he is
being sought, Luke 4:42 has "the people" come to Jesus. The
change was probably necessitated by the fact that in Luke's
Gospel Simon has not yet been called to follow Jesus. ·

Luke 5:1-3 agrees with Mark (#1) in portraying Simon
as a fisherman on the Lake of Gennesaret, but Luke omits all
mention of Andrew, Simon's brother, in this scene (cf. Mark
1:29). In the following verses of chapter 5 Luke mentions
Simon first among those who are to become disciples (Mark
#2); and, in fact, the call is much more personally directed to
Simon, for it is associated with a miraculous catch of fish from
Simon's boat. We shall have to discuss this miracle separately
since it has no parallel in Mark or Matthew; but here we may
note that it is to Simon alone that Jesus says, "Henceforth you
[singular] will be catching men." This forms an interesting contrast to Mark 1:17 (Matt 4:19), where Simon and Andrew
are addressed: "Follow me and I will make you [plural] become
fishers of men."

As in Mark (#5), Simon ("whom he named Peter") is

listed first among the Twelve whom Jesus "named apostles" (Luke 6:13-14). Yet neither the grammar of this reference nor the general pattern of the Lucan usage of names[244] suggests that Luke looked on the moment of the choice of the Twelve as the moment of the change of Simon's name to Peter. In ##6 and 8, the first two scenes involving the "inner group" of Peter, John, and James, Luke has no significant Petrine divergence from Mark.[245] But in #7, although Luke agrees with Mark in having Peter confess Jesus as the Messiah (of God), in having Jesus respond by commanding the disciples to be silent, and in Jesus' prediction of the suffering of the Son of Man, Luke *omits* all reference to Peter's refusal to accept this saying and to Jesus' rebuke of Peter. Thus, there is no unflattering portrait of Peter in the confessional scene. This is part of a deliberate Lucan decision to omit, as far as possible, all that was blameworthy in the career of Peter and, indeed, of the apostles as a whole.[246]

Luke substantially agrees with Mark #9 where Peter says, "We have left our homes [*ta idia*] and followed you," but omits Mark #10, the cursing of the fig tree and Peter's calling atten-

---

[244] Luke's overall pattern of using "Simon" and "Peter" is different from either Mark's or Matthew's. We saw (note 90 above) that "Simon" was infrequent in Acts. But in the Gospel, while Luke uses "Peter" eighteen times, he uses "Simon" eleven times and, thus, more than any other evangelist. It is true that most of the occurrences of "Simon" come before 6:14 where Luke places "Simon whom he named Peter" first in the list of the newly-called Twelve apostles, and that all uses of "Peter" (as distinct from "Simon Peter") come after 6:14. But that is largely because Luke follows Mark's practice when he depends on Marcan material. When he draws upon other material (22:31; 24:34), Luke shows no hesitancy about continuing to use the name "Simon" after 6:14. We note also that his one usage of "Simon Peter" (5:8) occurs before 6:14.

[245] In #8 (the Transfiguration) Peter's offer to make three booths for Jesus, Moses, and Elijah is still explained as Peter's lack of understanding (Luke 9:33=Mark 9:6); but Luke drops Mark's reference to the three disciples' being "exceedingly afraid." See note 254 below on the Lucan order "Peter, John, and James."

[246] H. Conzelmann, *Die Mitte der Zeit* (5th ed.; Tübingen: Mohr, 1964), p. 22, n. 2, theorizes that the omission of Mark 8:33 ("Get behind me, Satan!") was prompted by Luke's theology of a "Satan-free" age of Jesus, extending in the Gospel from 4:22 to 22:3. But would that explain the Lucan omission of the rest of the Marcan verse which condemns Peter for thinking the thoughts of men rather than of God?

tion to the withered remnant.[247] In #11, instead of having Peter, James, John, and Andrew ask when the Temple will be destroyed (Mark 13:3—a question that could be interpreted as a misunderstanding on the part of these disciples), Luke 21:7 has the question asked by an anonymous "they" (cf. "some" in 21:5).

It is in the Passion Narrative in particular that Luke softens the Marcan picture of Peter.[248] The prediction of Peter's denials (Mark #12) is preceded in Luke by a passage that assures Simon of Jesus' prayer that his faith shall not fail and that he shall turn again and strengthen his brethren (Luke 22:31-32, which we shall discuss below). In the course of the actual prediction of the denials Peter expresses his good intention to remain with Jesus only once (22:33), rather than twice as in Mark (14:29, 31), and then in a more nuanced form, "I am ready to go with you to prison and to death." Peter is not mentioned by name in the Gethsemane scene and so does not receive from Jesus special blame for his sleeping (as in Mark #13). Peter's denials of Jesus (Mark #14) are softened, for the Lucan Peter does not magnify the intensity of the denials by swearing or cursing (Jesus?), as does the Marcan Peter. Luke may wish us to think that Peter's denials were witnessed by Jesus; for he is the only evangelist to tell us that after the denials, "The Lord turned and looked at Peter," an implicit reproach that causes Peter to weep *bitterly* (compare Luke 22:62 to Mark 14:72).[249]

If Luke 24:5-7 omits all special reference to Peter from the message given by the "two men" to the women at the empty

---

[247] This omission is sparked more by Luke's tendency to soften the picture of Jesus than by any recognizable motif in Luke's outlook on Peter. Another possible explanation is that for Luke or for his tradition the story of the fig tree had been transmitted as a pure parable (Luke 13:6-9).

[248] In the Passion Narrative Luke may be following a non-Marcan account as his main source. See V. Taylor, *The Passion Narrative of St. Luke* (Society for New Testament Studies Monograph 19; Cambridge University, 1972) and the literature cited therein. If so, the Lucan differences from Mark in this area may be less significant than if Luke were deliberately changing Mark. Of course, one would still have to ask why Luke preferred his source to Mark.

[249] The human interest touch is typical of Lucan style, and probably reflects Lucan redaction. .

tomb (Mark #15), he has, as we shall see, a compensatory tradition that the risen Lord appeared to Simon (Luke 24:34).

In judging Luke's adoption and adaptation of the Marcan picture of Peter, clearly one would find it impossible to attribute to Luke any of the polemic against Peter that some exegetes (e.g., Weeden) find in Mark. Not only does Luke omit from the Gospel several Marcan scenes that might damage the memory of Peter; but the first half of the Book of Acts, as we have seen, gives to Peter a prominent and praiseworthy role in the early church. The latter fact reminds us that, in speculating about Luke's intentions in the Gospel, we must keep Acts in mind, for Luke is an orderly and reasonably consistent theologian.

Indeed, the Book of Acts throws light on one of three minor passages (Luke 8:45; 12:41; 22:8) where Lucan redaction has introduced Peter into a Marcan or "Q" pericope which did not originally mention him. In 22:8 Luke alone has Jesus send *Peter and John* (contrast "the disciples" in Mark 14:12ff.; Matt 26:17ff.) to prepare the Passover meal for himself and his disciples. The association between Peter and John will be a prominent feature in the story of Jerusalem church history in Acts 3:1ff.; 4:13ff.; and 8:14 (cf. Gal 2:9).

The other two minor passages simply highlight the role of Peter as spokesman, already well attested in the basic Marcan portrait. The first (Luke 8:45) occurs in a scene that is intimately yoked with the healing of Jairus' daughter (cf. Mark #6—the first "inner group" incident). As Jesus is on his way to Jairus' house, a woman with a hemorrhage touches him. Jesus asks, "Who was it that touched me?" In response, *Peter* [250] says, "Master, the multitudes surround you and press upon you." This somewhat patronizing reply that Luke 8:45 attributes to Peter is made by Jesus' disciples in Mark 5:31 and omitted by Matthew (see note 174 above). The second passage (Luke 12:41) occurs in material shared by Matthew and Luke, i.e., "Q" material (see note 27 above). When we studied Matt 18:21, we found that Matthew used a question by Peter to

---

[250] An important number of textual witnesses (Greek, Latin, and Bohairic) read: "Peter and those who were with him"—probably a scribal attempt to harmonize Luke and Mark; yet see Mark 1:36.

introduce a "Q" saying (p. 78 above), while the parallel in Luke 17:4 reported the "Q" material consecutively without interruption or need of interlocutor. Now, if we compare Luke 12:40-42 with Matt 24:44-45, we have exactly the same phenomenon with the editorial actions of the evangelists reversed. Missing from Matthew is any counterpart to Luke 12:41 where *Peter* asks about the parable concerning the thief who came when the householder did not expect him: "Lord are you telling this parable for us or for all?" The introduction of Peter is almost certainly Lucan redaction.

Moving on from the Lucan adaptation of the Marcan portrait of Peter and these few redactional passages that reinforce that portrait, we come to three Petrine scenes that are peculiar to Luke and may have come to him from pre-Lucan sources: (a) the miraculous catch of fish which serves as context for the call of Simon (5:1-11); (b) Jesus' prayer at the Last Supper that Simon's faith will not fail but that he will turn and strengthen his brethren (22:31-32); (c) the tradition that the risen Lord appeared to Simon (24:34). We shall discuss each in detail, but the consistency of the name "Simon" in each is worth noting (note 244 above).

B. The Call of Simon and the Miraculous Catch of Fish (Luke 5:1-11)

In Mark 1:16-20 and Matt 4:18-22 the call of the first disciples is narrated without much ado. Jesus sees two sets of brothers who are fishermen (Simon and Andrew; James and John); he urges them, "Follow me and I will make you become fishers of men"; they leave their nets and follow him. The story in Luke 5:1-11 is more complicated. As Jesus is preaching by the Lake of Gennesaret, the fishermen from two boats are washing their nets. Jesus gets into Simon's boat,[251] puts out from the land, and teaches the people from the boat. When Jesus finishes preaching, he tells Simon to put out into the deep water and to

---

[251] In the sequence in Luke's Gospel, Jesus has already met Simon in the preceding chapter when he healed Simon's mother-in-law.

lower the nets for a catch. Simon protests that they have toiled all night and caught nothing; but he lowers the net, and they catch so much that the nets are breaking. When the fishermen in the other boat come to help, both boats are so filled that they begin to sink. Peter falls at Jesus' knees and says, "Depart from me, for I am a sinful man, O Lord." Jesus replies, "Do not be afraid; henceforth you will catch men." Finally the boats are brought to land, and the fishermen leave everything and follow him.

Does Luke have an independent and fuller form of the story of the call of the first disciples than the one found in Mark/Matthew, or has Luke added to the call another narrative about Peter and a miraculous catch of fish? In a certain way the Lucan story is more logical: the miracle offers a reason why the fishermen would leave everything and follow Jesus. But this logic could well be a Lucan "improvement" of the Marcan storyline, and we must recognize that there are real inconsistencies in the present Lucan narrative. The details of the fishermen on the shore and of Jesus' teaching from the boat, which Luke uses as a setting for his narrative, are found in different places in Mark/Matthew (respectively in Mark 1:16-20 and 4:1-2 and par.); it is probably Luke who has joined them. Since Jesus asks only Simon to put out to sea, one would presume that the other unnamed fishermen stay on shore; but when the catch of fish takes place, the other boat is apparently at sea. Simon's action of falling down at Jesus' knees would be more appropriate on land than in a boat, as would his words, "Depart from me." Finally, the transition from Simon's reaction to the call of the disciples is awkward, e.g., two of the fishermen are belatedly identified as James and John; and yet, even after they are mentioned, Jesus addresses only to Simon the words, "Do not be afraid; henceforth you will catch men." All of this is best explained if the Lucan account of Simon's miraculous catch of fish belonged originally to a setting other than that of the call of the first disciples.

Is the story a Lucan creation or does it come to the evangelist from pre-Lucan tradition? That Luke did not create the substance of the narrative seems clear, for it bears a remarkable similarity to the account of Simon Peter's miraculous catch of fish in John 21:1-13. The following details are shared by both:

—The disciples have fished all night and have caught nothing.

—Jesus tells them to put out the net(s) for a catch.

—His directions are followed and an extraordinarily large catch of fish is made.

—The effect on the nets is mentioned.[252]

—Simon Peter (note the name [253]) is the one who reacts to the catch.

—Jesus is called Lord.

—The other fishermen take part in the catch but say nothing.

—Among the other fishermen are the sons of Zebedee.[254]

—When they return to land, the theme of following Jesus occurs (see John 21:19, 22).

---

[252] John 21:11 reports that the net was not torn (*schizein*); Luke 5:6 says, "Their nets were breaking" (*diaressein*). Although such scholars as Lagrange, Hoskyns, and Barrett judge Luke to mean that the nets broke, M. Zerwick, *Biblical Greek* (note 68 above), #273, interprets this as an instance where the imperfect tense indicates an attempt that was *not* carried into effect—the nets almost broke, but they did not in fact break.

[253] Luke 5:8 (see John 21:7) is the only instance in the Third Gospel of the name "Simon Peter." The Western textual tradition has just "Simon," but this is by way of harmonization with the usage in the rest of this story where Luke has "Simon" five times. As we have noted (see also note 244 above), in the three Petrine incidents peculiar to Luke (here; 22:31-32; 24:34), the name is always "Simon," never "Peter"; but that is less significant in the present instance, for Luke has not yet mentioned that Jesus named Simon "Peter" (6:14). While in both Luke 5 and John 21, Simon Peter is the one who reacts to the catch, John 21:7 mentions also the Beloved Disciple; but, as we shall see in the next chapter, this figure is probably a Johannine addition to the original story.

[254] The mention of these two men in John 21:2 marks their only appearance in the Fourth Gospel. The mention of them in Luke 5:10a is parenthetical and breaks up the sequence; and so it has been suggested that their names were not originally part of the pre-Lucan story of the catch of fish, but belonged to the context of the call of the disciples into which the story of the catch was inserted. On the other hand, it should be noted that here Luke mentions James before John; and that is not true in the two "inner group" (Peter, John, James) scenes that Luke shares with Mark (see Luke 8:51; 9:28 where Luke has changed the order found in Mark 5:37 and 9:2). Parenthetically, we may note that Luke probably prefers the order "Peter, John, and James" because Peter and John are associated in Acts.

—The same vocabulary is used for getting aboard, landing, net, etc.; but this may be coincidental since the technical vocabulary of fishing is limited.

These similarities [255] make it reasonable to conclude that *independently* Luke 5 and John 21 have preserved variant forms of the same miracle story—independently, because there are also many differences of vocabulary and detail that make borrowing, one from the other, an unlikely hypothesis.[256] Which Gospel is closer to the original version of the story? No unqualified answer can be given,[257] since in certain details Luke's version seems to have undergone more development (nets almost breaking; two boats almost sinking), while in other details it is apparently John's version that is more developed (perhaps the enumeration of 153 fish).

More significant for our purposes is the problem of the original localization of this miracle story involving Peter. Was it originally a story associated with Jesus' ministry, as Luke would have it (even if it was not part of the call of the first disciples)? Or was it part of a post-resurrectional appearance as

---

[255] There is another possible similarity if we interpret Simon Peter's statement in Luke 5:8, "Depart from me, for I am a sinful man, O Lord," as a reference to Peter's denials of Jesus—an interpretation that fits in with the suggestion, which we shall discuss, that the original locus of this fishing miracle was post-resurrectional. (In the post-resurrectional account in John 21:15-17, there is a similar implicit reference to Peter's denials in Jesus' triple demand to Simon Peter, "Do you love me?".) Yet, if the miracle story was not originally post-resurrectional, Simon Peter's exclamation in Luke 5:8 may be no more than an ordinary mortal's sense of unworthiness in the presence of one who has worked a stupendous miracle.

[256] An even more unlikely hypothesis is the harmonizing suggestion that the event happened twice, once during Jesus' ministry, as reported by Luke, and once after the resurrection, as reported by John 21 (a thesis defended in the commentaries on Luke by Plummer and Lagrange). Even if one were willing to accept the methodology implicit in such harmonization, one would still have to explain how in John 21 Peter could go through the same situation and much of the same dialogue without recognizing Jesus.

[257] That the answer is not simple is apparent from Bultmann's vacillation. In his *History* (note 26 above), pp. 217-18, he concludes that the Johannine account is a later version in some way derived from Luke's version; but in his *Gospel of John* (Philadelphia: Westminster, 1971; German, 1941), p. 705, he finds John more original in some features and in localization.

John 21 would have it? An impressive list of scholars can be lined up on each side of this issue,[258] and we cannot hope to solve it. It may be pointed out that in general there is more evidence for originally post-resurrectional stories having been retrojected into Jesus' ministry than vice versa.[259] If one examines Luke 5:4-9, 10b, and 11a for post-resurrectional features, a trace of the original recognition of the risen Jesus might be found in the "O Lord" of 5:8 (see note 199 above), while the equivalent of an apostolic mission might be found in 5:10b, "Henceforth you will catch men."[260] Also the "Do not be afraid" of 5:10b might be compared to the fear that greets the risen Jesus (cf. Matt 28:10; Luke 24:37-38). The suggestion of an original post-resurrectional setting of Peter's miraculous catch of fish would imply that Luke has independently followed the same course as Matthew who, as we have seen, may have formed the Petrine dialogue in 16:16b-19 from post-resurrectional material.

On the redactional level of what the scene means in its present location, Luke 5:10b makes it clear that the abundant catch of fish is symbolically related to Simon's future catching

---

[258] For a very complete discussion and survey of the literature see R. Pesch, *Der reiche Fischfang* (Düsseldorf: Patmos, 1969). Among those favoring a Lucan or pre-resurrectional localization are Wellhausen, Goguel, Macgregor, R. H. Fuller, and P. Seidensticker; among those favoring a Johannine or post-resurrectional setting are B. Weiss, von Harnack, H. Grass, and R. E. Brown. The last mentioned in his commentary on John (note 31 above), II, pp. 1089-92, argues that the miraculous catch of fish may have been part of the first appearance of the risen Jesus to Peter. Pesch himself thinks that both Luke and the Johannine redactor (i.e., the composer of ch. 21) took basically the same miracle story, preserved in slightly variant forms, and created a setting for it, so that we can trust neither Luke nor John for the original setting of the story. (Of course, in all of this we are debating about the setting of the earliest traceable form of the story, not about historicity which cannot be scientifically determined.)

[259] So G. Klein, p. 35 in the 1967 article cited in note 139 above.

[260] Because a similar statement, "I will make you [plural] (become) fishers of men," appears in the Marcan/Matthean account of the call of the first disciples, it would seem more logical to conclude that the promised commission to Simon in Luke 5:10b belonged originally to the calling rather than to the narrative of the catch of fish. However, Klein, *ibid*, p. 34, argues that it was part of the story of the catch and addressed only to Peter.

of men. Thus the apostolic sending of Peter and his success in missionary endeavor (of which we read in Acts) is grounded in the pre-Easter intention of Jesus.[261] Indeed, since Simon's own fishing has caught nothing and all the fish are caught through an acceptance of the power of Jesus, it is apparent that Simon as a fisher of men will have his success also through the power of Jesus. Of himself, he is a sinful man, and he needs Jesus to make him a catcher of men. Luke certainly means that Simon's partners, James and John, will also catch men; but in directing the Lord's promise to Simon alone, Luke is preparing for the dominant role that Simon will have among the Twelve in the Book of Acts.

C. Jesus' Prayer for Simon's Faith Not To Fail (Luke 22:31-32)

After the blessing of the bread and the cup by Jesus at the Last Supper, Mark 14:26-31 and Matt 26:30-35 present a scene wherein, on the way to Gethsemane, Jesus tells his disciples, "You will all stumble [*skandalizein*] (because of me this night), for it is written, 'I will strike the shepherd, and the sheep will be scattered.' " Peter then protests, "Even though all shall stumble, not I." This leads into Jesus' prediction of Peter's threefold denial.

Luke 22:24-38 has a much longer dialogue following the institution of the eucharist; and all of it, including the prediction of Peter's denials, is set in the upper room (see 22:12) where the Last Supper was eaten. He describes a dispute among the "apostles" (see 22:14) as to who will be the greatest, to which Jesus responds with a parabolic statement concerning the obligation of the leader to serve. But then he promises the apostles a place of honor because they have continued with him in his trials: "As my Father appointed a kingdom for me, so do I appoint for you, that you may eat and drink at my table in my kingdom, and sit on thrones judging the twelve tribes of

---

[261] H. Schürmann, *Das Lukasevangelium* (Herders theologischer Kommentar III, part 1; Freiburg: Herder, 1969), p. 264.

Israel" (22:29-30). Thus the preparation for the prediction of Peter's denials is quite different in Luke from what is found in Mark/Matthew. Not only is there no saying warning that all the disciples will stumble, but the opposite is indicated: "You are the ones who have continued with me in my trials" (22:28). The Lucan tendency to soften the failings of the disciples is evident here. Their falling away is only obliquely hinted at in the two verses (31-32) which are our principal concern and which form the immediate introduction to Jesus' prediction of Peter's denials. In these verses Jesus says:

[31]Simon, Simon, behold, Satan demanded you [plural] to sift like wheat. [32]But I have prayed for you [sing.] that your [sing.] faith may not fail. And you [sing.], when you [sing.] have turned again, strengthen your [sing.] brothers.

Our first question here, as elsewhere, concerns the origin of these verses. Is this dominical saying a tradition that came to Luke or did he fashion it himself? If it came to him, was it originally in its present context? The absence of the saying from Mark/Matthew does not immediately answer negatively the second of these two questions; for we have mentioned that in the Passion Narrative Luke may be following an independent source (note 248 above), and that source may have had a longer account of the Last Supper. Nevertheless, the fact that the immediately preceding verses in Luke (22:25-26 and 30) have parallels *elsewhere* in Matthew (20:25-26 and 19:28 respectively) suggests that Luke may have gathered here scattered material pertinent to the future of the apostles.

A hint that verses 31-32 have been inserted into the present context by Luke may also be found in the strange plural "you" in vs. 31, following an address to Simon, and preceding the many forms of the second person singular in vs. 32 (pronouns and verb forms). It has been suggested that in vs. 31 Simon is being addressed as a representative of the group of the apostles, but the awkwardness of the switch from "Simon" to a plural "you" remains disconcerting. Since the plural "you" is found in the preceding verses of this chapter [262] as part of Jesus' address to the apostles, could the clause "Behold, Satan demanded you to sift like wheat" have originally been addressed to the apostles? In that case, the awkwardness has resulted from Luke's attempt to combine it with a saying addressed to Simon which Luke has introduced. The demand of Satan to sift the apostles like wheat may have been the equivalent in the Lucan tradition to the Marcan/Matthean: "You will all stumble (because of me)."

What then of the section of verses 31-32 addressed to Simon in the second person singular: "Simon, Simon . . . I have prayed for you that your faith may not fail. And you, when you have turned again, strengthen your brothers"? Is this saying pre-Lucan? The double use of "Simon" would suggest that it is (notes 244, 253 above), especially when we contrast it with the prediction of *Peter's* denials that follows. Nevertheless, there is evidence of the Lucan hand, for instance, in the verb "strengthen" (*stērizein*).[263] In treating the Matthean Petrine passages we postulated several times that we were dealing with a tradition which antedated the evangelist but which he had reworked in his own style; the same may be true here. An interesting suggestion has been made that the pre-Lucan saying (minus the words "when you have turned again") represents an old tradition according to which Peter did not deny Jesus—rather, Jesus prayed for him and his faith did not fail.[264] The clause "when you have turned again" would then have been added by Luke to make the saying conform to the other tradition of the prediction of Peter's denials which follows immediately in Luke.[265] This is highly speculative, but in any case we are dealing with a saying very favorable to Simon and his role.

---

[262] Note the usage of the second person plural pronoun in 22:15, 16, 18, 19, 20, 26, 27, 28, 29, 31, 35, 37, not to mention the second person plural verb forms.

[263] *Stērizein* and its compound *epistērizein* occur three and four times, respectively, in Luke and in Acts, and never in the other Gospels. In Acts *epistērizein* is used to describe the activity of Christian prophets (15:32), of Paul and Barnabas (14:22), of Paul and Silas (15:41), and finally of Paul alone (18:23). Neither verb is used of Peter in Acts.

[264] This is the thesis of G. Klein, note 139 above.

[265] Bultmann, *History* (note 26 above), p. 267.

Moving from the question of the hypothetical pre-Lucan meaning of the saying to what it means on the redactional level as it is now found in Luke's Gospel, we face the fact that now Simon is part of the apostolic group (the plural "you") whom Satan demanded in order that he might sift them like wheat. Thus, even for Luke, the apostles can be tempted, and that includes Simon. Have we then a partial Lucan equivalent to Mark 8:33, "He rebuked Peter and said, 'Get behind me, Satan' "? This seems dubious precisely because, as we pointed out, Luke omitted that opprobrious charge from his account of the aftermath of Peter's confession, and he scarcely reintroduced the opprobrium here. Moreover, vs. 32 indicates that in Simon's case Jesus prayed for him, and so presumably Satan never got his demand as regards Simon.

The implied positive results of Jesus' prayer for Simon are, first, that his faith did not fail, and second, that when he turned again, he strengthened his brothers. That Jesus had to pray for Simon's faith which was liable to failure may have a distant relationship to the tradition in Matt 14:28-31 where Peter, a "man of little faith," has to be rescued by Jesus. It may also be related to a motif in the earlier Lucan story about Simon and the miraculous catch of fish, for there we saw that of himself Simon Peter was a sinner who had to be empowered by Jesus. As for vs. 32 it is not clear how Luke means to reconcile Jesus' prayer that Simon's faith would not fail and the hint that it did fail expressed in the clause "when you have turned again." Since the verse immediately precedes the prediction of Peter's denials, the "turning again" refers to the period after the denials. Luke may mean that through Jesus' prayer the lack of faith implicit in the denials did not become a permanent failure, and Peter's faith revived after the resurrection (cf. Luke 24:34).

More important for our purposes is the second result of Jesus' prayer: Simon's strengthening his brothers. Who are these "brothers"? At first glance, they would seem to be the apostles whom Satan has demanded, that he might sift them like wheat. Is the idea that, thanks to Jesus' prayer for him, Simon was the only one who was not given over to Satan? Consequently, since his faith did not fail (permanently), he had to strengthen the others whose faith did fail by restoring them to belief in Jesus the Messiah? Yet, as we have pointed out, Luke has never indicated such a failure on the part of the apostles. He has omitted from the Last Supper scene the Marcan/Matthean saying about the disciples stumbling and the sheep being scattered (Mark 14:27, citing Zech 13:7), and he has had Jesus tell the apostles three verses earlier: "You are the ones who continued with me in my trials" (Luke 22:28). Moreover, Luke does not tell us that all the disciples left Jesus to flee after he was arrested on the Mount of Olives (cf. Mark 14:50). Rather, Luke gives the impression that the disciples remained in Jerusalem through the crucifixion (see not only 24:33 but also 23:49 which has "all his acquaintances" watching the crucifixion).

We are thus led to conclude that Luke may mean Simon's "brothers" to include a wider group than the Twelve apostles [266] and that the command to "strengthen" them does not necessarily mean "restore to faith." In the Book of Acts "brothers" often has a wide meaning. For example, in Acts 1:15 Peter is depicted as standing "among the brothers (the company of persons was in all about a hundred and twenty)." In Acts 15:23 a letter is sent from "the brothers," i.e., the apostles and elders of Jerusalem "to the brothers who are of the Gentiles in Antioch, Syria, and Cilicia." The verb "to strengthen" in Acts (note 263 above) involves encouraging the Christian communities, especially through missionary preaching. Of interest is Acts 15:32: "Judas and Silas, who were themselves prophets, exhorted the *brothers* [at Antioch] . . . and *strengthened* them." Thus, Luke 22:32, with its directive to Simon to "strengthen your brothers,"[267] may be meant to prepare for the story of

---

[266] Of course, it is not impossible that in a pre-Lucan stage the saying did refer to the Twelve. Fuller, *Formation* (note 76 above), p. 35, theorizes that the original reference of the saying was to Peter's action after the (first) appearance of the risen Jesus to him—he proceeded to assemble the disciples for the second appearance.

[267] The fact that the verb form "strengthen" is an aorist imperative need not be pressed to the point of concluding that only one act of strengthening can be meant.

Peter's missionary career in chapters 1-15 of Acts where he will be a leading spokesman for the faith of the Jerusalem community (chapters 1-5), will go about visiting converts in Samaria (ch. 8), and Lydda and Joppa (9:32-43), and will take the significant step of commanding that the Roman Cornelius be baptized (chapters 10-11).

Yet if we interpret 22:32 through a reference to Acts, it should be noted that the Gospel passage singles out Simon for the task of strengthening the brothers, while in Acts many have the role of strengthening, e.g., Paul, Barnabas, Judas, and Silas. (And, indeed, in Acts when Peter is active, he is often not alone, but accompanied by John.) Why then does Luke 22:32 contrast Simon with the plural apostolic "you" of verse 31? Is this because Luke knew of the tradition that Simon was the first of the Twelve to see the risen Jesus (24:34)? Or is it because, of *the Twelve*, Peter will be the most active apostolic missionary in the Book of Acts? In any case, the prayer and promise of Jesus regarding Simon in Luke 22:31-32 is meant to anticipate Peter's post-resurrectional prominence, a preparation of the type that we detected also in our discussion of Simon's miraculous catch of fish in 5:1-11.

What relation does the dominical saying recorded by Luke have to the dominical saying regarding Simon Bar-Jonah recorded in Matt 16:17-19? This is a significant question precisely because, as we saw (note 195 above), Cullmann has proposed that the Lucan Last Supper verses were the original context of the Matthean promise to Peter. In both instances Peter's faith is not something for which he can claim personal credit—for Luke, it is because of Jesus' prayer that Simon's faith does not permanently fail; for Matthew, Simon's faith in Jesus as the Messiah, the Son of the living God, is a gift from the Father in heaven. But the role assigned to Peter in Luke is different from the role assigned to him in Matthew. In Luke, Simon's role of strengthening involves a hortatory, missionary function, while the role that Matthew gives to Peter as rock has the function of a foundation.[268] The former is continuing and ac-

---

[268] A partial resemblance might be developed if Jesus' founding the church on Peter the rock (cf. Matt 7:24-27) can be seen as the reason

tive;[269] the latter is once for all. Nor is Matthew's second image whereby Peter is promised the power of the keys and of binding and loosing particularly close to the Lucan image of strengthening, although both imply continuing activities. A closer parallel to the Lucan imagery might be found in John 21:15-17 where Simon, son of John, is told three times to feed Jesus' sheep. (We have already seen a connection between Simon's miraculous catch of fish in Luke 5:1-11 and John 21:1-13.) As will become evident in the next chapter, the Johannine three-fold command of Jesus to Simon may be an implicit corrective of Peter's threefold denial, the prediction of which immediately follows Luke 22:31-32.

D. The Appearance of the Risen Lord to Simon (Luke 24:34)

After the risen Lord had appeared to the two disciples on the road to Emmaus (24:13-32), they returned to Jerusalem and found the Eleven gathered together with others. The two disciples were immediately told, "The Lord has been raised indeed and appeared to Simon" (24:34).[270] Luke gives no information as to where or when this appearance occurred, but in the present Gospel sequence it must have occurred in the Jerusalem area between Peter's Easter morning visit to the tomb when he did *not* see Jesus (24:12, 24)[271] and the evening

---

why the gates of Hades cannot prevail against the church—this is a form of strengthening, but with a connotation different from the way Luke uses "strengthen" in Acts.

[269] Yet there is nothing in 22:32 that carries the picture beyond Peter's lifetime and suggests a successor after his death in the role of strengthening the brothers.

[270] We have not accepted the thesis that Simon was one of the two disciples who saw Jesus on the road to Emmaus, and that it was these two disciples who made the announcement in 24:34 to the Eleven. See J. H. Crehan, *Catholic Biblical Quarterly* 15 (1953), pp. 418-26.

[271] This visit is mentioned for the first time in Luke 24:12, a Western non-interpolation, i.e., a verse found in our best textual witnesses from the East but surprisingly missing from the Western textual tradition (which usually interpolates rather than omits). Today scholars are increasingly inclined to accept the authenticity of such verses; see K. Snod-

return of the two disciples to Jerusalem. Obviously this chronology is difficult since Jesus was with the two disciples for a considerable time in the afternoon (and this is only one of the difficulties inherent in Luke's presentation of all the appearances of the risen Lord on one day!). Indeed, the tradition that Peter did not see Jesus at the tomb and the tradition that the Lord appeared to Simon are two very different traditions. We may solve this tension best if we recognize that the announcement "The Lord has been raised indeed and has appeared to Simon" is a stray item of kerygmatic proclamation that Luke has fitted awkwardly into his condensed Gospel sequence.

That Luke received this formula from early preaching is suggested by a comparison with the formula in I Cor 15:4-5 which Paul says he received and passed on: "He was raised . . . and appeared to Cephas." The Greek of the two formulas is remarkably similar (Luke: *ēgerthē . . . kai ōphthē Simōni;* Paul: *egēgertai . . . kai . . . ōphthē Kēpha*). Moreover, the use of the name "Simon" in 24:34 stands out when, in the previous reference in the chapter (24:12), the name "Peter" was employed. But if Luke received the formula from early tradition, he may have known little about the appearance except that it was the first appearance of the risen Jesus to a member of the Twelve. That would explain why he has it mentioned in an artificial manner by the Eleven just before Jesus appears to them (24:36ff.). The setting that Luke gives to the formula, then, tells us nothing about where or when the appearance actually occurred and does nothing to discredit the probable indication in Mark 16:7 that Jesus appeared to Peter in Galilee (cf. also the apocryphal *Gospel of Peter,* 58-60).[272] The hypo-

---

grass, " 'Western Non-Interpolations,' " *Journal of Biblical Literature* 91 (1972), pp. 369-79. Nevertheless, Luke 24:12 which has Peter (alone) go to the tomb and Luke 24:24 which reports that "some of those who were with us went to the tomb" may stem from different layers of Lucan tradition and/or redaction.

[272] This touches on the very complicated problem of which Gospel tradition is more correct: that the risen Jesus first appeared to the remaining members of the Twelve in Jerusalem (Luke; John 20; Marcan Appendix) or that he first appeared to them in Galilee (Matthew; John 21 [critically corrected], and perhaps Mark 16:7). See the discussion in

thesis that it occurred on the shores of the Lake of Galilee and that the narrative of it is preserved partially in John 21:1-13 is of interest, for it would establish a relationship of all three special Petrine sections in Luke (5:1-11; 22:31-32; 24:34) with that post-resurrectional scene; but obviously this is highly speculative.

What is factual is that Luke gives us the only explicit Gospel reference to a special appearance of the risen Jesus to Peter. Yet he makes nothing of this appearance in the narrative that follows in chapter 24. Why then did he bother to mention it? Was it perhaps once more by way of preparing for the role of Peter as the most important member of the Twelve in the Book of Acts, a motive that we found in the preceding Petrine passages in Luke?[273]

In conclusion then, we see that Luke has presented a very favorable portrait of Peter to the (Gentile?) Christian community for which he writes toward the end of the century. Gone are many of the harsh judgments about Peter that we find in Mark and Matthew, so that Peter's career during the ministry of Jesus fits more smoothly with the picture of his career in the early church given in the Book of Acts. The Lucan Gospel portrait does not have the Matthean emphasis on Peter as the rock on which the church will be built, but does prepare the way for the image of Peter as the missionary and strengthener of the church. From his first call by Jesus he is uniquely destined to be a catcher of men. He enters his time of greatest crisis (Jesus' arrest and passion) with the assurance that Jesus has prayed that his faith will not fail and that he will turn again to strengthen the brethren. If his denials are narrated as the only blemish on his career. Luke takes pains to remind the

---

all the standard books on the resurrection, e.g., the work of Fuller cited in note 76 above.

[273] We have asked whether the tradition of an appearance of the risen Jesus to Simon prompted the singling out of Simon for the (post-resurrectional) role of strengthening the brothers in 22:32. Was the appearance to Simon also the original setting of the miraculous catch of fish now located in 5:1-11? See A. R. C. Leaney, "Jesus and Peter. The Call and Postresurrection Appearance (Lk V. 1-11 and XXIV. 34)," *Expository Times* 65 (1954), pp. 381-82.

reader that these denials were forgiven, for the risen Lord appeared to Simon. It is probably no accident that Peter is the last of the Twelve to be mentioned by name in the Gospel and the first of the Twelve to be mentioned by name in the Book of Acts. If for Luke the Twelve apostles are the bridge between the historical Jesus and the church, Simon or Peter plays that role par excellence.

CHAPTER EIGHT:
PETER IN THE
GOSPEL OF JOHN[274]

Simon Peter[275] is referred to more frequently than is any other disciple in the Fourth Gospel—even more frequently than the unnamed "disciple whom Jesus loved." As we shall see, John agrees with the Synoptic Gospels in many features concerning the role and character of Peter; yet much of the material that John reports about Peter is not the same as what is reported in the Synoptic Gospels. In discussing the general picture of Peter in the first three Gospels, we were able to use as a basic outline the fifteen Petrine passages or details in the Gospel of Mark. Of these, only part of #1 (Simon Peter fishes on the Sea of Tiberias[276]) and ## 12 and 14 (the denials of Peter) are clearly reproduced in John. This difference of material concerning Peter is part of the radical variance of Gospel outline which divides John from the Synoptics and which has caused scholars to suggest that the Fourth Evangelist drew

---

[274] The discussion for this chapter was led by R. E. Brown. Two sessions of the task force (May, September 1972) were devoted to the evidence of John.

[275] The combination "Simon Peter" is used more often by John than by any other New Testament writer. The custom begins with the first mention (1:40), even before Jesus has changed Simon's name to Cephas or Peter (1:42), and continues into chapter 21. The consistent pattern in scenes where Peter is named several times is to use "Simon Peter" at the beginning of the scene, even if just "Peter" is used later.

[276] This is indicated only in John 21. Andrew, Simon Peter's brother, is mentioned several times but is not named in the fishing scene of chapter 21.

upon a tradition independent of the Synoptics and/or their sources.[277] We have seen that the Gospels of Matthew and Luke give us portraits of Peter which circulated in two different communities (predominantly Jewish Christian and Gentile Christian respectively?) toward the end of the first century, but these are communities that would have been familiar with the same general Gospel material, especially the Marcan and the "Q" material. The Fourth Gospel was addressed to another Christian community at roughly the same period[278] but a community familiar with a markedly divergent Gospel tradition, stemming (at least by its own claim) from the "disciple whom Jesus loved" (John 19:35; 21:24). Let us see how Peter fares in this community's recollections and esteem.

It may prove helpful if we classify the Petrine passages in John, chapters 1-20, under two headings: (A) those where he appears without the Beloved Disciple, and (B) those where he appears with the Beloved Disciple. A third section (C) will deal with the role of Simon Peter in John 21, a chapter that is generally regarded as a later supplement to the Gospel (note 297 below).

A. The General Picture of Peter in John (John 1–20)

There are six passages in which John presents Simon Peter without mention of the Beloved Disciple: (1) 1:40-42: Jesus

---

[277] See Chapter Two, B, 7. For the complicated question of Johannine sources see the discussion in Brown, *John* (note 31 above), I, pp. xxviii-xxxiv. A theory gaining adherence is that the evangelist drew upon at least a collection of miracle stories and some basic sayings material, and may even have had an independent tradition of the passion.

[278] It is generally assumed that the final form of the Fourth Gospel is to be dated in the 90's, slightly later than the Gospels of Matthew and of Luke; but the composition of John may have stretched over a considerable period of time, especially if we posit a redaction by another hand (see note 297 below). We shall speak of a Johannine community, but little is known of its make-up or structure. Was it a group of communities? Was it more a religious fellowship than a church (a word that John does *not* use) in the sense(s) of that term in other New Testament works of the late first century? See note 36 above.

meets Simon and says that he will be called Cephas; (2) 6:67-69: Simon Peter confesses Jesus as the Holy One of God; (3) 13:6-11: Jesus washes Simon Peter's feet; (4) 13:36-38: Jesus predicts Simon Peter's denials; (5) 18:10-11: Simon Peter cuts off the servant's ear in the Garden; (6) 18:17-18, 25-27: Simon Peter denies Jesus three times.

The first two (1:40-42 and 6:67-69) may be discussed together, for they constitute a partial Johannine parallel to the Synoptic tradition that Jesus gave to Simon the name Peter, and that Peter was the one who spoke for the Twelve in confessing Jesus at a crucial time. In the Fourth Gospel the first two disciples who come to Jesus (in the Jordan valley, not at the Sea of Galilee, as in the Synoptic tradition) are disciples of John the Baptist, and one of them is "Andrew, Simon Peter's brother" (1:40). After spending part of a day with Jesus, Andrew seeks out his brother and announces to him, "We have found the Messiah." When Andrew leads Simon to Jesus, Simon is greeted with the dominical words: "So you are Simon, son of John? You shall be called Cephas (which means Peter)." Attention has already been called to the similarity of this to the saying in Matt 16:17-18: "Blessed are you Simon Bar-Jonah. . . . You are Peter."[279] It is interesting that this change of name in John, as well as in Matthew, occurs after the acknowledgment of Jesus as the Messiah; but here it is Andrew, not Peter, who has made the acknowledgment.[280] The Johannine parallel to

---

[279] See the discussion in relation to note 210 above. In both passages Simon's patronymic (respectively, son of John and son of Jonah) is given, as it is elsewhere only in John 21:15-17. John gives the Aramaic name "Cephas" (the only Gospel occurrence), the equivalent to Matthew's *"Petros."* The difference of tense (John: "You *shall be called* Cephas"; Matthew: "You *are* Peter") should not be pressed, as if one were a promise and the other a fulfillment. (Indeed, an older exegesis saw in John 1:42 a prediction of a name change; in Mark 3:16 the actual name-giving; and in Matt 16:18 a confirmation of the name.) The future tense is best understood as part of a literary style of name-changing, e.g., the future tense appears in the LXX of Gen 17:5 and 15, even though the author consistently uses the new name from that point on. So Brown, *John* (note 31 above), I, p. 80, against Bultmann.

[280] In John 1 a series of exalted titles is given to Jesus in the very first days of his ministry; Lamb of God (vss. 29, 35), Rabbi (38), Messiah (41), He of whom Moses and the prophets wrote (45), Son

the Synoptic tradition of Peter's confession of Jesus at Caesarea Philippi does not come until 6:67-69. There, after the evangelist has commented on the many who do not believe in Jesus, even some of his disciples (6:60, 66), Jesus is pictured as addressing the Twelve: "Will you also go away?"[281] Simon Peter answers for them: "We have believed and have come to know that you are the Holy One of God."[282] This confession of Jesus by Peter, however, does not play the decisive role in John that the Caesarea Philippi confession plays in Mark or, in a somewhat different way, in Matthew. Jesus has already been confessed in chapter 1 of the Gospel (note 280 above), and so Jesus' reaction to Simon Peter's confession in chapter 6 is much more neutral or noncommittal than his reaction in the Synoptic tradition. Jesus neither praises Simon, as in Matthew, nor ultimately speaks to him as Satan, as in both Mark and Matthew.[283] Thus, while the Johannine Simon Peter retains a certain prominence as a spokesman for the Twelve, he is not the first disciple to be called, and he is assigned no special precedence because of his confession of Jesus.

The third Johannine scene to mention Simon Peter is the washing of the feet at the Last Supper in John 13:6-11. At first Peter does not understand the significance or symbolism of having Jesus wash his feet, and so he resists: "You shall never wash my feet." But when Jesus stresses the necessity, Simon Peter overreacts with enthusiastic acceptance, "Lord, not my feet only, but also my hands and my head." Jesus has to insist that only the washing of the feet is necessary. This scene has no parallel in the Synoptic tradition, but it agrees with that

---

of God and King of Israel (49), and Son of Man (51). This reflects the Johannine theological view that Jesus' glory was apparent from the beginning (1:14; 2:11).

[281] Note the similarities to the Caesarea Philippi setting where there is also a distinction between the inadequate things that men say about Jesus and what his disciples believe: "But who do you say that I am?" This is the first of the rare mentions of the Twelve in John, and the use of the term may indicate pre-Johannine tradition. See note 36 above.

[282] A number of Greek and other textual witnesses have heightened the similarity to Matt 16:16 by reading in John 6:69: "the Messiah, the Son of (the living) God." See note 148 above.

[283] See note 153 above.

tradition's image of an impulsive figure who often misunder-
stands the real thrust of Jesus' demands.

If we may jump ahead to the fifth general Petrine scene in
John (18:10-11), we find even more dramatic evidence of the
impulsiveness of Peter. Although the first three Gospels mention that the ear of the servant of the high priest was cut off
during the arrest of Jesus in Gethsemane (Mark 14:47 and
par.), only John identifies the swordsman as Simon Peter. Thus,
it is Peter who has to be told to put his sword back, for Jesus
must drink the cup that the Father has given to him (John
18:11). We are distantly reminded of Peter's failure to understand when Jesus spoke of the suffering of the Son of Man
after the Caesarea Philippi confession, and of Jesus' reprimand
to him (Mark 8:31-33; Matt 16:21-23).

The fourth and sixth general Petrine scenes in John involve
the prediction of the denials (13:36-38) and the actual three
denials (18:17-18, 25-27). They are very much the same in
substance as the Synoptic accounts, with minor variations in
detail. The only verse for which the Synoptic Gospels have no
parallel is John 13:36, where Jesus tells Simon Peter, "Where
I am going, you cannot follow me now, but you shall follow
afterward." This verse may be connected with the reference
in John 21:18-19[284] to Peter's following Jesus by being put
to death.

B. Simon Peter and the Beloved Disciple (John 13–20)

If the general picture of Simon Peter in John thus far is not
markedly distinct from the Synoptic portrait (and, indeed, is
somewhat less highlighted), Peter's relationship to the "disciple
whom Jesus loved" is highly distinctive and constitutes a critical
question for evaluating the Johannine attitude toward Peter.
Just what are we to think of this Beloved Disciple who makes

---

[284] This connection may have been made by the redactor who wrote
21:18-19 in light of 13:36. Or the evangelist (i.e., the writer of 13:36)
may already have known of Peter's death and hinted at it.

his initial appearance at the Last Supper, in the second half of the Fourth Gospel?[285] Was he merely a symbol for the Christian disciple whom Jesus loves, or was he a real person associated with Jesus?[286] If the latter, was he a well-known figure, e.g., a member of the Twelve (see notes 31 and 281 above)? Or was he a minor figure whose career during the lifetime of Jesus was magnified precisely because he was a hero or even a founding-father of the Johannine community and/or its tradition?[287] We cannot answer these disputed questions with certitude, but we accept as the most likely working hypothesis that for the Johannine community the Beloved Disciple was a real person whom they thought to have been a companion of Jesus and whose career was dramatized so that he could serve as a model for all disciples or believers.

With this hypothesis, how does the Johannine estimation of the Beloved Disciple compare with other Christian views attested in the New Testament that give a priority to Peter? Is there any hint in John of a rivalry between Simon Peter and the Beloved Disciple—a rivalry that might reflect later Christian disputes about the importance to be attributed to these two men or to their memories?[288] In an attempt to answer these questions we shall study the three scenes in John 13–20 that associate Simon Peter and the Beloved Disciple: (1) 13:23-26

---

[285] Some have thought that the unnamed disciple of John the Baptist who appears in 1:37-40 is the Beloved Disciple. This suggestion has been influential in identifying him as John, son of Zebedee; for then the Beloved Disciple, Andrew, and Simon Peter would be the first three disciples called, comparable to Simon and Andrew, James and John in the Synoptic traditon.

[286] Some who think that the Beloved Disciple is only a symbolic figure in chapters 13-20 admit that the redactor responsible for ch. 21 (mistakenly) thought he was a real person (21:24). Such a suggestion depends on the thesis that the redactor had only a distant relationship to the evangelist and the Johannine community. See Bultmann, *John* (note 257 above), pp. 700-18.

[287] So R. Schnackenburg, "On the Origin of the Fourth Gospel," *Jesus and Man's Hope,* vol. 1 (Pittsburgh Theological Seminary; *Perspective* 11 [1970]), pp. 223-46.

[288] If the Beloved Disciple was not a real person but simply a model Christian, a comparison with Simon Peter becomes complicated. Would the evangelist want to tell us that any disciple whom Jesus loves ranks with Peter in importance?

at the Last Supper; (2) 18:15-16 in the courtyard of the high priest; (3) 20:2-10 at the empty tomb of Jesus.

The "disciple whom Jesus loved" appears in the Gospel for the first time in the setting of the Last Supper (13:23-26). All the Gospels report the Supper incident where Jesus predicts that one of those eating at table with him will betray him (Mark 14:18 and par.). This prediction gives rise to a question among those at table as to who the betrayer might be. But only John gives names to two figures involved in this questioning: Simon Peter and the Beloved Disciple. The latter is so close to Jesus at table that he is "reclining on Jesus' bosom" (13:23)—a position indicative of Jesus' affection for him. Simon Peter is at a distance and has to signal to the Beloved Disciple to ask whom Jesus means. It is in response to the Beloved Disciple's question that Jesus gives an answer identifying the traitor (while in Mark 14:20 and Matt 26:23 Jesus' answer is in response to the general question from the disciples). This first scene already indicates that in the Fourth Gospel the Beloved Disciple enjoys a primacy in Jesus' love and that Jesus favors him. The fact that Simon Peter has at least a secondary part in this intimate scene suggests that he too was an important figure in the community's memory of the career of the historical Jesus —indeed, the most prominent among the named disciples. The following scenes will confirm that for the Johannine community the two most prominent disciples of Jesus were the Beloved Disciple and Simon Peter, but that the former was closer to Jesus' heart and affections than the latter.

The scene involving Peter's denials of Jesus is again found in all four Gospels, but the Synoptic tradition introduces the scene in a simple manner: after Jesus' arrest, Peter followed him at a distance, even into the courtyard of the high priest (Mark 14:54 and par.). In John 18:15-16 the situation is more complicated. There is another disciple, known to the high priest, who accompanies Jesus into the courtyard or palace. Simon Peter is left standing outside at the gate and is admitted only when the other disciple comes out and speaks to the girl at the gate. As Peter enters, the girl questions him; and this sets the scene for the first denial in which Peter says he is not one of Jesus' disciples. Is this mysterious disciple who was known to the high priest the Beloved Disciple?[289] One reason for thinking so is that the Beloved Disciple is the only male disciple of Jesus who on the next day stands at the foot of the cross, along with Jesus' mother (19:25-27). Clearly then John portrays the Beloved Disciple as one who did not deny Jesus or flee during the passion. He is the one clear exception[290] to Jesus' prediction: "An hour is coming and, indeed, has already come, for you to be scattered, each on his own, leaving me all alone" (16:32). Moreover, the close association with Simon Peter in 18:15-16 is another reason for assuming that the disciple known to the high priest is the Beloved Disciple. In any case, a disciple of Jesus who does not deny him in the courtyard of the high priest is contrasted with Simon Peter who seeks admission to follow Jesus, only immediately to deny his discipleship. And at the foot of the cross Simon Peter is noticeably absent, so that the mother of Jesus is entrusted not to him but to the Beloved Disciple.[291] Thus, while Peter's denials are no more graphically portrayed than in the other Gospels,[292] the Beloved Disciple, especially at the cross, emerges in John as the true follower of Jesus who was faithful to him.

---

[289] For a negative response, see B. Lindars, *The Gospel of John* (New Century Bible; London: Oliphants, 1972), p. 548. That a disciple of Jesus would be an acquaintance of the high priest is very curious. The girl's question indicates that Peter would probably not have been admitted if he had said that he was one of Jesus' disciples. Why then was the other disciple admitted, especially if he was a disciple who was particularly close to Jesus (the Beloved Disciple)? While there are such difficulties about the identity of the unnamed disciple and the historicity of the scene, there is an even greater problem of why the scene would have been invented, since it serves no particular theological purpose. See Brown, *John* (note 31 above), pp. 822-23, 841.

[290] If the disciple known to the high priest was someone other than the Beloved Disciple, then there were two disciples who were exceptions and did not desert Jesus in the hour of his passion.

[291] This scene could be indicative of the ecclesiastical importance of the Beloved Disciple if we were certain of the symbolic significance of the mother of Jesus. Is she a symbol of the people of God? Of the church?

[292] On the one hand the Johannine Simon Peter does not curse and swear in denying Jesus (cf. Mark/Matthew). On the other hand, his denials show greater vacillation, since shortly before this he had struck with the sword in Jesus' defense (18:10-11).

The scene on Easter morning when the women go to the tomb and find it empty is common to the four Gospels; but only in John 20:2-10 and in Luke 24:12, 24 (see note 271 above) does their report prompt a visit by male disciples of Jesus who also find it empty. Luke 24:24 speaks of "some of our company" going to the tomb. Luke 24:12 (a Western non-interpolation—note 271 above) has Peter alone run to the tomb, stoop down, see the burial wrappings, and wonder what has come to pass. John 20:2-10 has Simon Peter and "the other disciple, the one whom Jesus loved,"[293] run side by side toward the tomb. The other disciple outruns Peter and reaches the tomb first; he looks in at the burial wrappings but does not enter until Peter arrives and goes in. Inside, Peter observes the wrappings and the cloth that covered the head, rolled up by itself. When the other disciple finally enters, we are told: "He saw and believed (for as yet they did not know the Scripture that he must rise from the dead). Then the disciples went back home" (20:8-10).

A host of questions is raised by the possible symbolism of the Johannine narrative. Simon Peter is named first (20:2) and the other disciple waits and allows Peter to enter the tomb first. Are these indications of precedence for Peter? Or is the other disciple given precedence because he outruns Peter and thus is more eager to discover the mystery of the empty tomb? Such questions cannot be answered with any certainty. A much more substantial issue arises from the fact that in 20:8 the Beloved Disciple sees and *believes*,[294] while nothing is said about Simon Peter's having come to faith.[295] This leads us to

---

[293] This is the only time in the story that "the other disciple" (mentioned four times) is identified as the "disciple whom Jesus loved." Was "the other disciple" a more original title for this figure? Does Luke 24:12 indicate a pre-Johannine form of the story in which Peter alone figured?

[294] The verb *pisteuein*, "to believe," can also mean "to be convinced"; and it has been proposed that John 20:8 means no more than that the Beloved Disciple became convinced that Mary Magdalene had spoken the truth when she reported that the tomb was empty (Augustine, von Dobschütz, Nauck). This would render the climax of the scene trite, and does not do justice to the invocation of Scripture in 20:9 as something that would implicitly confirm this belief. See Lindars, *John* (note 289 above), p. 602.

[295] The sudden switch from "*He* saw and believed" in 20:8 to "*They*

suspect that for the Johannine community the first one to have come to resurrection faith was the Beloved Disciple—a suspicion that will be strengthened when we discuss 21:7. This would stand in striking contrast to the implication of I Cor 15:5 and Luke 24:34 that Peter was the first of the major companions of Jesus' ministry to have seen the risen Lord.[296]

Before passing on to the supplementary chapter (21), how may we summarize the relationship of Simon Peter to the Beloved Disciple from what we have seen in the second half of the Gospel? Should we speak of rivalry in a sense whereby Peter would be deliberately depreciated in order to exalt the Beloved Disciple? Probably not. For the Johannine community the Beloved Disciple was the basic source of their tradition about Jesus (19:35) and was highly revered. It was important that he be shown close to Jesus in the crucial events that have become part of the Christian tradition, e.g., the Last Supper, the passion, the crucifixion, and the aftermath of the resurrection. Yet the Johannine community knew also that one could not talk about the career of Jesus without also talking about Simon Peter. Thus, both figures played a prominent role in the Johannine tradition: the Beloved Disciple because he was of intimate internal importance to the community; Simon Peter because he was integral to the Jesus tradition. To speak of rivalry is probably an exaggeration, if it implies polemic or

did not know the Scripture" in 20:9 has led some to think that John meant to suggest that Simon Peter also believed. W. Marxsen, *The Resurrection of Jesus of Nazareth* (Philadelphia: Fortress, 1970), p. 58, says that "we are certainly intended to suppose" this. However, 20:9 is most likely meant to explain why Simon Peter did *not* come to faith— none of the followers of Jesus expected the resurrection. It may have been inserted precisely to highlight the extraordinary insight of the Beloved Disciple who alone saw the implications of the empty tomb and the burial clothes.

[296] Of course, in 20:8 John does not have the Beloved Disciple see the risen Lord. This happens in 21:7; and if that chapter is treated independently (so that the appearance of Jesus on the shore of the Sea of Tiberias becomes the first appearance of the risen Lord), the Beloved Disciple is the first to see the risen Lord. Yet this treatment of chapter 21 is a critical reconstruction, and in the present Gospel sequence the appearance in chapter 21 is explicitly designated as the third appearance of the risen Lord (21:14). In the Johannine tradition, Mary Magdalene was the first to see the risen Lord; then came the disciples together.

animosity, since that would not be true to the Johannine portrait of Simon Peter. At most, we might say that this community has placed its apostolic figure (the Beloved Disciple) on a pedestal by showing him to be of competitive importance with Simon Peter, the most famous figure from the ministry of Jesus known to the church at large.

C. Simon Peter and the Beloved Disciple in John 21

The appearance of the risen Jesus to Thomas in John 20:24-28 is narrated in a way that would mark it as the last appearance the evangelist intended to recount, since in verse 29 Jesus turns from Thomas to bless those who have *not* seen and yet believe. The evangelist reinforces this impression by supplying a conclusion immediately afterwards (20:30-31), explaining why he has written the book and not included all of Jesus' signs. It is quite startling, then, to turn the page and find another chapter narrating an appearance of the risen Jesus in Galilee, an appearance in which his disciples act as if they had never seen him before. Small wonder that chapter 21 is commonly considered an addendum to the completed Gospel! Stylistic differences [297] further suggest that its author (called the redactor) was not the evangelist who wrote the rest of the Gospel. What scholars do not agree upon is whether the redactor was a disciple of the evangelist, favorable to his thought, who added stray Johannine material to the Gospel lest it be lost, or whether he was one who disagreed with basic thrusts of the evangelist's thought and sought to correct him by additions. We shall not attempt to solve such a question here; but in working with the hypothesis that chapter 21 was an addendum

---

[297] These are discussed in painstaking detail by M.-E. Boismard, "Le chapitre xxi de saint Jean: essai de critique littéraire," *Revue Biblique* 54 (1947), pp. 473-501. The bibliography of critical scholarship on this chapter is large; see Brown, *John* (note 31 above), II, pp. 1131-32. The redactor or author of chapter 21 is thought to have made other significant additions to the body of the Gospel, and it is around the theology of those additions that the debate about the nature of the redaction has centered.

by the redactor, we keep an open mind on two points. First, even if the chapter was added, it may contain old and valuable material—in fact, at times, an older tradition than is found in the Gospel itself.[298] Second, the chapter's theological outlook is not necessarily the same as that found in John 1–20.

All of this is important for our discussion since the whole of chapter 21 is built around Simon Peter and the Beloved Disciple. It will facilitate our discussion if we divide the chapter into three sections: (1) The appearance of the risen Jesus and the miraculous catch of fish (21:1-14); (2) The risen Jesus instructs Simon to feed his sheep (21:15-17); (3) Jesus speaks of the destinies of Simon Peter and of the Beloved Disciple (21:18-23).

(1) As for the miraculous catch of fish (21:1-14), we remind the reader that we have already discussed the relationship of this scene to Luke 5:1-11, where Simon is called to be a catcher of men. We encountered the difficulty of deciding whether the original context of the miracle story was the ministry of Jesus (as in Luke) or the time after the resurrection (as in John). In dealing with the pre-Gospel history of the scene we may also mention the possibility that 21:1-14 is composite, combining the stories of two appearances of the risen Jesus (his first appearance to Simon Peter at the Sea of Tiberias; a later appearance to the disciples at a meal).[299]

Be this as it may, our chief interest must be in the present form of the Johannine story. If Simon was the only figure of importance alongside Jesus in the core of the Lucan narrative (5:4-10), here he is accompanied by six other disciples whose names are given after his in a list in 21:2.[300] However, Simon Peter still has the most important role in the fishing narra-

---

[298] The redactor struggles to explain the significance of two obscure sayings of Jesus (21:18, 22), and in the case of 21:22 he has to correct a broadly circulated interpretation of the saying. He scarcely invented a saying that caused him difficulty; rather he was working with older traditions known to the Johannine community.

[299] The scene is dissected in one way or another by such scholars as Wellhausen, Bauer, Loisy, Schwartz, and Bultmann. See Brown, *John* (note 31 above), II, pp. 1084-95.

[300] This is the closest the Fourth Gospel comes to the Synoptic tradition of naming Peter first in the list of the Twelve.

tive. He takes the initiative in going out fishing; he jumps into the sea to go to meet Jesus; and he hauls the net of fish ashore. The ecclesiastical significance of this prominence would be clearer if we could be certain that the symbolism of the miraculous catch of fish was the same for the Johannine redactor as it was for Luke—a sign of the future missionary catch of men, bringing them to Jesus.[301] But the redactor does not make this explicit as does Luke 5:10b.

What is strikingly Johannine is the contrast between the Beloved Disciple[302] and Simon Peter. While both see the stranger on the shore, only the Beloved Disciple recognizes that it is the Lord; and it is he who passes this information on to Peter. This is quite harmonious with the thrust of 20:8 where the Beloved Disciple, not Simon Peter, sees the significance of the empty tomb and believes. Love gives the Beloved Disciple insight. Peter's impetuosity in jumping from the boat to go to Jesus is consistent with the portrait in 18:10-11 where he rushes to defend Jesus with a sword. Thus, there is a continuity in chapter 21 with the picture of these two figures in the body of the Fourth Gospel. Simon Peter remains important, but he is not the one really attuned to Jesus.

(2) It is in 21:15-17 that the full attention of Jesus is turned to Simon Peter. The threefold question, "Simon, son of

---

[301] There are some possible indications of this motif in John 21. The verb *helkein (helkyein)* used for "hauling in" the fish in 21:6 and 11 is the same verb that appears in the promise of Jesus in 12:32: "When I am lifted up from the earth, I shall *draw* all men to myself." The detail that the net which traps the fish is not torn *(schizein)* may symbolize the unity of the Christian missionary endeavor, for throughout Jesus' ministry men are constantly divided *(schizein)* over Jesus, as we see in 7:43; 9:16; 10:19. The number 153 in the catch of fish (21:11) is said by Jerome (PL 25:474C) to be the total number of species of fish recognized by the Greek zoologists, so that it may represent the totality and range of the Christian mission. Obviously these interpretations are increasingly speculative.

[302] It is curious that the Beloved Disciple is not mentioned among the seven disciples in 21:2, and his presence seems to be an afterthought. He is absent in the Lucan parallel in 5:1-11 (we saw a similar situation when we compared John 20:2-10 and Luke 24:12). Of course, the redactor may want us to identify him with one of the seven disciples, e.g., with one of the sons of Zebedee (John?) or with one of the other two unnamed disciples. See note 31 above.

John, do you love me?", is generally thought to reflect Peter's threefold denial, and so the scene is often described as a rehabilitation of Peter.[303] But our main interest is in the corresponding threefold command to feed Jesus' sheep.[304] This is pastoral imagery, but what is implied in it by way of an ecclesiastical role for Peter? Often the scene is interpreted in terms of the shepherd imagery in John 10 (which, of course, is applicable to all who have the role of pastors in the Christian community). The shepherd feeds his sheep by leading them out to pasture, and they immediately know him and follow him (10:3-5). This could be symbolic for nourishing the Christian flock through preaching and teaching. The good shepherd protects his sheep from the wolf even if it means laying down his life for the sheep (10:11ff.). This could be symbolic for protecting them from heresy (Acts 20:28-30). That some connection between the imagery of John 21:15-17 and 10:1-18 is intended may be seen from what follows in chapter 21—the command to feed the sheep is followed by a prediction of how Peter will die (laying down his life for the sheep).

The threefold command to feed the sheep also seems to imply an authority over the sheep, especially if we recall that in the Old Testament the king was described as a shepherd.[305]

---

[303] The Beloved Disciple is not mentioned in 21:15-17, but one can scarcely imagine the Johannine Jesus three times asking the disciple whom he loved, "Do you love me?" This disciple has not denied Jesus and does not need to be rehabilitated. Of course, the rehabilitation of Simon Peter is only by implication, and such scholars as Spitta, Goguel, and Bultmann have rejected this motif. Most recently Lindars, *John* (note 289 above), p. 633, accepts it.

[304] P. Gaechter, "Das dreifache 'Weide meine Lämmer,'" *Zeitschrift für Katholische Theologie* 69 (1947), pp. 328-44, considers the threefold character of the command separately from the threefold question. He cites the ancient Near Eastern legal custom of saying something three times before witnesses in order to solemnize it or make it legal, e.g., in a contract conferring rights. However, a threefold repetition automatically has an air of solemnity without the suggestion of such a legal parallel.

[305] The fact that King David had been a shepherd helped to make this common Oriental imagery more appropriate for the monarchy of Judah. See especially Ezek 34 which is often cited as the background for the shepherd imagery of John 10. The commands in John 21:15-17 use two Greek verbs for "feed" in the sequence: *boskein, poimainein, boskein*. In the Greek Bible both these verbs translate Hebrew *rā'āh*, "to feed,

But what kind of authority is the Johannine Jesus giving to Simon? There is little in John 21 to suggest that it is the authority of the secular king. It is a pastoral authority that is rooted in Simon Peter's love for Jesus; for before Jesus commissions Simon to feed the sheep, he asks whether Simon loves him. It is a pastoral authority that does not make the sheep belong to Simon—he is instructed to feed *Jesus'* sheep. It is a pastoral authority that (as we have seen by way of comparison to chapter 10) puts the primary obligation on Simon, not on the sheep: he has to lead them out to pasture; he has to protect them; he has to lay down his life for them. Nevertheless, it is noteworthy that in the Johannine tradition this command to feed the sheep is specifically addressed to Peter and not to the Beloved Disciple (or to anyone else).[306] Was this command recorded simply as part of the story of Peter's rehabilitation after his denials? Or does it reflect a situation where the figure

---

pasture," and so we can be dubious about attempts to find a sharp distinction between them. Nevertheless, *poimainein* covers a somewhat broader field of meaning, for it describes not only feeding the flock, but also guarding and guiding them; equivalently it can mean "to rule, govern" (II Sam 7:7; Ps 2:9; Matt 2:6). Note the distinction in Philo, *Quod deterius* VIII 25: "Those who feed [*boskein*] supply nourishment ... but those who tend [*poimainein*] have the powers of rulers and governors."

[306] On the one hand, the fact that the imagery involves a shepherd and sheep means that the Johannine community knows of different roles. If Peter can feed the sheep only because he loves Jesus, that does not mean that everyone who loves Jesus becomes a shepherd. Peter has to be appointed to that by Jesus. On the other hand, the uniqueness of the command to Peter in 21:15-17 must be set over against the other postresurrectional command to all the disciples in 20:21, "As the Father has sent me, so do I send you." We are reminded of the way Matthew deals with the power of the keys and the power of binding/loosing: both (if they are distinct) are promised to Peter alone in Matt 16:19, while in Matt 18:18 the power of binding/loosing is given to all the disciples (see note 231 above). A limitation on any authority given to Simon Peter in the Johannine tradition would be implied in John 13:16: "Amen, amen, I say to you, a servant is not greater than his master; nor is he who is sent [*apostolos*] greater than he who sent him." An even further limitation is seen by G. F. Snyder, "John 13:16 and the Anti-Petrinism of the Johannine Tradition," *Biblical Research* 16 (1971), pp. 5-15, who thinks that this Johannine saying with its reference to *apostolos* belongs to the debate at the end of the first century about the authority of the apostles.

of Simon Peter had become a symbol of pastoral authority in parts of the Christian world?

This last query leads us into a discussion of parallels for John 21:15-17. It is interesting that, while the best Gospel parallel for 21:1-14 with its fishing (missionary?) motif is Luke 5:1-11, we must turn to Matt 16:18-19 for a parallel to 21:15-17.[307] Peter is not only a missionary fisher of men (the earlier Christian image?), but also a pastor who has a responsibility for and authority over those who already believe. But the emphasis on authority is stronger in Matthew (cf. the power of the keys). In addition, the Matthean imagery of binding and loosing is more legalistic in background and lacks the Johannine overtones of love and obligation (e.g., protecting the sheep; laying down one's life for them).

A somewhat closer New Testament parallel for the conception of Peter as a pastoral figure would be I Peter 5:1-4, a passage to be discussed in the next chapter. There, Peter speaking as a presbyter (or elder) urges his fellow presbyters: "Tend the flock of God that is in your charge, exercising oversight [episkopein—missing in some manuscripts] not by constraint but willingly . . . not as domineering over those in your charge but being examples to the flock. And when the Chief Shepherd is manifested, you will obtain the unfading crown of glory." In this passage from the epistle there is a clear note of authority, but a clearer note of obligation to the flock, even as in John 21. Moreover, the implicit patterning of Peter the shepherd on Jesus the Good Shepherd which we drew from a comparison of John 21 and John 10 becomes explicit in the epistle where Peter and the other presbyters are to tend the flock of God until the Chief Shepherd's appearance.

---

307 We do not think of these as variant forms of the same saying of Jesus; rather they are scenes involving a similar attitude toward Simon and his ecclesiastical role. We hypothesized that the original setting of Matt 16:16b-19 was also post-resurrectional. In both, Jesus takes the initiative in giving Simon Peter a role of authority, a role that still enables Jesus, however, to speak of "my church" and "my sheep." Yet the wording of the commission is quite different. (Rough parallels to the wording of Peter's confession and Jesus' promise in Matt 16:16b-19 would be found in John 1:42; 6:69; 20:23.)

(3) Since being a shepherd involves laying down one's life for the sheep (John 10:11), the command to Simon to feed Jesus' sheep leads into the next section of the scene (21:18-23) where Peter's death is predicted in terms suggestive of martyrdom.[308] The little dialogue after the prediction, where Jesus says to Peter, "Follow me," reminds us that there was a following of Jesus at the end of the Lucan account of the miraculous catch of fish (Luke 5:11). Moreover, it echoes the sentence peculiar to the Johannine form of the prediction of Peter's denials: "Where I am going, you cannot follow me now, but you shall follow afterward" (13:36). Jesus said those words on his way to death; and his command to follow, addressed to Peter in 21:19, is most probably an invitation to martyrdom.

Once again the Beloved Disciple appears by way of contrast. He has not died a martyr's death. Does that mean he is inferior to Simon Peter? No, because his destiny was also willed by Jesus.[309] And so even without a martyr's death, he is still entitled to bear witness (*martyrein*—21:24), and it is on his witness that the community's tradition rests. Thus, the roles of Simon Peter and of the Beloved Disciple are partially different and partially the same. Simon Peter is specifically commissioned by Jesus as a shepherd, and this is done after Jesus has drawn from him a threefold confession of love that compensates for

---

[308] In itself the imagery of 21:18 is obscure (stretching out one's hands; having a belt fastened around one; being led where one does not wish to go); it is capable of interpretations other than the one given to it by the redactor in 21:19. This suggests that an earlier prediction is being clarified and interpreted *post eventum*, namely, in terms of the death of Peter which has already occurred. The hint of martyrdom is found in the redactor's claim that the saying "indicated the sort of death by which Peter was to glorify God." These last words echo Christian terminology for martyrdom; see I Peter 4:16; *Martyrdom of Polycarp* 14:3; 19:2. The idea that the martyrdom was by crucifixion appears in a reference to this verse in Tertullian, *Scorpiace* 15 (PL 2:151B). Also cf. the references to Jesus' crucifixion ("the sort of death he was to die") in John 12:33 and 18:32.

[309] The saying pertinent to the Beloved Disciple is not much clearer than the saying pertinent to Peter. The redactor takes pains to clarify that the saying does not necessarily mean what the words seem to imply, and his effort is best explained if the Beloved Disciple had already died. It would then have been imperative for the redactor to show that his death did not falsify Jesus' promise.

his denials—a confession that will have to be tested by a willingness to die. No confession of love needs to be drawn from the Beloved Disciple who has never denied Jesus, but neither does he receive a specific commission as a shepherd.[310] In a certain sense he needs no special commission to be what he is, for he is the Beloved of Jesus. Yet both these men are witnesses. Simon's martyrdom is a witness consonant with his shepherd's duty of laying down his life. The form of the Beloved Disciple's witness is different: he "remained" as Jesus wished, i.e., he lived out a long life in the love of Jesus. But this witness is not inferior, and neither is the community that depends on his witness.

We wondered at the beginning of our discussion of this chapter whether the portrait of Simon Peter and the Beloved Disciple drawn by the redactor was essentially different from the picture painted by the evangelist in the body of the Gospel. The very fact that, in order to interpret chapter 21, we have constantly needed to refer back to the earlier chapters suggests that the thought pattern is not so markedly different. It is true that Simon Peter is more prominent in this chapter than he is in any other chapter of the Gospel, but that does not mean that he is aggrandized beyond Johannine bounds. In characteristically Johannine manner the Beloved Disciple is placed alongside Peter. It is he and not Peter who first recognizes the risen Jesus. Peter's denials are indirectly recalled. He is rebuked when he asks about the future of the Beloved Disciple who is also promised a special destiny by Jesus, so that he is not inferior to Peter. If Simon Peter is commissioned with a pastoral role as shepherd of the sheep, this is probably not to be attributed to the peculiar interests of the redactor but may reflect a wider New Testament tradition about the special dealings of the risen Jesus with Peter. Thus it is not clear that the redactor's attitude is much more pro-Petrine than the evangelist's.

On the other hand, we have not found in chapter 21 any animosity against Peter.[311] We saw in the body of the Gospel

---

[310] Perhaps he was not eligible to be a model shepherd because he did not die a martyr's death.

[311] We have not accepted the thesis of S. Agourides, "The Purpose of John 21," *Studies in the History and Text of the New Testament—in*

that the Johannine community accepted the fact, attested in the other Gospels as well, that one could not narrate the story of Jesus' ministry without talking about Simon Peter. The community secured its own position by placing its hero, the Beloved Disciple, alongside Simon Peter and showing his primacy in love. Similarly we may surmise that the Johannine community acknowledged that one could not tell the story of the Christian church (at least by the end of the century) without mentioning Peter's importance in a missionary and in a pastoral role.[312] Once again the community secured its own position by placing the Beloved Disciple alongside Simon Peter. He too saw the risen Jesus, indeed before Simon Peter recognized him. If he was not known as a shepherd of the flock who laid down his life for Jesus' sheep, he bore a different witness no less valid since it was willed by Jesus. Chapter 21 is not an attack on the pastoral authority of Peter; it is a demand for the recognition of another type of discipleship, just as authentic as that of the best known of the traditional apostles.[313]

Honor of K. W. Clark, ed. B. L. Daniels and M. J. Suggs (Salt Lake City: Univ. of Utah, 1967), pp. 127-32, that the redactor's intention was to counteract an exaggerated honor or authority being attributed to Peter within certain Christian circles in the Province of Asia. See also Snyder's article mentioned in note 306 above.

[312] We neither imply nor deny that the historical Peter exercised a role of pastoral authority over a particular church (e.g., as its presbyter) or over a series of churches. But clearly by the end of the century pastoral roles were being justified by relating them to the great apostles —a good example is found in the Pastoral Epistles of Paul which have the Apostle of the Gentiles give pastoral directives to Timothy and Titus and to the churches supervised by them. It is not unnatural that Peter, the best known of the Twelve, would become the focus of such pastoral authentication. His appearance in this role in Matthew, I Peter, and John 21 shows the wide currency of the view.

[313] The Johannine tradition has its own approach to some features associated elsewhere with apostolic authority. The fact that the Gospel speaks favorably of Simon Peter's feeding the flock shows that it was not opposed to the idea of a major apostle serving as a vehicle of tradition passed down to the faithful (since "feeding" certainly implies teaching). Yet, in the Johannine view, the teacher par excellence was not an apostle or the apostles but the Paraclete who guaranteed that the authentic Jesus tradition would be properly understood, preserved, and communicated (John 16:13-14). This Paraclete was given to all believers who loved Jesus and kept his commandments (14:15-16).

donymous (written by someone invoking Peter's name, authority, and memory), a possible date of composition would be the last decades of the first century.[316] Our task force has taken no position on this question, although we found that the epistle's attitude toward Peter is closer to that of the later works of the New Testament. However, even if a later Christian wrote the epistle in Peter's name, presumably he hoped that the ideas he was presenting could gain acceptance as Peter's ideas in the communities he was addressing. This hope implies a certain conception of Peter, of the nature and extent of his influence, and of the kind of ideas that might be associated with him.

Within I Peter the points of concern for our study of Peter include: (1) Implications from the origin and nature of the epistle; (2) The portrait of Peter as shepherd in 5:1-4.

(1) *Implications from the origin and nature of the epistle.* It is significant that I Peter is addressed to predominantly Gentile Christians in areas of Asia Minor (Pontus, Galatia, Cappadocia, Asia, and Bithynia), some of which had been evangelized by Paul.[317] Was it that Peter had worked in these areas, or did he gain influence there through the activities of his co-workers and disciples? We cannot answer this question with assurance. Activity by Peter in Asia Minor would reinforce the picture of

---

[316] It has been observed that I Peter stands in a close relation to *I Clement,* a letter written from Rome *ca.* A.D. 95. If a dependency of *I Clement* on I Peter could be shown, we would have a date before which I Peter must have been composed. However, it may be that the resemblances are to be explained, not by dependence, but by similarity of milieu. See J. N. D. Kelly, *The Epistles of Peter and of Jude* (Harper's New Testament Commentaries; New York: Harper & Row, 1969), p. 12.

[317] That Gentile Christians are involved is suggested by passages such as 1:14 and 2:10 which describe the addressees in terms of former ignorance and lack of status as a people—terms scarcely applicable to the people of Israel. The areas of Asia Minor are listed in 1:1. (The peculiar order of the list need not concern us here.) The address of the epistle is much more specific than the address of the Epistle of James to "the twelve tribes of the dispersion." A comparable address to specific churches would be found in the seven letters of the Book of Revelation (Apocalypse), also directed to congregations in the Pauline missionary territory. Of the areas mentioned by I Peter, Galatia was addressed by a Pauline letter; and Galatia and the Province of Asia (Ephesus) had been visited during the Pauline missionary journeys (Acts 16:6; 18:23; 19:1).

Peter as a missionary and apostle, not only to the circumcised (Gal 2:8), but also to the uncircumcised. The epistle would reflect his authority even in areas where another apostle had worked—an indication all the more significant if Paul was still alive.[318] If neither Peter nor his co-workers had been active in Asia Minor, it is even more impressive that his name could be thought to carry weight in this area. Moreover, if the letter is pseudonymous and Peter had been dead for some twenty or thirty years, it is noteworthy that his name could still be invoked to instruct Christian churches.

We should add to this discussion the important indication in 5:13 where I Peter conveys greetings from "the woman who dwells in Babylon" to the churches addressed in Asia Minor. It is generally thought that "Babylon" is a symbolic name for Rome;[319] in fact, this reference has been used as New Testament evidence for Peter's ultimately going to Rome (Chapter Two, D, above). And so, in I Peter, to what extent is the authority of Peter associated with the authority of the Roman church? Do the addressees already accept Peter's (or Rome's?) authority? Or is the epistle an attempt to speak in Peter's name to Christians who have been outside the orbit of Peter's influence during his lifetime, and thus to establish Petrine and even Roman influence over them? A dating of I Peter toward the end of the first century reminds us that in *I Clement,* which has resemblances to I Peter (note 316 above), a presbyter of the Roman church writes and instructs the church at Corinth which had been founded by Paul.

The problem of a Petrine letter addressed to a Pauline area

---

[318] The best known Christian tradition dates the deaths of Peter and of Paul to persecution in Rome in the 60's.

[319] "Babylon" has this symbolic function in Revelation (Apocalypse) 17:5. The Rome/Babylon equation need not mean that I Peter was actually sent from Rome—both authorship and localization may have been pseudonymous. But it would mean that Peter and Rome were closely associated in Christian thought. A less frequent suggestion is that "Babylon" designates a military colony in the Nile delta bearing that name (Josephus, *Antiquities* II, 15:1; #315). In his *Essays* (note 49 above), E. M. Merrill, pp. 267-333, contends that Peter labored only in the East, and so takes "Babylon" to refer to the famous ancient city in Mesopotamia.

is heightened by the observation that elements of Pauline theology are found in I Peter. Similarities of I Peter to Romans and Ephesians [320] are not such as to indicate direct borrowing but rather mutual dependence on a common catechetical tradition.[321] We shall see more of the interaction of Petrine and Pauline thought when we consider II Peter 3:15-16.

(2) *The portrait of Peter as shepherd in I Peter 5:1-4.*[322] In 5:1 the author of I Peter, addressing himself to the presbyters (elders)[323] of the communities of Asia Minor, assumes the title of "fellow presbyter" or "co-presbyter." We should not be deceived by this modest stance as if the author were presenting himself as their equal. He has already identified his authority as apostolic (1:1); and so the use of "fellow presbyter" is a polite strategem of benevolence, somewhat as when a modern bishop of a diocese addresses his "fellow priests."

---

[320] For eight passages in Romans that show affinity to I Peter, see W. Sanday and A. C. Headlam, *The Epistle to the Romans* (International Critical Commentary; New York. Scribner's, 1895), pp. lxxiv ff. For Ephesians, see C. L. Mitton. "The Relationship between I Peter and Ephesians," *Journal of Theological Studies*, n. s., 1 (1950), pp. 67-73.

[321] In his commentary (note 37 above), pp. 9-24, Selwyn attributes the Pauline similarities to the fact that Silvanus was secretary for the author of I Peter (5:12) even as he (Silas) had been a companion of Paul. For arguments to the contrary, see Beare's commentary (note 38 above), pp. 188-92.

[322] In our discussion we did not commit ourselves to any specific structural analysis of I Peter and thus to whether it was an original composition in its entirety and/or whether it drew upon and quoted earlier liturgical hymns and catechetical material. The view that behind I Peter there was originally a self-contained hortatory discourse (now represented in 1:3—4:11), and that the pseudonymous author of the epistle adapted this by adding an opening salutation (1:1-2) and a final admonition (4:12—5:14) has gained fresh support in K. P. Donfried. *The Setting of II Clement in Early Christianity* (Leiden: Brill, 1973). This analysis would imply that the passage we are about to discuss was part of the primary concern of the author of the epistle.

[323] Theoretically this passage needs to mean no more than that Peter, an old man, was addressing those of similar age (cf. 5:5); but the whole context implies that elder or presbyter denotes a position of authority rather than simply serving as a designation of age (whether or not, *de facto*, such a position was held mostly by older men). Some have related the function of the Christian presbyter/bishop to that of the *mebaqqēr* or "overseer" of the Qumran community, a functionary for whom "shepherd" terminology was also employed. See R. E. Brown, *Priest and Bishop* (New York: Paulist, 1970), pp. 65-69.

Writing as Peter, the author has the authority to address the Asian presbyters because he has been a "witness to Christ's sufferings" or passion as well as "a partaker in the glory that is to be revealed" (5:1). If the work is pseudonymous and written after Peter's death, the reference to being a witness (*martys*) to Christ's sufferings may be all the more persuasive[324] because the recipients know that Peter was a martyr (*martys*) for Christ. If the reference to partaking in the glory is not to the glorious parousia (cf. 1:7, 11; 2:12), it may be a recollection that Peter was the first to see the risen Jesus.[325]

The instruction to the presbyters about tending the flock,[326] not by constraint but willingly, not for gain but generously, not by domineering but by being examples (5:2-3), is by implication based on Peter's own example as a witness (*martys*), as a presbyter, and as a shepherd. Elements in this portrait echo late first century works. In John 21 (*possibly* associated with the Province of Asia, since tradition would locate the composition of the Fourth Gospel at Ephesus) Simon Peter is given a commission to tend Jesus' sheep, and this is said to involve his death as a martyr (John 21:15-19). Peter's charge to his fellow presbyters to "tend the flock of God" (*poimainein*) in I Peter would take on added significance if the tradition were known that he himself had been charged to tend (*poimainein*) the sheep of Jesus. The similarities between John 21 and I Peter [327]

---

[324] It must be remembered that the epistle is written to encourage the hearers to bear suffering and persecution as Christ did (4:1, 12-13; cf. 2:21).

[325] However, the author of II Peter (1:16-18) seems to have taken it as a recollection of Peter's witnessing the Transfiguration.

[326] It is noteworthy to find the "flock" symbolism employed in an epistle that also describes Christians as a royal priesthood (2:9) and a brotherhood (2:17).

[327] The use of the verb *poimainein* in John 21:16 gives Simon Peter a certain authority over the sheep; and authority is also implicit in Peter's instruction to the presbyters who *exercise oversight*—in many early mss. the verb *episkopein*, "to exercise oversight," is found in I Peter 5:2. The authority of Simon Peter in John 21 is conditional upon his loving Jesus, a condition not unlike what is implicit when the author of I Peter instructs the presbyters of Asia not to be domineering. In John 21 (interpreted in the light of John 10) the model of shepherdship is Jesus himself whom I Peter 5:4 calls the "Chief Shepherd."

are not such that we would have to posit dependence of one on the other; rather the two would seem to reflect a common tradition about Peter. We should also note the account in Acts (written near the end of the century) of Paul's instructions to the presbyters of Ephesus: "Take heed ... of all the flock in which the Holy Spirit has made you overseers [*episkopoi*] to feed [*poimainein*] the church of the Lord" (Acts 20:28). The task that Paul assigns to these shepherds includes being guardians of orthodoxy (20:29ff.), helping the weak (20:35), and being ready for the imprisonment and afflictions that may await them in their ministry (20:23-27). We see, then, that in areas of Asia Minor "shepherd" had become the ideal figure of comparison for those who were presbyters in the churches,[328] and that in some writings pertinent to the region Peter had assumed the image of a principal presbyter-shepherd.

In I Peter the portrait of Peter as a presbyter-shepherd is one of caring for the flock by overseeing them and by bearing personal witness to Jesus' sufferings. Historically, we have no reliable evidence that Peter ever served as a presbyter for a particular congregation, not even for the Roman congregation. But there is respectable evidence that Peter died a martyr's death. One might surmise that, because shepherds of the flock were challenged to imitate Jesus by laying down their lives as martyrs for the sheep in their care, Peter's death as a martyr at Rome made him a model for the presbyter-shepherds. Subsequently, by simplification, he may have been spoken of as if he were historically a presbyter-shepherd, especially at Rome. But much of this theorizing reflects the judgment that I Peter is pseudonymous. If the epistle is Peter's own, directly or through a secretary, then, although Peter has apostolic authority (1:1), he presents himself in 5:1 on the level of a "fellow presbyter" whose special witness is to point to the sufferings of Christ.

B. The Second Epistle of Peter

This letter seems to address the same audience (even though

---

[328] It is also found in Ignatius' letters to the *Philadelphians* 2:1 and *Romans* 9:1.

the opening lines do not list the areas of Asia Minor), for in 3:1 the author speaks of it as "the second letter that I have written to you." However, we have accepted the virtually unanimous judgment of critical scholars that II Peter really is the work of another hand and is surely pseudonymous. If it is dated to the first half of the second century (and thus made the latest work in the New Testament), it may have been written anywhere from twenty-five to fifty years after I Peter.

The community is now troubled, not so much by persecution as by false teaching and doctrinal and moral confusion. The authority of Simeon Peter[329] is called upon to correct such abuses. If once more he is presented as a witness, indeed, as an eyewitness (1:16), his witness is not to the sufferings of Jesus (as in I Peter 5:1) but to the moment, presumably of the Transfiguration, when Jesus received honor and glory from God the Father (1:17). This emphasis may be meant to counteract the claim of the false teachers that there will be no future coming of Jesus in glory (3:1-10)—Peter should know authoritatively since he saw the first coming of Jesus in glory. Against the false prophets (2:1) Peter can speak with surety, for he was one of those for whom the prophetic word was made more sure (1:19). He has the authority to interpret the words of Scripture, especially the prophecies (1:20-21). In particular he can correct the ignorant and the unstable who are twisting and misconstruing the difficult writings of Paul (3:15-16). Obviously, in II Peter the shepherdship of Peter is being applied in a different way from that encountered in I Peter; and the primary emphasis is now on Peter as the guardian of orthodox faith—a possible facet of the presbyter-shepherd, as we saw in Acts 20:28-30. His apostolic authority enables him to judge interpretations of Scripture, even the writings of another apostle. We can now speak of a "Petrine magisterium,"[330] perhaps related to an application of the binding/

---

[329] It is interesting to find in this late New Testament work (1:1) the archaizing spelling "*Symeōn*," which also occurs at Acts 15:14 (see note 119 above). There is some Greek manuscript evidence in II Peter for the more usual "*Simōn*" spelling.

[330] Peter's role in correcting an exegesis of the Pauline writings (II Peter 3:15-16) can be seen as an example of the development of the

loosing power we saw in Matthew.

If we study the Pastoral Letters of Paul (perhaps post-Pauline, just as the Petrine Epistles may be post-Petrine), we find that we may speak of a "Pauline magisterium" as well. In II Timothy 1:13 Paul tells Timothy: "Follow the pattern of the sound words which you have heard from me." Thus, in the later parts of the New Testament we have the development of a view of apostolic authority, and not just of Peter's authority, especially as a protection against false teaching (II Timothy 4:3-4). The names of several apostles may have been invoked, e.g., the magisterium of James by the Jewish Christians. But in the canonical New Testament Peter and Paul are the most important figures in the developing trajectory of apostolic authority.[331] By the time II Peter was written and in the circles it represented, the Petrine trajectory was beginning to outstrip the Pauline one. The catalyst for this may have been the fact that the troublesome opponents, gnostics probably,[332] were arguing on the basis of Paul. The author felt that recourse to the authority of Peter would be persuasive in correcting their appeal to Paul.[333]

---

teaching office of the church (which is what we mean by "magisterium"), according to E. Käsemann, "An Apologia for Primitive Christian Eschatology," *Essays on New Testament Themes* (Studies in Biblical Theology, 41; London: SCM, 1964), p. 190. He describes the mentality of the author of II Peter thus: "It [exegesis] must therefore be regulated; this is done by tying it to the Church's teaching office." Käsemann regards this as a manifestation of "early Catholicism."

[331] II Timothy purports to have been written in Rome (1:17), even as does I Peter (note 319 above) and presumably II Peter (by implication in 3:1). Since both Peter and Paul were thought to have died in Rome, they were looked upon as the great apostles of the Roman church.

[332] See Käsemann, "Apologia" (note 330 above), pp. 170-72.

[333] It may be asked why the author did not compose a deutero-Pauline letter to correct his opponents. One reason may have been that there was an already fixed collection of Pauline letters ("all his letters"—II Peter 3:16).

CHAPTER TEN:
CONCLUSIONS FROM
THE STUDY[334]

The title page of our study of Peter in the New Testament speaks of it as a collaborative assessment prepared as "background for ecumenical discussions of the role of the papacy in the Universal Church." We shall keep that ultimate purpose in mind as we sum up the results, and yet we are aware that the governing factor of the study has been to do justice to the New Testament outlook and not necessarily to solve later problems. The complexity of relating the New Testament evidence to later problems has been recognized by scholars of all Christian confessions. A perceptive passage from the Roman Catholic exegete, Wolfgang Trilling,[335] illustrates a sensitivity about the questions that must be answered:

---

[334] This chapter was drafted in preliminary form by R. E. Brown with the help of important material supplied by R. H. Fuller. The draft was circulated for reactions which were then correlated and discussed at the (final) March 1973 meeting of the task force.

[335] The German of this citation appeared in Trilling's article, "Ist die katholische Primatslehre schriftgemäss? Exegetische Gedanken zu einer wichtigen Frage," *Zum Thema: Petrusamt und Papsttum* (Stuttgart: Katholisches Bibelwerk, 1970), p. 55. It appears in English translation in R. Pesch, "The Position and Significance of Peter in the Church oꞋ the New Testament," *Concilium* 64, entitled *Papal Ministry in the Church* (New York: Herder & Herder, 1971), pp. 32-33.

Does the witness of the New Testament as a whole justify us in concluding that there is a function of guidance and leadership applicable to the entire Church and attached to a particular person (and therefore to his "successors")? Does this witness imply that there really is such a function in which an individual is empowered to have this leadership, a function which may possibly be realized in various forms according to the circumstances of particular periods and particular situations in history? Already within the New Testament itself, do we find Peter's function set apart from other similar functions (the apostolate of Paul, cf. Gal 2:11-14) as though it represented the opposite pole to them, or was it rather one among a whole complex of different "forms" through which the Church was administered? Already in the New Testament itself can we establish a change of form taking place between two distinct levels of tradition belonging to two different periods, representing the first and second generations of the Church (cf. Acts 1 and 2 Peter)? Can we establish any integral continuity in the Petrine function between the three other levels which have been mentioned? ("the historical Jesus," the Palestinian-Syrian communities, the later level of the Church as a universal whole), or which developments within these levels or strata are to be discerned?

We believe that our study offers an approach to answering such questions, at least in part. Perhaps this will become apparent if we gather our conclusions under two headings: first, the historical career of Simon Peter in the ministry of Jesus and in the early church; second, the images of Peter and the roles attributed to him in New Testament thought.

A. The Historical Career of Simon Peter

We shall be concerned with two phases in Simon Peter's life: his role in the ministry of Jesus, and his role in the early church. Our chief information concerning the former comes from the Gospels, although in reading them we are aware that the prominence which Peter later gained may have been retrojected into Jesus' ministry. Our chief information concerning the latter comes in a more direct form from the Pauline letters and Acts and indirectly from the Gospels. Our conclusions represent a cautious minimum, and we may be sure that there was more to the career of Simon Peter than we can know from our sources.

1. **Simon during the ministry of Jesus.** We may state the following conclusions:

(a) *Simon was one of the first called* among those who would become the regular companions of Jesus and who would remain active followers after the resurrection. It is doubtful that he was the very first, for in both the Synoptic and the Johannine traditions his call is associated with that of others.[336] Moreover, we can compare Simon's priority only to that of the others who remained active followers after the lifetime of Jesus and whose memory, therefore, was preserved.

(b) *Simon was very prominent* in this same group of regular companions and subsequent followers. So prominent was he, in fact, that as far as we know the story of the ministry of Jesus was not told without mention of Simon.[337] Yet here we must be very wary of possible retrojection into the Gospel picture. For instance, it is difficult to know whether Simon really was a spokesman for the intimate companions of Jesus during his lifetime or whether the instances of such spokesmanship in the Gospels are the reflection of his later role as the spokesman for the Twelve in the Jerusalem church. Yet his role as a spokesman is attested in all the primary strata of the Gospel tradition with the possible exception of "Q" (see note 27 above). Similarly it is hard to evaluate the import *in the ministry* of Simon's always being named first in the lists of the Twelve (indeed with the specification "first," *prōtos,* in Matt 10:2). Simon is not remembered to have functioned in solitary splendor, for in the Gospel story he is frequently associated with other prominent disciples: e.g., with James and John (and sometimes Andrew)

---

[336] In the Synoptic tradition he is called at the Lake of Galilee along with Andrew (not mentioned by Luke), James, and John; in the Johannine tradition he is called in the Jordan valley but only after two other disciples of John the Baptist have followed Jesus (Andrew and one unnamed).

[337] Simon is the most frequently mentioned disciple in all four Gospels. Moreover, even the distant Gentile converts of Paul in Galatia know of Peter.

as an inner group in the Synoptic tradition, and with the Beloved Disciple in the Johannine tradition.

(c) *Simon probably made a confession of Jesus,* in terms of a known Jewish expectation. In the common Synoptic tradition he is said to have confessed Jesus as the Messiah, while in the Johannine tradition his confession is of Jesus as the Holy One of God. It might be judged that in such instances we have a retrojection of Peter's later role as a spokesman of the Christian faith in Jerusalem after the resurrection, but this inference is not so simple. The suspicion that Simon may have made such a confession during Jesus' lifetime does not imply that it was an adequate or satisfactory evaluation of Jesus or that Jesus accepted it. Indeed, a critical analysis of Mark (wherein 8:33 is taken to have referred originally to 8:29b) indicates that Jesus did not accept the confession of Peter, and this indication constitutes an argument for the historicity of the confession. Ultimately the early church did find satisfactory the confession of Jesus as the Messiah,[338] and so it is not easy to attribute to church creation a scene where Jesus reacted unfavorably to such a confession by one of his followers.[339]

(d) Equal probability must be given to the thesis that *Simon failed, at least partially, to understand Jesus.* The likelihood that Jesus did not accept Peter's confession; the tradition that Jesus rebuked him as Satan; the reported acts of misplaced enthusiasm on Simon's part; the story of his denials of Jesus—it is difficult to be certain of the historicity of all these details, but taken together they bear impressive witness to an incomplete understanding on Simon's part.

---

[338] "Christ" became part of Jesus' name. But, of course, this church attitude was made possible by a Christian reinterpretation of "Messiah" in a less nationalistic sense and with the modification of attributing to the Messiah a career of suffering and rejection. Thus, if Simon did confess Jesus as the Messiah, the meaning that he gave to the term and which Jesus found unsatisfactory presumably differed considerably from the understanding of the term that subsequent Christians found satisfactory.

[339] We are less certain of the designation of Jesus as Messiah by his enemies, for instance, by the high priest during his trial. It is more likely that the early church would attribute a false understanding of the term to an enemy than to a disciple.

2. **Peter in the early church.** We may state the following conclusions:

(a) *Simon came to be known as Cephas (Peter),* probably because Jesus himself gave him this name. The fact that the naming occurs in different contexts in three Gospels (Mark 3:16; Matt 16:18; John 1:42) raises a question about the original setting of the incident. Therefore, we cannot be sure whether this naming occurred during Jesus' ministry or after the resurrection (with subsequent retrojection into the accounts of the ministry).

(b) *Simon (Cephas) was accorded an appearance of the risen Jesus,* probably the first appearance.[340] This is supported by the ancient pre-Pauline tradition cited in I Cor 15:5, by Luke 24:34, and perhaps by Mark 16:7. Moreover, it might explain the prominence of Peter in the early church, not all of which is explicable in light of his role during Jesus' ministry.

(c) *Peter was the most important of the Twelve* in Jerusalem and its environs. (This phrasing liberates us from an almost impossible decision about Peter's importance relative to two other figures who were *not* members of the Twelve, namely, James the brother of the Lord, and Paul the apostle.) That Peter served as a spokesman for the Twelve is clear in Acts, perhaps implied in Gal 1:18, and certainly implied in the Gospel accounts of Peter's having this function during Jesus' ministry. Yet, in reference to the Twelve, Peter's position was nuanced; and special authority over the others is not clearly attested. Rather, in Acts he is presented as consulting with "the apostles" and even being sent by them (8:14); he and John act almost as a team (3:1ff.; 4:1ff.; 8:14).

(d) *Peter had a missionary career,* at least among the circumcised and perhaps among Gentiles. (Such a missionary career is not widely attested in the New Testament for other members of the Twelve, unless by implication in passages like Matt 28:19-20 and Mark 16:15 where the missionary command of

---

[340] In speaking of "first appearance" here and elsewhere, we are thinking only of the appearances to those who would become official proclaimers of the resurrection. We have not discussed the question of possible previous appearances to women followers of Jesus.

the risen Jesus is addressed to the Eleven.[341]) Although Paul
speaks explicitly of Cephas as "entrusted with a gospel *to the
circumcised*" (Gal 2:7), the evidence for Peter's wider missionary ministry is impressive. Acts 10 attributes to Peter an
important step in commanding the baptism of the Gentile
Cornelius, and both I Cor 1:12 and I Peter 1:1 imply Petrine
influence in largely Gentile areas.[342]

(e) *Peter's theological stance probably was intermediary* between that of James and that of Paul, at least in the religious
questions of which we have knowledge. While Acts 15:25 portrays the leaders as all of one mind *(homothymadon)*, it is
clear, if we read between the lines of the account of the Jerusalem "council," that a more stringent position with regard to
the observance of the Law was advocated by James than by
Peter,[343] an observation in harmony with the implication of
Gal 2:12. On the other hand, Gal 2:11 indicates a difference
between Peter and Paul, with Peter pictured as a somewhat
more conservative figure.

B. The Images of Peter in New Testament Thought

Although we have listed the minimal facts about Simon
Peter of which we have some historical certitude, this does not
do justice to the whole New Testament picture. Peter became

---

[341] We do not know whether the Twelve would be included in Paul's
reference to "the other apostles" (I Cor 9:5), who are obviously
missionaries—see the distinction made between "the Twelve" and "all
the apostles" in the formula that Paul records in I Cor 15:5, 7 (note
77 above).

[342] Another trace of Peter's taking a benevolent attitude toward non-
enforcement of Jewish customs on Gentiles (a theme implicit in Peter's
vision about eating unclean foods in Acts 10) may be found in Matt
15:15 where it is to Peter that Jesus explains that a person is not ren-
dered impure by what he eats.

[343] According to both Acts and Paul, the three figures, James, Peter,
and Paul, are all representative of a moderate or centrist position on
the Gentile question, as opposed to the extreme represented by the
Christian Pharisees or the false brethren. In particular, the closeness
of Peter to Paul is stressed by Cullmann, *Peter* (note 45 above), p. 48.
But despite their harmony, there were shades of diversity.

a symbol for Christian thought, so that during his lifetime and afterwards he was portrayed as playing many roles in church life. Some of these were surely founded on his historical career; some of them may have been influenced by Christian idealization. Adapting the language of current New Testament scholarship, we may seek to trace a *trajectory* of the images of Peter.[344]

In discussing the historical career of Simon Peter, we have already seen several roles played by Peter: an early and perhaps the first witness of the risen Jesus, the leader and spokesman of the Twelve, the missionary. It is in reference to the last mentioned that we can begin to trace our trajectory.

Because Peter was the most prominent missionary among the Twelve and, perhaps also, because he had been a fisherman, the image of *Peter as the great Christian fisherman (missionary)* developed. In Luke 5 the apostolic call to become fishers of men (which in Mark is directed to Peter and Andrew, and implicitly to James and John) is addressed in the singular to Simon who is told, "Henceforth you will be catching men." Similarly, in the first part of John 21 (a passage that has many parallels to Luke 5), in the post-resurrectional period Simon Peter is described as initiating a fishing expedition that with Jesus' help and direction makes an astounding catch. This catch is numbered, symbolically but obscurely, at 153 fish, and Simon Peter is the one who hauls it ashore without the net breaking. Whether or not the historical Peter did have a mission to the uncircumcised, the emphasis in Acts on the significance of his commanding the baptism of the Roman Cornelius is another step in the dramatization of Peter's role in the Christian mission. He is the one destined by Jesus to strengthen his fellow Christians ("your brothers" in Luke 22:32) through his continued missionary preaching.

If the first half of John 21 portrays Simon Peter as the fisherman, the second half portrays him as *the shepherd (pastor) of the sheep*—a shift in imagery that seems to reflect a shift in the concerns of church life.[345] In the latter part of the first

---

[344] The terminology comes from J. M. Robinson and H. Koester, *Trajectories through Early Christianity* (Philadelphia: Fortress, 1971).

[345] We do not mean to imply that the image of Peter the missionary

century the main Christian problems seem no longer to be just those of the scope and manner of the mission; they are also the problems of settled communities: local leadership; care of the faithful; supervision against dangerous innovations, etc. In short the concerns are shifting toward the pastoral, and Peter can be portrayed as the model shepherd/pastor whose role and authority is based on his love for Jesus and whose primary duty is to feed the sheep. Since at this time the presbyterate has come to the fore in many churches as the institution entrusted with pastoral care, Peter is presented as a model presbyter who can instruct other presbyters on how to care for the flock (I Peter 5). Related to the image of Peter as exercising pastoral authority are the powers of the keys of the kingdom and of binding and loosing entrusted to him by Jesus in Matt 16:19.[346] As we saw, the power of the keys *may* be evocative of the authority of the major-domo over the royal household, and the power of binding and loosing is a Christian adaptation of rabbinic authority.

Closely connected with the theme of Peter the shepherd/pastor is the image of *Peter the Christian martyr*. From sources outside the New Testament we have respectable evidence that Peter died a martyr's death in Rome in the 60's (see Chapter Two, D, above); and John 21, in retrospect, sees this as a glorious witness to which Jesus had destined Simon Peter. It is the ultimate step in following Jesus (John 13:36), and it conforms him to the example of the Good Shepherd who laid down his life for his sheep (John 10:11). If I Peter was written after Peter's death, then the "Peter" who speaks there speaks from experience when he tells his fellow presbyter-shepherds: "When the Chief Shepherd is manifested, you will obtain the unfading crown of glory." He has truly been a witness *(martys)* of the sufferings of Christ (I Peter 5:1).

This last point leads us to another theme that emerged as

fisherman is dispensed with once he begins to be portrayed as a shepherd. The former image has its own life in subsequent Christian thought.

[346] Another Matthean passage associated with Peter's pastoral role is Matt 17:24-27 where Peter gets the answer from Jesus whether the Temple tax is to be paid. A problem posed to the Christian church is here answered through Peter.

part of the trajectory: *Peter the receiver of special revelation.*[347] We cannot say with certainty that the root of this image is in the important tradition about Peter having been the first of the major companions of Jesus' ministry to have seen the Lord after the resurrection (see above p. 161). But, as we have found, it is very likely that such a tradition provided the original context or catalyst for much of the New Testament material about Peter. Thus, Peter is pictured as one of the three disciples who witnessed Jesus' Transfiguration (Mark 9:2ff. and parallels), a visionary scene which in II Peter 1:16-18 is used to bring Petrine authority to bear on a later church situation. Through knowledge presumably revealed to him in a special way, Peter is able to confront Ananias and Sapphira (Acts 5:1ff.). He takes the initiative in the baptism of the Roman Cornelius on the basis of visionary guidance (Acts 10:9-16), and the vision of an angel accompanies his miraculous release from prison (Acts 12:7-9).

An image directly related to Peter the receiver of special revelation is that of *Peter the confessor of the true Christian faith.* We have stressed the historical likelihood that during the ministry of Jesus, Simon made a confession of Jesus (which may have reflected a quite inadequate grasp of the mystery of Jesus). We have also seen that Peter did function as a spokesman for the Twelve in Jerusalem and that he was a missionary preacher. Eventually all of this combined, and Peter is portrayed even during Jesus' ministry as the one who gave voice to a solemn revelation granted to him by God about who Jesus was: the Messiah and the Son of the living God (Matt 16:16-17).[348] In the light of the post-Easter events it becomes clear to the Christian community that with this faith Peter is the rock

---

[347] This theme is greatly developed in the apocrypha; see note 47 above.

[348] The account of Simon Peter's confessing Jesus as the Holy One of God in John 6:69 is less exuberant in describing Peter as the spokesman of divine revelation. But even in John, the Twelve are contrasted with those who have abandoned Jesus; and it is as their spokesman that Peter makes his confession, as a part of his recognition that Jesus has the words of eternal life (6:66-68).

on whom Jesus has founded his church against which the gates of Hades[349] shall not prevail.

Not only is Peter presented as a confessor of the Christian faith; eventually he can be seen as a *guardian of the faith against false teaching*. Some hints of this aspect may be implied in the power of binding and loosing, if that is a power of excommunication; but it comes to the fore in II Peter. Here Peter speaks as a magisterial voice that can interpret the prophecies of Scripture (1:20-21) and can correct misinterpretations based on the authority of other apostles such as Paul (3:15-16).

This high view of Peter's function does not, however, eliminate the dark side in the image of the Apostle, the image of *Peter the weak and sinful man*. In the New Testament trajectory he can be portrayed as being reproached by Paul (Gal 2:11ff.), as misunderstanding Jesus' words and intentions (e.g., Mark 9:5-6; John 13:6-11; 18:10-11), as being rebuked by Jesus as "Satan" (Mark 8:33; Matt 16:23). In the Passion Narrative he can be singled out as the one who denied the Lord (Mark 14:66-72 and parallels). But his very tears at the end of this scene show that, while being portrayed as a weak, sinful man, Peter is seen as a truly repentant sinner. Thus, even if Simon once denied Jesus, he has been rehabilitated—a rehabilitation doubtlessly to be connected with the appearance of the risen Jesus to him (as hinted in John 21:15-17). The man of little faith has been saved from sinking by Jesus (Matt 14:28-31); the sinful, unworthy fisherman has been spiritually empowered by Jesus (Luke 5:8-10); and now that he has turned again, he has become a source of strength (Luke 22:32).

Thus in early Christian thought, as attested by the New Testament, there is a plurality of images associated with Peter: missionary fisherman, pastoral shepherd, martyr, recipient of special revelation, confessor of the true faith, magisterial protector, and repentant sinner. When a trajectory of these images is traced, we find indications of development from earlier to later images. However, we must not think that it is only Peter's image that goes through such a trajectory. For instance, a com-

---

[349] See note 208 above.

parison of the earlier Pauline letters with the Pastoral Epistles shows a developing image of Paul: at first he is a missionary concerned with the growing pains of newly founded communities; later he is a type of super-presbyter concerned with the appointment and pastoral qualities of presbyters in long established churches and becomes indeed "*the* Apostle." The image of the Twelve also has its own trajectory. If originally they were seen in an eschatological perspective (a symbolic number related to the renewal of Israel and God's fulfillment of His plan), they too would eventually be portrayed as wide-ranging missionaries (especially in post-New Testament Christian legend), as exercising pastoral care (already in Matt 18:18 where they have the power of binding and loosing), as rulers of churches, as martyrs, as spokesmen of the Christian faith (implied in Acts with its notion of apostolic tradition), and even as the foundation stones of the church (Eph 2:20; Rev 21:14). Our concentration on the various images of Peter in this book should not blind us to the same or similar images applied to others in the New Testament.

But, and this is why we have concentrated on Peter, in Christian history after the New Testament period, and especially in the West, the Petrine trajectory eventually outdistanced the other apostolic trajectories (e.g., of the Twelve and even of Paul). We may see this at least incipiently in II Peter[350] where the image of Peter is evoked to correct those appealing to Paul. But such further tracing of the Petrine trajectory and the factors that influenced it is really the task of a Patristic study (note 4 above). That we end our New Testament investigation on a note providing an entree into the Patristic period is not indicative of a spirit of frustration but of accomplishment. In our study we have faced the same historical difficulties encountered

---

[350] To have a complete picture one would have to trace the trajectories of Peter and Paul further into Christian history. If II Peter seems to rank Peter over Paul, that evaluation is catalyzed by the fact that his opponents are advocating Paul. A very similar situation is reflected in the early strata of the Pseudo-Clementine literature. But as will be clear in the Patristic study (note 4 above), it was quite possible in later tradition for Peter and Paul to be placed side by side again without one dominating the other.

by our predecessors and have understood only too well how the limited factual material about Peter in the New Testament made it possible for Christians to differ in evaluating the career of the historical figure. But precisely because we have discovered the importance of the trajectory traveled by Peter's image, a trajectory that even in the New Testament is not coterminous with his historical career, it has become clear to us that an investigation of the historical career does not necessarily settle the question of Peter's importance for the subsequent church. The ecumenical discussion must involve not only the historical figure but also the continuing trajectory of his image in the New Testament and beyond. To what extent is such a trajectory determined by the historical figure? To what extent is the subsequent trajectory determined by the New Testament trajectory itself? And to what extent is it determined by the accidents of later history?[351] And whatever way we answer these questions, how does God's providence and His will for His church enter into the trajectory? By shifting the focus to these questions, we think we have fulfilled the promise on our title page of preparing a "background for ecumenical discussions of the role of the papacy in the Universal Church."

---

[351] Obviously there is another related question: To what extent has the later trajectory of Peter's image influenced the various Christian interpretations of Peter's roles in the New Testament? In short, the question of the effect of theological retrojection upon exegesis.

Select Bibliography[352]

I. Bibliographies

Arató, P., "Petrus," in the bibliographical section of *Archivum Historiae Pontificiae* (Rome: Facultas Historiae Ecclesiasticae in Pontificia Universitate Gregoriana), each year, since 1963.

D'Aragon, J.-L., "Bibliographie," *L'Église dans la Bible: Communications présentées à la XVIIe réunion annuelle de l'Association Catholique des Études Bibliques au Canada,* ed. C. Matura *et al.* (Studia. Recherches de philosophie et de théologie publiées par les facultés SJ de Montréal, 13; Bruges-Paris: Desclée de Brouwer, 1962), pp. 169-202.

Ghidelli, C., "Bibliografia Biblica Petrina," *La Scuola Cattolica, Supplemento Bibliografico* 96 (1968), pp. 62*-110*.

Nober, P., "Petrus," in "Elenchus Bibliographicus," *Biblica* (Rome: Pontificium Institutum Biblicum), each year, since 1955.

II. Summary Surveys

Braun, F.-M., "Die Kirche als Stiftung Jesu. Tu es Petrus," *Neues Licht auf die Kirche: Die protestantische Kirchendogmatik in ihrer neuesten Entfaltung* (Einsiedeln: Benziger, 1946), pp. 57-90.

Dinkler, E., "Die Petrus-Rom-Frage," *Theologische Rundschau,* Neue Folge 25 (1959), pp. 189-230; 289-335; 27 (1961), pp. 33-64; 31 (1965-66), pp. 232-53.

Kretschmar, G., "St. Peter's Place in the Apostolic Church," *The Ecumenical Review* 9 (1956-57), pp. 85-90.

Linton, O., "Die neueste Literatur über den Kirchengedanken des Urchristentums. Geschichtliches," *Das Problem der Urkirche in der neueren Forschung. Eine kritische Darstellung* (Uppsala Universitets Årsskrift, Teologi 2; Uppsala: Almqvist and Wiksell, 1932), pp. 157-85.

Pesch, R., "The Position and Significance of Peter in the Church of the New Testament. A Survey of Current Research," *Papal Ministry in the Church,* ed. H. Küng (*Concilium* 64; New York: Herder and Herder, 1971), pp. 21-35.

Rigaux, B., "Saint Peter in Contemporary Exegesis," *Progress and De-*

---

[352] The bibliography was prepared by J.A. Burgess. Recommendations were made by members of the task force, especially by K. Froehlich who readied the bibliography for publication. In regard to the entries pertaining to the New Testament books, the standard commentaries on the respective books are presupposed.

cline in the History of Church Renewal, ed. R. Aubert (*Concilium* 27; New York: Paulist, 1967), pp. 147-79.

Schulze-Kadelbach, G., "Die Stellung des Petrus in der Urchristenheit," *Theologische Literaturzeitung* 81 (1956), cols. 1-14.

III. General Works

Bea, A. *et al., San Pietro.* Atti della Settimana Biblica. Associazione Biblica Italiana (Brescia: Paideia, 1967).

Benoit, P., "La primauté de saint Pierre selon le Nouveau Testament," *Istina* 2 (1955), pp. 305-34; reprinted in *Exégèse et Théologie,* vol. II (Paris: Cerf, 1961), pp. 250-84.

Blank, J., "The Person and Office of Peter in the New Testament," *Truth and Certainty* (*Concilium* 83; New York: Herder and Herder, 1973), pp. 42-55.

Bourke, M.M., "The Petrine Office in the New Testament," *Proceedings of the 25th Annual Convention of the Catholic Theological Society of America* (1970), pp. 1-12.

Cullmann, O., *Peter: Disciple, Apostle, Martyr. A Historical and Theological Essay* (2nd ed.; Philadelphia: Westminster, 1962).

Cullmann, O., "Petros," *Theological Dictionary of the New Testament,* ed. G. Kittel and G. Friedrich, vol. 6 (Grand Rapids: Eerdmans, 1968; from German, 1959), pp. 100-12.

Denzler, G., Christ, F., Trilling, W., Stockmeier, P., *Zum Thema Petrusamt und Papsttum* (Stuttgart: Katholisches Bibelwerk, 1970).

Dreyfus, P., "La primauté de Pierre à la lumière de la théologie biblique du reste d'Israël," *Istina* 2 (1955), pp. 338-46.

Gächter, P., *Petrus und seine Zeit. Neutestamentliche Studien* (Innsbruck: Tyrolia, 1958).

Garofalo, S., Maccarone, M., *et al., Studi Petriani* (Rome: Istituto di Studi Romani, 1968).

Gewalt, D., *Petrus. Studien zur Geschichte und Tradition des frühen Christentums* (Theological dissertation; Heidelberg, 1966; typescript); cf. *Theologische Literaturzeitung* 94 (1969), cols. 628f.

Goetz, K.G., *Petrus als Gründer und Oberhaupt der Kirche und Schauer von Gesichten nach den altchristlichen Berichten und Legenden. Eine geschichtlich-exegetische Untersuchung* (Untersuchungen zum Neuen Testament, 13; Leipzig: Hinrichs, 1927).

Journet, Ch., *The Primacy of Peter from the Protestant and from the Catholic Point of View* (Westminster, Md.: Newman, 1954).

Karrer, O., *Peter and the Church: An Examination of Cullmann's Thesis* (Quaestiones Disputatae, 8; New York: Herder, 1963; English translation of Part 3 of *Um die Einheit der Christen: Die Petrusfrage;* Frankfurt: Knecht, 1953).

Karrer, O., "Simon Petrus, Jünger-Apostel-Felsenfundament," *Bibel und Kirche* 23 (Stuttgart: Katholisches Bibelwerk, 1968), pp. 37-43.

Klink, J.L., *Het Petrustype in het Nieuwe Testament en de oud-christelijke letterkunde* (Proefschrift; Leiden: E. Ijdo, 1947).

O'Connor, D.W., *Peter in Rome, The Literary, Liturgical, and Archaeological Evidence* (New York: Columbia University, 1969).

Porúbčan, S. "The Consciousness of Peter's Primacy in the New Testament," *Archivum Historiae Pontificiae* 5 (1967), pp. 9-39.

Rimoldi, A., *L'Apostolo San Pietro, fondamento della Chiesa, principe degli apostoli ed ostiario celeste nella Chiesa primitiva dalle origini al concilio di Calcedonia* (Analecta Gregoriana, 96; Series Facultatis Historiae Ecclesiasticae, sectio B (n.18); Rome: Gregorian University, 1958).

Schelkle, K.H., "Petrus in den Briefen des Neuen Testaments," *Bibel und Kirche* 23 (Stuttgart: Katholisches Bibelwerk, 1968), pp. 46-50.

Schmid, J., "Petrus 'der Fels' und die Petrusgestalt der Urgemeinde," *Begegnung der Christen. Studien evangelischer und katholischer Theologen*, eds. M. Roesle and O. Cullmann (*Festschrift* O. Karrer; Stuttgart: Evangelisches Verlagswerk, 2nd ed., 1960), pp. 347-72.

Schnackenburg, R., "Das Petrusamt. Die Stellung des Petrus zu den anderen Aposteln," *Wort und Wahrheit. Zeitschrift für Religion und Kultur* 26 (1971), pp. 206-15. English summary version: "The Petrine Office. Peter's Relationship to the Other Apostles," *Theology Digest* 20 (1972), pp. 148-52.

Trilling, W., "Zum Petrusamt im Neuen Testament. Traditionsgeschichtliche Überlegungen anhand von Matthäus, 1. Petrus und Johannes," *Theologische Quartalschrift* 151 (1971), pp. 110-33.

Vögtle, A., "Petrus, Apostel," *Lexikon für Theologie und Kirche*, 2nd ed., vol. 8 (Freiburg: Herder, 1964), cols. 334-40.

IV. The Pauline Epistles

A. GENERAL

Barrett, C.K., *The Signs of an Apostle* (The Cato Lecture; Philadelphia: Fortress, 1970).

Holl, K., "Der Kirchenbegriff des Paulus in seinem Verhältnis zur Urgemeinde," *Gesammelte Aufsätze*, vol. II: *Der Osten*, ed. H. Lietzmann (Tübingen: Mohr, 1928), pp. 44-67.

B. GALATIANS

Barrett, C.K., "Paul and the Pillar Apostles," *Studia Paulina in honorem J. de Zwaan septuagenarii* (Haarlem: Bohn, 1953), pp. 1-19.

Blinzler, J., "Petrus und Paulus. Über eine angebliche Folge des Tages von Antiochien," *Aus der Welt und Umwelt des Neuen Testaments. Gesammelte Aufsätze* 1 (Stuttgarter Biblische Beiträge; Stuttgart: Katholisches Bibelwerk, 1969), pp. 147-55.

Eckert, J., *Die urchristliche Verkündigung im Streit zwischen Paulus und seinen Gegnern nach dem Galaterbrief* (Biblische Untersuchungen, ed. O. Kuss, 6; Regensburg: Pustet, 1972), esp. pp. 163-228.

Eckert, J., "Paulus und die Jerusalemer Autoritäten nach dem Galaterbrief und der Apostelgeschichte. Divergierende Geschichtsdarstellung im Neuen Testament als hermeneutisches Problem," in *Schriftauslegung. Beiträge zur Hermeneutik des Neuen Testaments und im Neuen*

Testament, ed. J. Ernst (Paderborn: Schöningh, 1972), pp. 281-311.

Kilpatrick, G.D., "Galatians 1:18: *Historēsai Kēphan,*" *New Testament Essays,* ed. A.J.B. Higgins (*Festschrift* T. W. Manson; Manchester University, 1959), pp. 144-49.

Klein, G., "Galater 2, 6-9 und die Geschichte der Jerusalemer Urgemeinde," *Zeitschrift für Theologie und Kirche* 57 (1960), pp. 275-95; reprinted with an additional note in *Rekonstruktion und Interpretation* (Beiträge zur Evangelischen Theologie, 50; Munich: Kaiser, 1969), pp. 99-128.

Lönning, I., "Paulus und Petrus. Gal. 2, 11ff. als kontroverstheologisches Fundamentalproblem," *Studia Theologica. Scandinavian Journal of Theology* 24 (1970), pp. 1-69.

Tyson, J.B., "Paul's Opponents in Galatia," *Novum Testamentum* 10 (1968), pp. 241-54.

C. CORINTHIANS

Barrett, C.K., "Cephas and Corinth," *Abraham unser Vater, Juden und Christen im Gespräch über die Bibel,* ed. O. Betz *et al.* (*Festschrift* O. Michel; Arbeiten zur Geschichte des Spätjudentums und Urchristentums, 5; Leiden: Brill, 1963), pp. 1-12.

Barrett, C.K., "Paul's Opponents in II Corinthians," *New Testament Studies* 17 (1970-71), pp. 233-54.

Hurd, J.C., *The Origin of I Corinthians* (New York: Seabury, 1965).

Manson, T.W., "The Corinthian Correspondence. 1.," *Bulletin of the John Rylands Library* 26 (1941-42), pp. 101-20; reprinted in *Studies in the Gospels and Epistles,* ed. M. Black (Philadelphia: Westminster, 1962), pp. 190-209.

V. The Acts of the Apostles

Dupont, J., *Études sur les Actes des Apôtres* (Lectio Divina, 45; Paris: Cerf, 1967), esp. pp. 163-242.

Haenchen, E., "Petrus-Probleme," *New Testament Studies* 7 (1960-61), pp. 187-97; reprinted in *Gott und Mensch. Gesammelte Aufsätze, Band* 1 (Tübingen: Mohr, 1965), pp. 55-67.

Ridderbos, H.N., *The Speeches of Peter in the Acts of the Apostles* (London: Tyndale, 1962).

Sanders, J.N., "Peter and Paul in the Acts," *New Testament Studies* 2 (1955-56), pp. 133-43.

VI. The Gospels in General

Klein, G., "Die Berufung des Petrus," *Zeitschrift für die neutestamentliche Wissenschaft* 58 (1967), pp. 1-39; reprinted with an additional note in *Rekonstruktion und Interpretation* (Beiträge zur Evangelischen Theologie, 50; Munich: Kaiser, 1969), pp. 11-48.

Klein, G., "Die Verleugnung des Petrus. Eine traditionsgeschichtliche

Untersuchung," *Zeitschrift für Theologie und Kirche* 58 (1961), pp. 285-328; reprinted with additional material in *Rekonstruktion und Interpretation* (Beiträge zur Evangelischen Theologie, 50; Munich: Kaiser, 1969), pp. 49-98. Cf. also *Zeitschrift für die neutestamentliche Wissenschaft* 58 (1967), pp. 39-44 (answer to Linnemann).

Linnemann, E., "Die Verleugnung des Petrus," *Zeitschrift für Theologie und Kirche* 63 (1966), pp. 1-32; reprinted in revised form in *Studien zur Passionsgeschichte* (Forschungen zur Religion und Literatur des Alten und Neuen Testaments, 102; Göttingen: Vandenhoeck, 1970), pp. 70-108.

Merkel, H., "Peter's Curse," *The Trial of Jesus. Cambridge Studies in Honour of C.F.D. Moule,* ed. E. Bammel (Studies in Biblical Theology, second series, 13; London: SCM, 1970), pp. 66-71.

Refoulé, F., "Primauté de Pierre dans les Évangiles," *Revue des sciences religieuses de l'université de Strasbourg* 38 (1964), pp. 1-41.

VII. Mark

Bultmann, R., "Die Frage nach dem messianischen Bewusstsein Jesu und das Petrusbekenntnis," *Zeitschrift für die neutestamentliche Wissenschaft* 19 (1919-20), pp. 165-74; reprinted in *Exegetica. Aufsätze zur Erforschung des Neuen Testaments,* ed. E. Dinkler (Tübingen: Mohr, 1967), pp. 1-9.

Dinkler, E., "Peter's Confession and the 'Satan Saying': The Problem of Jesus' Messiahship," *The Future of Our Religious Past. Essays in Honour of R. Bultmann,* ed. J.M. Robinson (New York: Harper, 1971; from German, 1964), pp. 169-202.

Haenchen, E., "Die Komposition von Mk. VII [read: VIII], 27-IX, 1 und Par.," *Novum Testamentum* 6 (1963), pp. 81-109.

Schille, G., "Der Beitrag des Evangelisten Markus zum kirchenbildenden (ökumenischen) Gespräch seiner Tage," *Kerygma und Dogma* 12 (1966), pp. 135-53.

Trocmé, E., *La formation de l'Évangile selon Marc* (Études d'histoire et de philosophie religieuses, 57; Paris: Presses Universitaires, 1963), pp. 96-109.

Weeden, T.J., "The Heresy That Necessitated Mark's Gospel," *Zeitschrift für die neutestamentliche Wissenschaft* 59 (1968), pp. 145-58.

Weeden, T.J., *Mark—Traditions in Conflict* (Philadelphia: Fortress, 1971).

Wilcox, M., "The Denial Sequence in Mark XIV 26-31, 66-72," *New Testament Studies* 17 (1970-71), pp. 426-36.

VIII. Matthew

A. GENERAL

Bornkamm, G., Barth, G., Held, H.J., *Tradition and Interpretation in Matthew* (The New Testament Library; Philadelphia: Westminster, 1963; from German, 1960).

Braumann, G., "Der sinkende Petrus: Matth. 14, 28-31," *Theologische*

Zeitschrift (Basel) 22 (1966), pp. 403-14.

Hummel, R., "Die Perikope von der Tempelsteuer," *Die Auseinandersetzung zwischen Kirche und Judentum im Matthäusevangelium* (Beiträge zur Evangelischen Theologie, 33; Munich: Kaiser, 1963), pp. 103-6.

Kilpatrick, G.D., *The Origins of the Gospel According to St. Matthew* (Oxford: Clarendon, 1946), pp. 37-44 ("Peculiar Narratives, b. Petrine Stories").

Strecker, G., *Der Weg der Gerechtigkeit: Untersuchung zur Theologie des Matthäus* (Forschungen zur Religion und Literatur des Alten und Neuen Testaments, 82; 3rd ed.; Göttingen: Vandenhoeck, 1971), pp. 198-206 ("Petrus").

Trilling, W., *Das wahre Israel. Studien zur Theologie des Matthäus-Evangeliums* (3rd ed.; Munich: Kösel, 1964), pp. 154-63 ("Die Kirche").

Trilling, W., "Amt und Amtsverständnis bei Matthäus," *Mélanges bibliques en hommage au R. P. Béda Rigaux,* eds. A. Descamps and A. de Halleux (Gembloux: Duculot, 1970), pp. 29-44.

B. MATTHEW 16

Allen, E.L., "On This Rock," *Journal of Theological Studies,* New Series, 5 (1954), pp. 59-62.

Betz, J., "Christus—petra—Petrus," *Kirche und Überlieferung,* eds. J. Betz and H. Fries (*Festschrift* R. Geiselmann; Freiburg: Herder, 1960), pp. 1-21.

Betz, O., "Felsenmann und Felsengemeinde. Eine Parallele zu Mt. 16, 17-19 in den Qumranpsalmen," *Zeitschrift für die neutestamentliche Wissenschaft* 48 (1957), pp. 49-77.

Bornkamm, G., "The Authority to 'Bind' and 'Loose' in the Church in Matthew's Gospel," *Jesus and Man's Hope. Pittsburgh Festival on the Gospels,* vol. 1 (Pittsburgh Theological Seminary; *Perspective* 11 [1970]), pp. 37-50.

Burgess, J., *A History of the Exegesis of Matthew 16:17-19 from 1781 to 1965* (Theological Dissertation; Basel, 1965).

Bultmann, R., "Die Frage nach der Echtheit von Matth. 16, 17-19," *Theologische Blätter* 20 (1941), pp. 265-79; reprinted in *Exegetica. Aufsätze zur Erforschung des Neuen Testaments,* ed. E. Dinkler (Tübingen: Mohr, 1967), pp. 255-77.

Cullmann, O., "L'apôtre Pierre, instrument du diable ou instrument de Dieu? La place de Mt. 16.16-19 dans la tradition primitive," *New Testament Essays,* ed. A.J.B. Higgins (*Festschrift* T.W. Manson; Manchester University, 1959), pp. 98-103; re-published in German in *Oscar Cullmann: Vorträge und Aufsätze 1925-1962,* ed. K. Froehlich (Tübingen and Zurich: Mohr and Zwingli, 1966), pp. 202-13.

Da Spinetoli, O., "La portata ecclesiologica di Mt. 16, 18-19," *Antonianum* 42 (1967), pp. 357-75.

Dubarle, A.-M., "La primauté de Pierre dans Matthieu 16, 17-19. Quelques références à l'Ancien Testament," *Istina* 2 (1955), pp. 335-38.

Emerton, J.A., "Binding and Loosing—Forgiving and Retaining," *Journal of Theological Studies,* New Series 13 (1962), pp. 325-31.

Froehlich, K., *Formen der Auslegung von Matthäus 16, 13-18 im lateinischen Mittelalter* (Theological dissertation; Basel, 1961; typescript); partly published under the same title, Tübingen: Präzis, 1963.

Fuller, R.H., "The 'Thou Art Peter' Pericope and the Easter Appearances," *McCormick Quarterly* 20:4 (1967), pp. 309-15.

Grundmann, W., *Das Evangelium nach Matthäus* (Theologischer Hand-Kommentar zum Neuen Testament, 1; Berlin: Evangelische Verlagsanstalt, 1968), pp. 392-96 ("Exkurs zu Mt. 16, 17-19").

Hahn, F., "Die Petrusverheissung Mt 16, 18f.," *Materialdienst des Konfessionskundlichen Instituts Bensheim* 21 (1970), pp. 8-13.

Kahmann, J., "Die Verheissung an Petrus: Mt. 16, 18-19 im Zusammenhang des Matthäusevangeliums," *L'Évangile selon Matthieu. Rédaction et théologie,* ed. M. Didier (Journées Bibliques de Louvain, 1970; Bibliotheca Ephemeridum Theologicarum Lovaniensium, 29; Gembloux: Duculot, 1972), pp. 261-80.

Knoch, O., "Die Deutung der Primatstelle Mt. 16 im Lichte der neueren Diskussion," *Bibel und Kirche* (Stuttgart: Katholisches Bibelwerk) 23 (1968), pp. 44-46.

Ludwig, J., *Die Primatworte Mt XVI, 18-19 in der altkirchlichen Exegese* (Neutestamentliche Abhandlungen, 19:4; Münster: Aschendorff, 1952).

Obrist, F., *Echtheitsfragen und Deutung der Primatstelle Mt. 16, 18f. in der deutschen protestantischen Theologie der letzten dreissig Jahre* (Neutestamentliche Abhandlungen, 21:3-4; Münster: Aschendorff, 1961).

Oepke, A., "Der Herrenspruch über die Kirche, Mt. 16, 17-19, in der neuesten Forschung," *Studia Theologica* II, 2 (1948), pp. 110-65.

Pia, K., *Matth. 16, 18 (Tu es Petrus, etc.) bei Luther* (Theological dissertation; Freiburg i.B., 1954; typescript).

Ringger, J., "Das Felsenwort. Zur Sinndeutung von Mt. 16, 18, vor allem im Lichte der Symbolgeschichte," *Begegnung der Christen. Studien evangelischer und katholischer Theologen,* eds. M. Roesle and O. Cullmann (*Festschrift* O. Karrer; Stuttgart: Evangelisches Verlagswerk, 2nd ed., 1960), pp. 271-346.

Vögtle, A., "Messiasbekenntnis und Petrusverheissung: Zur Komposition Mt 16, 13-23 par.," *Biblische Zeitschrift,* Neue Folge 1 (1957), pp. 252-72; 2 (1958), pp. 85-103; reprinted in *Das Evangelium und die Evangelien: Beiträge zur Evangelienforschung* (Düsseldorf: Patmos, 1971), pp. 137-70.

Vögtle, A., "Zum Problem der Herkunft von Mt. 16, 17-19," *Orientierung an Jesus. Zur Theologie der Synoptiker,* ed. P. Hoffmann *et al.* (*Festschrift* J. Schmid; Freiburg: Herder, 1973), pp. 372-93.

Von Campenhausen, H., "The Power of the Keys in the Primitive Church," *Ecclesiastical Authority and Spiritual Power in the Church of the First Three Centuries* (Stanford University, 1969; from German, 1953), pp. 124-48.

IX. Luke

Delorme, J., "Luc V. 1-11. Analyse structurale et histoire de la rédaction," *New Testament Studies* 18 (1971-72), pp. 331-50.

Dietrich, W., *Das Petrusbild der lukanischen Schriften* (Beiträge zur Wissenschaft vom Alten und Neuen Testament, 94; Stuttgart: Kohlhammer, 1972).

Hilgert, E., *The Ship and Related Symbols in the New Testament* (Assen: Royal Vangorcum, 1962), pp. 105-23 ("The Stories of a Miraculous Draft of Fish").

Leaney, A.R.C., "Jesus and Peter. The Call and Post-Resurrection Appearance (Lk. V. 1-11 and XXIV. 34)," *Expository Times* 65 (1954), pp. 381-82.

Pesch, R., *Der reiche Fischfang, Lk. 5, 1-11/Joh. 21, 1-14. Wundergeschichte—Berufungserzählung—Erscheinungsbericht* (Kommentare und Beiträge zum Alten und Neuen Testament; Düsseldorf: Patmos, 1969).

Prete, B., *Il primato e la missione di Pietro. Studio esegetico critico del testo di Lc 22, 31-32* (Supplementi alla Rivista Biblica, 3; Brescia: Paideia, 1969).

Schürmann, H., "Der Dienst des Petrus und Johannes. Lk. 22, 8," *Trierer Theologische Zeitschrift* 60 (1951), pp. 99-101; reprinted in *Ursprung und Gestalt. Erörterungen und Besinnungen zum Neuen Testament* (Kommentare und Beiträge zum Alten und Neuen Testament; Düsseldorf: Patmos, 1970), pp. 274-76.

Schürmann, H., "Die Verheissung an Simon Petrus. Auslegung von Lk. 5, 1-11," *Bibel und Leben* 5 (1964), pp. 18-24; reprinted in *Ursprung und Gestalt. Erörterungen und Besinnungen zum Neuen Testament* (Kommentare und Beiträge zum Alten und Neuen Testament; Düsseldorf: Patmos, 1970), pp. 268-73.

Schürmann, H., "Eine Anfügung: Die Brüder im Glauben stärken (Lucas 22, 21-32)," in *Der Abendmahlsbericht Lucas 22, 7-38 als Gottesdienstordnung, Gemeindeordnung, Lebensordnung* (Paderborn: Schöningh, 1957), pp. 54-69; reprinted in *Ursprung und Gestalt* (see preceding item), pp. 128-31.

Schürmann, H., *Jesu Abschiedsrede, Lk. 22, 21-38. III. Teil einer quellenkritischen Untersuchung des lukanischen Abendmahlsberichtes, Lk. 22, 7-38* (Neutestamentliche Abhandlungen, 20:5; Münster: Aschendorff, 1957), pp. 99-116 (Luke 22:31f.).

Zillessen, K., "Das Schiff des Petrus und die Gefährten vom andern Schiff (Lk. 5, 1-11)," *Zeitschrift für die neutestamentliche Wissenschaft* 57 (1966), pp. 137-39.

X. John

Agourides, S., "The Purpose of John 21," *Studies in the History and Text of the New Testament,* ed. B.L. Daniels and M.J. Suggs (*Festschrift* for K. W. Clark; Salt Lake City: University of Utah, 1967), pp. 127-32.

Glombitza, O., "Petrus, der Freund Jesu. Überlegungen zu Joh. 21, 15ff.", *Novum Testamentum* 6 (1963), pp. 277-85.

Snyder, G.F., "John 13:16 and the Anti-Petrinism of the Johannine Tradition," *Biblical Research* 16 (1971), pp. 5-15.

XI. The Petrine Epistles

Hunzinger, C.-H., "Babylon als Deckname für Rom und die Datierung des 1. Petrusbriefes," *Gottes Wort und Gottes Land,* ed. H. Graf Reventlow (*Festschrift* H.W. Hertzberg; Göttingen: Vandenhoeck, 1965), pp. 67-77.

Käsemann, E., "An Apologia for Primitive Christian Eschatology," *Essays on New Testament Themes* (Studies in Biblical Theology, 41; London: SCM, 1964; from German, 1952), pp. 169-95.

Schelkle, K. H., "Spätapostolische Briefe und Frühkatholizismus," *Wort und Schrift. Beiträge zur Auslegung und Auslegungsgeschichte des Neuen Testaments* (Kommentare und Beiträge zum Alten und Neuen Testament; Düsseldorf: Patmos, 1966), pp. 117-25.

Index of Authors

179